INFIRM GLORY

Shakespeare and
the Renaissance
Image of Man

INFIRM GLORY

*Shakespeare and
the Renaissance
Image of Man*

SUKANTA
CHAUDHURI

CLARENDON PRESS · OXFORD
1981

Oxford University Press, Walton Street, Oxford OX2 6DP

London Glasgow New York Toronto
Delhi Bombay Calcutta Madras Karachi
Kuala Lumpur Singapore Hong Kong Tokyo
Nairobi Dar es Salaam Cape Town
Melbourne Wellington
and associate companies in
Beirut Berlin Ibadan Mexico City

Published in the United States by
Oxford University Press, New York

© *Sukanta Chaudhuri 1981*

British Library Cataloguing in Publication Data
Chaudhuri, Suzanta
Infirm glory.
1. Shakespeare, William — Criticism and
interpretation
I. Title
822.3'3   PR2976   80–41785

ISBN 0-19-812801-0

set by Hope Services, Abingdon
and printed in Great Britain
at the University Press, Oxford
by Eric Buckley
Printer to the University

To

my Mother
and Father

Preface

I began writing this book to clarify to myself certain features of Renaissance thought. As I worked, I grew more and more interested in the formal or 'literary' qualities of the poems and plays that came to be my central concern. In moments of confidence, I feel I may have been able to show how literary criticism and the history of ideas may be placed at each other's service. But I have mainly written about works very different from those normally used by historians of ideas. My 'historical' conclusions must stand or fall by my analysis of form and language in the imaginative works of Shakespeare and his contemporaries. I hope that even those who cannot grant my conclusions may agree with some of my analysis.

I need hardly point out that the first two chapters, on the continental Renaissance, do no more than sketch in the roughest of backgrounds. To a lesser extent this is also true of Chapter III, on Elizabethan and Jacobean authors. Of innumerable omissions, perhaps the most obvious is that of Machiavelli and his influence. It is some consolation to assume that such matters will be generally familiar to my readers. I should also point out that my studies of Shakespeare's plays are guided by certain special concerns about heroism and the nature of man. This explains, though in the eyes of some it will not excuse, my concentration on the central character in some of the plays.

This book was conceived and almost entirely written in Calcutta, though completed at Oxford. The academic resources of Calcutta are richer than the world suspects; but it remains a hectic place to work in, and I must thank my colleagues and students for making my path as smooth and happy as lay in their power.

There are some more particular debts as well. In all matters of Renaissance studies, I owe Mr Arun Kumar Das Gupta more than I can say. Professor Kitty Scoular Datta gave me valuable advice in the early stages of my work, as did Professor

Nigel Alexander and Dr Stanley Wells towards the end. I am also grateful to Mrs Betty Radice, Mrs Barbara Taylor, the Revd Christopher Dent and Timothy Radcliffe OP for answering queries or reading over sections of the typescript. My debt to Mr John Buxton is less specific but no less real. These teachers, friends, and advisers have saved me from many errors. For those that remain, I alone am responsible.

The generosity of the Inlaks Foundation enabled me to work at Oxford during the final stages of composition. It also helped me directly with the preparation of the typescript.

My wife Supriya has provided me with acute criticism and unfailing support. I must pay her the thanks she will never demand.

Presidency College, Calcutta   SUKANTA CHAUDHURI
New College, Oxford

Contents

List of Works Cited	xi
A Note on Secondary Works	xv
INTRODUCTORY	1
I. VARIETIES OF SCEPTICISM	5
1. Cornelius Agrippa	5
2. Rabelais	13
3. Montaigne	18
II. HUMANISTS AND REFORMERS	25
1. Neoplatonism: Nicholas of Cusa, Ficino, Pico della Mirandola	25
2. Sin and Fall: Erasmus and other Humanists	35
3. The Theologians: Scholastic and Protestant	42
III. THE ENGLISH RENAISSANCE	52
1. The Condition of Humanity: Sidney and Some Other Writers	52
2. Francis Bacon	66
3. Burton's *Anatomy*	76
4. Cross-Purposes in Spenser's Poetry	84
5. Greville and Donne: the Experience of Love	96
IV. MARLOWE AND SHAKESPEARE	113
1. Marlowe and the Problem of the Tragic Hero	113
2. Falstaff and the King	122
3. *Hamlet*	134
4. *Troilus and Cressida*	146
5. *Measure for Measure*	154
6. *King Lear*	164
7. *Macbeth*	173
8. *Coriolanus; Antony and Cleopatra*	184
9. The Last Plays	193
EPILOGUE: MILTON	211
Notes and References	217
Index	229

List of Works Cited, with Short Titles

The following bibliography lists the primary texts and translations that I have quoted or referred to closely. Short titles used in the body of the book have been placed within square brackets at the end of each entry.

When quoting from old books, I have modernized the spelling and punctuation and silently expanded printer's contractions. Quotations from modern critical editions have been taken as they stand.

Agrippa, Cornelius: *Henrici Cornelii Agrippae ab Nettesheym, De incertitudine & vanitate scientiarum declamatio inuectiua, denuo ab autore recognita, & marginalibus annotationibus aucta* (No place or date of publication).

    Henrie Cornelius Agrippa, of the Vanitie and vncertaintie of Artes and Sciences: Englished by Ia. [mes] *San* [ford] *Gent....Imprinted at London, by Henrie Bynneman, . . . 1575.*

A Kempis, Thomas: *The Imitation of Christ*, anonymous twentieth-century translation (Everyman's Library, London, 1960).

Aquinas, St. Thomas: *Summa contra Gentiles*, translated by the English Dominican Fathers, 4 vols. in 5 (London, 1923-9).

    Summa Theologica, Latin text with English translation, introductions etc., 60 vols. (Blackfriars, 1964-76). [Blackfriars.]

Aristotle: *On the Art of Poetry*, translated by Ingram Bywater (Oxford, 1920).

Augustine, St.: *The City of God*, translated by Marcus Dods *et al.* (Modern Library, New York, 1950).

    Confessions, translated by E. B. Pusey (Everyman's Library, London, 1907).

Bacon, Francis: *The Advancement of Learning*: the text of William Aldis Wright's edition (1868) as reprinted in *The Advancement of Learning and New Atlantis*, ed. Arthur Johnston (Oxford, 1974). [Johnston.]

    Essays, edited by E. A. Abbott, 2 vols. (London, 1879). [Abbott.]

    All other works from the *Works* edited by J. Spedding, R. L. Ellis, and D. D. Heath, 7 vols. (London, 1857-9). The translations of Latin works are also those given in this edition. [ES.]

Burton, Robert: *The Anatomy of Melancholy*, edited by Holbrook Jackson, 3 vols. (Everyman's Library, London, 1932; reprinted, 1948). [EL.]

Calvin, Jean: *Institutio Christianae Religionis*, Latin edition of 1559, in *Opera Selecta*, edited by P. Barth and W. Niesel (Munich, 1926-52). [Munich.]
  Institutes, translated by Ford Lewis Battles (Library of Christian Classics, Vol. XX-XXI: Philadelphia, 1960). [Battles.]
Castiglione, Baldassare: *The Book of the Courtier*, translated by Sir Thomas Hoby (Everyman's Library, London, 1928).
Chaucer, Geoffrey: *Works*, edited by F. N. Robinson (2nd edition, Oxford, 1966).
Colet, John: *Enarratio in Epistolam S. Pauli ad Romanos: An Exposition of St. Paul's Epistle to the Romans*, with a translation etc. by J. H. Lupton (London, 1873). [Lupton.]
  Super Opera Dionysii: Two Treatises on the Hierarchies of Dionysius, with a translation etc. by J. H. Lupton (London, 1869).
Cusanus, Nicholas: *Opera Omnia: iussu et auctoritate Academiae Litterarum Heidelbergensis*:
  Vol. I: *De Docta Ignorantia*, ed. E. Hoffmann & R. Klibansky (Leipzig, 1932);
  Vol. III: *De Coniecturis*, ed. J. Koch & K. Bormann (Hamburg, 1972);
  Vol. V: *Idiota*, ed. L. Baur (Leipzig, 1937).
  I have referred to all three of the above editions as 'Heidelberg': the context makes clear which work I am referring to.
  The translations from Cusanus are my own.
Davies, Sir John: *The Poems*, edited by Robert Krueger with Ruby Nemser (Oxford, 1975).
De Meung, Jean (with De Lorris, Guillaume): *The Romance of the Rose*, translated into English verse by Harry W. Robbins (New York, 1962).
Donne, John: *The Elegies and The Songs and Sonnets*, edited by Helen Gardner (Oxford, 1965).
  The Epithalamions, Anniversaries and Epicedes, edited by W. Milgate (Oxford, 1978).
Eckhart, Meister: *Meister Eckhart: a Modern Translation* by Raymond Bernard Blakney (New York, 1941).
Erasmus, Desiderius: *Colloquia*, ed. L.-E. Halkin, F. Bierlaire, and R. Hoven in *Opera Omnia* (Amsterdam), Vol. I Pt. 3 (1972). [Amsterdam.]
  All other works as in *Opera*, 10 vols. in 11 (Leyden, 1703-6, reprinted, London, 1962). [Leyden.]
  The following translations have been used:
  Colloquies, translated by Craig R. Thompson (Chicago, 1965). [Thompson.]
  Enchiridion militis Christiani, translated by Raymond Himelick (Bloomington, 1963). [Himelick.]
  On the Freedom of the Will, translated by E. Gordon Rupp in collaboration with A. N. Marlow in *Luther and Erasmus: Free Will and Salvation* (Library of Christian Classics, Vol. XVII: London, 1969). [Rupp.]

Paraclesis, translated by John C. Olin in *Christian Humanism and the Reformation: Desiderius Erasmus, Selected Writings* (New York, 1965).

The Praise of Folly, translated by Hoyt Hopewell Hudson (Princeton, 1941). [Hudson.]

The translations from Erasmus' letters are my own.

Ficino, Marsilio: *Commentary on Plato's Symposium, the Text and a Translation*, by Sears Reynolds Jayne (University of Missouri Studies Vol. XIX no. 1: Columbia, 1944). [Jayne.]

Quaestiones quinque de mente from *Epistolarum liber II*, as in *Opera*, Vol. I (Basle, 1576). [Basle.]

Five Questions concerning the Mind, translated by Josephine L. Burroughs in *The Renaissance Philosophy of Man*, edited by E. Cassirer, P. O. Kristeller, & J. H. Randall Jr. (Chicago, 1948; reprinted, 1971). [Burroughs.]

Fletcher, Phineas: *The Purple Island*, from the *Poetical Works* of Giles and Phineas Fletcher, edited by Frederick S. Boas, Vol. II (Cambridge, 1909). [Boas.]

Greville, Fulke: *Caelica* and *A Treatie of Humane Learning* from *Poems and Dramas of Fulke Greville*, edited by Geoffrey Bullough, Vol. I (Edinburgh, 1939).

Luther, Martin: *Liber de Christiana libertate:* as in *Epistola Lutheriana ad Leonem Decimum Summum Pontificem. Liber de Christiana Libertate* (Wittenberg, 1521). [Wittenberg.]

The Freedom of a Christian, translated by W. A. Lambert and revised by Harold J. Grimm in Vol. 31 of Luther's *Works* (General Editor, Helmut T. Lehmann: Philadelphia, 1957). [Lambert.]

Malory, Sir Thomas: *Works*, edited by Eugène Vinaver (2nd one-vol. edition, Oxford, 1971).

Marlowe, Christopher: *The Complete Works*, edited by Fredson Bowers, 2 vols. (Cambridge, 1973).

Melanchthon, Philip: *Loci Communes Theologici* (Basle, 1561).

The translation is my own.

Milton, John: *The Poems*, edited by John Carey and Alastair Fowler (Annotated English Poets, London, 1968).

Mirandola: See under 'Pico'.

Montaigne, Michel de: *Œuvres complètes*, edited by Albert Thibaudet and Maurice Rat (Bibliothèque de la Pléiade, Paris 1962, reprinted, 1976). [Pléiade.]

The Complete Works, translated by Donald M. Frame (London, no date). [Frame.]

More, Sir Thomas: *A Dialogue of Comfort.*

Utopia, translated by Ralph Robinson.

Both texts as given in the Everyman's Library edition (revised: London, 1951).

Nicholas of Cusa: See under 'Cusanus'.

Ockham, William of: *Philosophical Writings*, selected, translated, and edited by Philotheus Boehner (London, 1957).

Pico della Mirandola: *De hominis dignitate, Heptaplus, De ente et uno* etc., edited by Eugenio Garin (Florence, 1942). [Garin.]
   Oration on the Dignity of Man, translated by Elizabeth Livermore Forbes in *The Renaissance Philosophy of Man* (see 'Ficino' for details). [Forbes.]
   ⎰*On Being and the One,* translated by Paul J. W. Miller. [Miller.]
   ⎱*Heptaplus,* translated by Douglas Carmichael. [Carmichael.]
   Both as published, with *On the Dignity of Man,* in one volume from. Indianopolis in 1965.
Rabelais, François: *Œuvres complètes,* edited by Guy Demerson *et al.* (Paris, 1973). [Demerson.]
   Gargantua and Pantagruel, translated by J. M. Cohen (Penguin Classics, Harmondsworth, 1955).
Ralegh, Sir Walter; *Works,* with the lives of Ralegh by Oldys and Birch, 8 vols. (Oxford, 1829).
   The earlier part of the *History of the World* appears in Vol. II and *The Sceptic* and *A Treatise of the Soul* in Vol. VIII of this edition.
Ruysbroek, Jan van: *The Book of the Sparkling Stone,* translated by Edmund Colledge in his collection, *Medieval Netherlands Religious Literature* (Leyden, 1965).
Scotus, Duns: *Duns Scotus: a Selection,* translated and edited by Allan Wolter (Edinburgh, 1962).
Shakespeare, William: *The Complete Works,* edited by Peter Alexander (London, 1951; reprinted, 1978).
Sidney, Sir Philip: *Miscellaneous Prose,* edited by Katherine Duncan-Jones and Jan van Dorsten (Oxford, 1973). [MP: References are to the page number followed, after a stop, by the line number.]
Spenser, Edmund: *Poetical Works,* edited by J. C. Smith and E. de Selincourt (Oxford, 1912; reprinted, 1970).
Tasso, Torquato: *Jerusalem Delivered,* translated by Edward Fairfax (Centaur Press edition, London, 1962).

A Note on Secondary Works

All direct references to secondary works have been documented in the notes. A bibliography of all the books I have used would be tedious, and one of all relevant books available, a task beyond my powers. My subject, after all, is a complex and wide-ranging one.

However, I feel I should mention a few works in particular. Every student of such subjects is familiar with Hiram Haydn's *The Counter-Renaissance* (New York, 1950) and Margaret Wiley's *The Subtle Knot* (London, 1952) and *Creative Sceptics* (London, 1966). I have also been stimulated by some chapters in Erich Auerbach's *Mimesis* (translated by Willard R. Trask: Princeton, 1953); by Charles G. Nauert Jr.'s *Agrippa and the Crisis of Renaissance Thought* (Urbana, 1965); by Stanley E. Fish's *Self-Consuming Artifacts* (Berkeley, 1972), especially the section on Burton; by Murray Roston on Donne (*The Soul of Wit*, Oxford, 1974); and by Wilbur Sanders on *Doctor Faustus* and *Macbeth* in *The Dramatist and the Received Idea* (Cambridge, 1968). Some of these works figure briefly in the notes, others not at all. Indeed there is relatively little that I have directly absorbed from these authors; but their interests and approaches have helped to shape my own.

Introductory

The chief purpose of this book is to illustrate some aspects of Shakespeare's achievement. But they are aspects that take on meaning only in the context of his times. The material needed to define this context is readily available. Perceptive studies have been made of most of the major authors individually, pointing to certain persistent conclusions. But seldom has this range of authors been studied collectively to present a coherent account of the age, or at least of certain well-defined trends within it.

I shall set out from the relatively firm ground of orthodox Scepticism. To the philosopher, 'Scepticism' is the distrust of man's capacity to attain to certain knowledge. (I have used the word in this exact philosophic sense all through the book.) This distrust was the unlikely basis of a school of philosophy traditionally founded by Pyrrho in the fourth century BC and best known today from the works of Sextus Empiricus (second to early third century AD).

The Sceptical tradition flourished in the Renaissance. The *Hypotyposes* of Sextus Empiricus appeared in Latin translation from Paris in 1562, and was republished, with his *Adversus mathematicos,* from Paris and Antwerp in 1569. Direct knowledge of Sextus is found as early as 1520, when Gianfrancesco Pico della Mirandola, nephew of the renowned Giovanni Pico, published his *Examen vanitatis doctrinae gentium.* This line of thought found its most famous Renaissance spokesman in Montaigne, and continued in the seventeenth century.

It seems, moreover, that this Sceptical tradition drew not only upon the orthodox classical sources, but also on important currents in Christianity. In one way or another, much medieval thought denied the possibility of spiritual knowledge through the exercise of reason, and proposed instead a total reliance upon faith. These anti-rational and Fideistic tendencies prove to have 'survived' into the Renaissance so strongly as to constitute a major factor in its intellectual climate.

This Sceptical strain may seem to provide an interesting contrast to the optimism and expansion of knowledge conventionally associated with the Renaissance. But in fact, it increasingly appears that such Scepticism stands to the general spirit of the age not in contrast but in association. It is the tip of an iceberg of doubt and self-distrust. More and more evidence may be gathered to suggest that the Renaissance was not simply a glorious 'rebirth' but an age of collapsing values and systems, of disturbance, exhaustion, and deep humility. 'Baroque man' of the early seventeenth century has long been known as a prey to gloom and fear. What is perhaps still inadequately realized is that this is the climax to a process of a hundred years and more.

The Revival of Learning entailed a vast task of assimilation and synthesis, with inevitable fears and failures. This disruption of the intellectual order is part of a still wider spirit of doubt and gloom. The Renaissance is afflicted with the distrust of all human faculties, the sense of man's ignorance and sinfulness, with perhaps a turning to revelation and divine mercy. Even at its most radiant, the age lays down firm limits to human prowess. If it idealizes an individual figure, this is generally offset by reflections upon common human nature. If it conceives of a well-defined world-order, man is permitted only restricted development within it. Such is the nature of the optimistic end of the spectrum; at the other, increasingly as the age progresses, we find the dissolution of traditional systems and a deep sense of the feebleness and foulness of man.

Among the works of the continental Renaissance, we have the writings of a Pico or an Erasmus, the art of a Leonardo or a Michelangelo, where, despite all the admissions of limitation and failure, we find a basic promise of achievement, an excited absorption in the play of the human faculties. The writings of Montaigne and Cervantes, the art of Il Rosso and El Greco, lie beyond the watershed: they are all in doubt about the capacities of man and his importance in the universe, though such doubt may lead them to a deeper and subtler engagement with the state of man. The same transition may be observed in the English Renaissance: a movement represented in travesty by the text-book simplism of 'Elizabethan exuberance' subsiding into 'Jacobean gloom'.

It is indeed remarkable how this unpromising standpoint fosters a new interest in man. Many authors are led by their sense of inadequacy to confine themselves to purely human concerns. The human state and human values thus take on a new if restricted importance.

This concentration upon the state of man must be distinguished from the simple celebration of human powers in a direct and single-minded way. In fact the new approach can make for a firmer, more valid celebration. A full admission of weakness, folly, and evil is accompanied by an interest in the working of the faculties, in what man *can* achieve. Again, as the age progresses, we find a new sense of the wonder and significance of human achievement, if no longer its absolute worth. The fruits of experience are prized for their own sake, although they so lamentably fall away from objective truth. Once again, man acquires power and dignity, this time by standards which refer only to himself and therefore cannot fail. There is obviously something precarious about this reinstatement, unsupported or even opposed by the external order. But this very self-sufficiency can generate a tragic heroism; it can also foster an untroubled sense of fulfilment, a total absorption in the experience. All these possibilities are most fully realized in the work of Shakespeare.

But as I have said, it seems necessary to take a European perspective. I am not trying to demonstrate the presence of a clear 'world-picture' in the age. Such pictures are difficult to draw if we adequately consider even a single country during a restricted period of time. My aim is wider and less clear: to note certain general tendencies in the thought of the age—not always the same conclusions, but certain assumptions and mental processes behind a wide range of systems and conclusions. They are to be found in philosophy as well as theology, works of art and 'pure literature'. Such a study can easily degenerate into a vague and even fanciful account of an alleged *Zeitgeist*; but obviously, the greater the range of material, the smaller the risk of such a failure.

In my opening survey of the continental background, I

shall emphasize the elements of doubt and collapse. Even in today's changed context of Renaissance studies, the matter has not received the importance it demands. But I shall also indicate the origins of the new concern with man; and my third chapter, on the English Renaissance, should reveal more clearly the intricate mingling of gloom and hope in a spirit of cautious and paradoxical enterprise. This will serve to lead us, in Chapter Four, to the nature of this compound in the greatest author of them all.

I. Varieties of Scepticism

1. Cornelius Agrippa

There appeared from Antwerp in 1530 a classic indictment of human learning entitled *De incertitudine et vanitate scientiarum*. It had in fact been written around 1526. The author, Heinrich Cornelius Agrippa von Nettesheim, was a noted scholar of the age. He had a degree in the liberal arts. He laid plausible claim to doctorates in law and medicine, as well as to special knowledge of theology. Above all, he was learned in the occult sciences, thus acquiring a certain notoriety as a magician. He came to be associated with Faust, and his fabled career provided much material for the Faust legend.

This was the unlikely man who in *De . . . vanitate* launched a bitter attack on the world of learning, practically dismissing the possibility of knowledge and preaching a complete reliance on the word of God.

To be scrupulously exact, Agrippa does not project a total Scepticism in this work. Even where he declares the impossibility of knowledge, he phrases this in a slightly hesitant way: 'difficilis, ne dicam impossibilis . . . ' (Ch. 1: *De inc.*, a3ᵛ). In fact, considering the subject of the book, *De . . . vanitate* is quite perversely erudite. It is designed as an encyclopaedic survey, proceeding from one field to another, dividing each into its component disciplines. Within this structure Agrippa marshals a considerable array of facts. Most of them are used to subvert the cause of learning; we shall soon see how. But some at least seem to be presented purely for the sake of information. Not infrequently he quotes authority for the view that learning is of no avail. This is not so much parody as paradox: an end being achieved by means that partly serve to disprove that end. There are passages which hint at a broader facetiousness: whimsical page-long catalogues of examples, a hyperbolic chapter showing how all learning is subverted by panders and bawds. The final praise of the ass is in the tradition of the paradoxical encomium.

Yet there is no question of Agrippa's basic seriousness. In those very passages where we may be tempted to doubt it, the substance fits in perfectly with the leading themes of the whole work. We wonder if we really ought to laugh; we may not even want to.

We have already been trapped by that cunning weapon of Renaissance Scepticism, as common and as various as Scepticism itself: a sort of extended, comprehensive paradox, the ironic circular treatment of a subject that makes us question the basis of this or any other intellectual operation.[1] In Agrippa's case, as this questioning is his avowed purpose, he cannot lose. Whether we take him seriously or not, he has won his point.

Whatever reservations he may make at times, the current of Agrippa's arguments draws us towards a total Scepticism. His very first chapter explains the basic reason for this:

And so large is the liberty of the truth, and the largeness thereof so free, that it cannot be perceived with the speculations of any science, nor with any strait judgement of the senses, nor with any arguments of the art of logic, nor with any evident proof, with no syllogisms of demonstration, nor with any discourse of man's reason, but with faith only: . . . (Ch. 1)[2]

Our intellectual methods are inadequate. Reality is too vast and various to be contained within the crude framework of human disciplines.

Agrippa can therefore make great play with a favourite weapon of all Sceptics: a simple catalogue of citations that exposes the changes, uncertainties, and contradictions of so-called knowledge. This is even true of physical or 'scientific' matters: Agrippa demonstrates how geographers and astronomers disagree among themselves (Chs. 27, 30). In moral and social matters the problem is quite insoluble, as there cannot be a single absolute truth. Societies and individuals differ among themselves:

. . . whereof it cometh to pass that that which at one time was vice, another time is accounted virtue: and that which in one place is virtue, in another is vice: that which to one is honest, to another is dishonest: that which to us is just, to other(s) is unjust, according to the opinion or laws of time, of place, of estate and of men. (Ch. 54)[3]

Hence moral philosophy builds on sand, and so does law: '. . . it be altogether made of nothing else but of frail and very weak inventions and opinions of men, which things be of all other(s) the weakest, and is altered at every change of time, of the state, and of the prince . . .' (Ch. 91).[4]

Even the letters of the alphabet change, and languages themselves. In Ch. 100 we have an eloquent passage on this theme.

The systems to which men subscribe hold their power not by intrinsic merit but merely by authority. Sceptics can show a peculiarly dual response to authority: they expose its hollowness but also admit its necessity. We shall see this clearly when we come to Montaigne. Agrippa too can grant the need for law, ceremony, and accepted codes; but by and large, he is concerned to expose and overthrow them. Learned opinion constitutes a mere tyranny born of pride: 'For they are so stiff and obstinate in their opinions, that they leave no place for the Holy Ghost, and do so assure themselves, and trust in their own strength and proper wit, that they yield to nor allow no truth . . .' (Ch. 101).[5]

In intellectual inquiry, authority impedes the search for truth. In his Preface to the reader, Agrippa seems to admit, in a guarded and negative manner, that the quest for knowledge is a valid and feasible pursuit. This is couched as a protest against the authority of Aristotle, Aquinas, and others, which thwarts the search for truth: '. . . what a wicked tyranny it is, to bind the wits of students to certain appointed authors, and to take from scholars the liberty to search and trace out truth' (Preface to the Reader).[6]

The tenets of authority do not embody truth. They are arbitrary self-secure artefacts—nothing better than the mere opinions of men, 'decreta et opiniones hominum' (Ch. 1). He repeats the point specifically when treating of 'judicial astrology' (Ch. 31) and natural philosophy (Ch. 49). It is present by implication through most of his work. In fact, there is more than authority at stake here. All intellectual pursuits are undermined by the classic premiss of Scepticism that first principles are themselves unproved.

For every science hath in it some certain principles, which must be believed, and cannot by any means be declared: which if any will

obstinately deny, the philosophers have not wherewith to dispute
against him, and immediately they will say, that there is no disputation
against him which denieth the principles: . . . (Ch. 1)[7]

From another direction, the intellect is discredited by the
standard Sceptical assault upon logic. The basis of logic is uncertain: a logical conclusion must be confirmed by authority
or by sensory experience—and both these are thoroughly
unreliable. Unlike his successor Montaigne, Agrippa says little
about the fallibility of the senses; but he discusses the matter
in his chapter on dialectic (Ch. 7).

It is if anything a graver indictment that logical definitions
bear no relation to actual experience. They traffic in abstractions, take us away from truth: 'But if any say to an unlearned
man, a mortal living creature reasonable, for a man, he will
less understand it than if he had said simply a man' (Ch. 7).[8]
We are brought back to common sense and common experience. So too in grammar, the arbitrary rules bear no relation
to actual usage. Mathematics is irrelevant because a perfect
shape like a circle is not to be found in nature. In all these
cases, human ingenuity has passed outside nature to its own
brain-spun abstractions.

In fact, art must be subordinate to nature: '. . . no art can
surmount nature, but doth imitate and follow it aloof off,
and the force of nature is far stronger than of art' (Ch. 90).[9]
Man can indeed obtain some control over nature's forces.
Agrippa grows quite enthusiastic over the mechanical arts and
'natural magic'. But even here man merely guides or exploits
the forces of nature. He does so, moreover, at grave moral
risk: mechanical inventions foster pride and luxury, magic
passes beyond the 'natural' into increasingly dangerous realms
and finally into plain traffic with the devil. Where man tries
to deny or reverse the power of nature, he is sure to fail, as
with alchemy. The moral danger, of course, remains as great
as ever.

De . . . vanitate has a strong moral bias. Agrippa continually
passes beyond strictly Sceptical issues to a wider indictment
of learning. Knowledge is not merely difficult or impossible;
it is spiritually unprofitable.

He then which knoweth all other things . . . yet he knoweth nothing,
except he know the will of God's word, and execute the same: he that

hath learned all things, and hath not learned this, he hath learned in vain, and knoweth all things in vain: . . . (Ch. 100)[10]

Agrippa is deeply aware that the arts and sciences are morally neutral. Their goodness, such as it is, consists in the use to which they are put by man. Man's moral motives are crucial: there is no science 'that of it self deserveth praise, but that which it getteth [more exactly, 'borrows'] of his honesty that professeth the same' (Ch. 1).[11] Among the few arts for which Agrippa finds a good word are geometry, architecture, and mechanical inventions; but these may be practised for the sake of pomp and vanity, or war and destruction. Political systems are less important than the men who implement them: 'For very well one, very well a few, very well the people do govern, if they be virtuous: and most naughtily, if they be wicked' (Ch. 55).[12]

The perversion of knowledge to evil purposes is exposed in greatest detail in the chapter on bawdry (Ch. 64). Undoubtedly this is a *tour de force*. Among the prostituted sciences are 'geometric architecture', which devises ladders and other mischiefs that lovers may misuse; medicine, which provides an excuse for a pander's errands; even *arithmetici ludi*, whose dangers (and indeed nature) are not clearly explained. Agrippa runs through his entire list of disciplines. While such anxiety for total proof may be suspect, his basic purpose is clear enough. Knowledge can be turned to great evil, and in man's fallen state will most often be so used.

Man's greatest task is therefore to acquire self-knowledge leading to salvation. Profane knowledge profits nothing towards this. In fact, self-knowledge consists precisely in an admission of the futility of learning, of man's basic ignorance. This in turn is owing to the sinfulness of man. Folly and ignorance are the consequences of moral decay.

Man's diseased faculties are constantly associated with original sin:

. . . God created all things very good, that is to say in the best degree wherein they might abide: even as he then hath created trees full of fruits, so also hath he created the souls as reasonable trees full of forms and knowledges, but through the sin of the first parent all things were reveled [i.e. veiled, concealed], and oblivion the mother of ignorance stept in. (Conclusion)[13]

Agrippa is not entirely consistent in this matter. At times (as above) it seems the faculty of knowledge, potentially effective and beneficent, has been corrupted by man's Fall. Elsewhere it appears that the quest for knowledge itself constitutes the Fall: in other words, that such a quest is essentially sinful. Needless to say, this is a much more radical denial of the intellect: a positive rejection, not merely a regretful surrender.

. . . this is the very pestilence, that putteth all mankind to ruin, the which chaseth away all innocency, and hath made us subject to so many kinds of sin, and to death also: which hath extinguished the light of faith, casting our souls into blind darkness: which condemning the truth, hath placed errors in the highest throne. (Ch. 1)[14]

But whatever the precise nature of this denial of learning, the duty of denial remains clear. Man must disclaim all wisdom and independence, relying on absolute faith in God and unquestioning acceptance of revelation. Agrippa typifies all those authors who cut through the knot of sin, folly, and ignorance by exhortation to a *docta ignorantia*: a 'wise ignorance' that repudiates proud knowledge of the world to acquire salvation through the knowledge vouchsafed by God:

It is better therefore and more profitable to be idiots and know nothing, to believe by Faith and Charity, and to become next unto God, than being lofty and proud through the subtleties of sciences to fall into the possession of the Serpent. (Ch. 101)[15]

This is the leading theme of Agrippa's final chapters, culminating in an attack on the 'Masters of the Arts' and a paradoxical encomium on the ass, much as Erasmus ends *The Praise of Folly* with the exaltation of holy or divine folly. In neither case should the intricacies of the paradox conceal the basic seriousness of purpose.

Agrippa thus seems to afford a simple instance of a process we shall observe in most Renaissance thinkers who question man's powers. They pass from an intellectual to a moral analysis, with a basic admission of man's imperfect moral nature. The admission is made in various modes, pointing to various conclusions. In this book I shall survey a range of reactions, showing how the same basic view of man can support very different concepts of his achievement and importance.

Agrippa's concept, as I have said, appears to be simple and direct. He resorts to an orthodox Christian standpoint, even to the utter abnegation of reason and reliance on faith. But let us see how he describes his position:

And finally all these laws of religion are laid upon no other foundation than on the ordinances of such as instituted them: and moreover, they have no other rule of certainty, but very incredulity. Consider how many opinions there be in religion, and how many there have been since the beginning of the world, how many ceremonies, how many worshippings . . . and yet the religion of the Lord God which hath continued so many years past cannot bring men to the right faith without the Word of God: . . . (Ch. 56)[16]

Agrippa is scarcely the only Christian thinker who leaves matters of faith outside the probings of his epistemology. But in his specially Sceptical context, we may be tempted to extend his arguments even to these matters. If the *religio dei* cannot prevail over the rest without postulating revelation, could it conceivably be just another voice in the babel of vain opinion? If the mysteries of faith are held on authority alone, may we not be reminded of Agrippa's strictures upon all authority?

Such doubts are admittedly irrelevant to the mysteries of the Word; but when Agrippa elaborates on the subject in his final chapters, he raises a new and more stubborn set of difficulties. To begin with, the preserved text of Holy Writ may not be whole and authentic. Many books are manifestly missing, as we see from references in works that do survive. Even of these latter, 'very few of many remain true and certain' (Ch. 99).[17]

Needless to say, this is the underlying premise of all humanist Biblical studies. But Agrippa follows it up with a truly devastating idea: even the Prophets and Evangelists made mistakes, so that what they recorded is not uniformly the Word of God. They wrote under the inspiration of the Holy Ghost, which comes and goes: 'Neither be the Prophets always prophets: nor always see, nor always foretell; nor a continual habit is prophecy, but a gift, a passion and a spirit that passeth: . . .' (Ch. 99.)[18] Even what was revealed by inspiration may have been misinterpreted or wrongly recorded by the human error of the authors: 'aut humanitus lapsos, aut mutata dei sententia deficientes' (Ch. 99; *De inc.*, z4ᵛ). Finally, a prophecy may be rendered invalid by some change in the matter to which it relates, so that the revelation is no longer valid.

In other words, Agrippa does *not* place matters of faith beyond the searchings of Scepticism. The inviolable Word of God is granted a purely theoretical existence, placed in a sort of epistemological limbo. In the only form in which man can apprehend that Word, it is subject to doubt and error.

These doubts lie fresh in our minds as we take up the next chapter, on the Word of God. The single-minded eloquence of this chapter is so persuasive that we may easily forget what went before; or again we may not. In any case, we may go back to the earlier chapter, and it must take its place in our total assessment of the work.

It is impossible to sort out this tangle beyond fear of contradiction. It seems to me, however, that these doubts concerning the scriptures do not undermine Agrippa's faith but rather reinforce it. It is the final and most disturbing proof of man's ignorance, his infinite capacity for error. It ensures that we do not approach the scriptures with proud confidence of assimilating their message and being saved thereby, but with utter humility and surrender of the understanding. The scriptures cannot be comprehended by any human power: 'nulla scientia, nulla speculatione, nulla contemplatione, nullis denique humanis viribus . . .' (Ch. 100; *De inc.*, z7ᵛ). The central truth of scripture has 'one constant, plain and holy meaning' (ibid.).[19] This cannot be distorted by errors of transmission or exegesis, but shines all the more clearly when we recognize and discount such error.

Although Agrippa's arguments are radically disturbing, they are in one sense extremely conservative. They follow the path of traditional Christian meditation on human weakness and the vanity of the world. Agrippa's contempt of profane and worldly matters may have been sharpened by reaction to the new learning that he himself espoused; but his view of man has hardly been modified by that learning.

Other Sceptics of the sixteenth century bring in new methods of enquiry and refutation. More important, they discover new interests and even virtues in the human state while accepting man's basic weakness. They may subscribe to the set moral or divine order, but it becomes less of a binding force. They cannot merely discount man in terms of the set values: he becomes important in his own right, and this importance prompts a fresh approach to the problem of survival in an uncertain universe.

In the following accounts of Rabelais and Montaigne, I shall note the Scepticism and moral doubt, particularly from aspects not prominent in Agrippa. I shall also point out important elements drawn from orthodox morals and religion. But my main purpose will be to describe the new concern with man, the humble but firm acceptance of his nature and predicament.

2. *Rabelais*

In Rabelais, the humility is indeed not much in evidence at first. His celebration of natural man is so lusty and full-throated, the passions and appetites so magnified, as to obscure much of the underlying uncertainty. Even the patent fragmentation of learning appears as the obverse of a positive assertion of basic humanity. With Rabelais's work, one needs to stand back from the canvas. Then the figures fall into perspective, the background opens out behind them, and the view proves essentially the same as in Agrippa or Montaigne.

Rabelais declares the folly of man stridently, almost with exultation:

Everyone is foolish, and it is quite right that the village of Foul in Lorraine is close to Toul . . . All are fools. Solomon says that the number of fools is infinite; nothing can be added to infinity, and nothing can be subtracted from it, as Aristotle proves. (III. 46: Cohen, pp. 414-15)[20]

This is spoken by Panurge, a man of eccentric views; but the reader inclined to dismiss it as Panurge's particular ranting should compare Rabelais's discourse in his own person on the *fat* or 'gormless' state of the world—to be cured by Pantagruelism alone (Prologue to Book V). Again, quite how ironical is Épistémon's defence of Judge Bridoye's action in deciding lawsuits by the throw of dice? It avoids the yet more preposterous mischiefs of law and judgement. Épistémon plays upon many serious premisses of Sceptical thinkers:

For he doubted his own knowledge and capacity, knew the inconsisten-cies and contradictions of the laws, edicts, customs, and ordinances, and was aware of the deceptions of the eternal Calumniator . . . Thus, avoiding the dangers and perplexities of a definite decision, he would by the throwing of dice discover the divine will and pleasure, which we call the final judgment. (III. 44: Cohen, pp. 410–11)[21]

This sense of inadequacy accompanies a 'simplicity and plain kindness'[22] in the magistrate. We begin to approach an ideal not uncommon among Sceptics, of the ripe wisdom of humble virtue.

Rabelais's mode does not permit too many explicit avowals of doubt and ignorance. But these do emanate implicitly from every point of the work. The five books together surely represent the greatest-ever fragmentation of the world of Renaissance learning.

Over and over in Rabelais, authorities whirl madly, dis-jointed from their orbits. Bridoye's defence of his own conduct (III. 42) is the most egregious welter of references. In a more pleasing oratorical style, Rondibilis the physician juggles with authorities in his discourse on marriage and cuckoldry (III. 31–2). A volley of derived knowledge, largely mythical, illustrates the possibility of cures and deterrents for calamities (IV. 62). We may also consider the instances of deaths from sudden accidents (IV. 17); Pantagruel's discourse on immortality (IV. 27); or the author's own justification of the manner of Gargantua's birth by instancing parallels (I. 6). The fact that such citations may be tongue-in-cheek merely heightens the irony.

Again, as in Agrippa, authorities contradict one another. Rabelais shows how one may propose infinite, and infinitely contradictory, interpretations of the same text or pheno-menon. 'Who is telling you that white stands for faith and blue for steadfastness? A mouldy book, you say . . . Who made it? . . . I do not know which surprises me more, his presumption or his stupidity . . .' (I. 9: Cohen, p. 57).[23] Every prognostication concerning Panurge's marriage is interpreted differently by Panurge and by his companions, so that the very possibility of interpretation seems absurd. It is the same with Panurge's consultation of a theologian, a doctor, a lawyer, and a philosopher (III. 29 ff.).

This serves to illustrate the endless ingenuities of argument, and may be related to the explicit indictments of logic itself. Here is Gargantua mourning the death of his wife Badebec in giving birth to Pantagruel:

'Shall I weep?' said he. 'Yes. Why then? Because my wife who was so good is dead.' . . .

And as he spoke he bellowed like a cow. But when Pantagruel came into his mind, he suddenly began laughing like a calf. . . . 'Ho, ho, ho, ho! How glad I am. Let's drink, ho, and banish all melancholy! . . .'

As he said this he heard the litanies and dirges of the priests who were carrying his wife to the grave. (II. 3: Cohen, pp. 177-8)[24]

So that 'On either side he found sophistical arguments which took his breath away. For he framed them very well *in modo et figura*, but he could not resolve them' (II. 3: Cohen, p. 177).[25] This dilemma illustrates more than the two-edged nature of logic; it brings out the intractability of experience, never to be confined within a set formulation or response.

The same sense of futility underlies Rabelais's treatment of grammar and the knowledge of languages. Panurge is a fluent linguist; but this does not help him to ask for food and obtain it (II. 9). Nor does scientific knowledge prove of much avail; witness the cuckolded astronomer Her Trippa:

There he was, peering into every ethereal and terrestrial concern without his glasses, discoursing of all events past and present and predicting the entire future. But one thing he entirely failed to see, and that was the jig his wife was dancing . . . (III. 25: Cohen, p. 356)[26]

We here approach the very basis of Rabelais's criticism of human learning: the fact that it is an empty brain-spun fabric, neither fostering our understanding of the world nor teaching us to live in it happily and virtuously.

The episodes of Panurge asking for food, and Her Trippa oblivious of his wife, illustrate the two main channels through which Rabelais's natural humanity flows: food and drink, and sex. Some (like Frère Jean des Entommeures) might prefer the first, others (like Panurge) the latter; but the legitimate pattern of human life seems to consist of these two alone. Messer Gaster is the 'first master of arts in this world' (IV. 57).[27]

'From good wine you cannot make bad Latin' (I. 19: Cohen, p. 77).[28] When Pantagruel's companions in voyage assail him with vain speculative queries, he answers them with action: he calls for food and drink (IV. 63–4). It is worth noting, too, how Rabelais's own book, the work that will banish 'gormlessness' from the earth, is continually likened to wine, and its readers to tipplers. The Oracle of the Holy Bottle, the goal of the voyagers' quest, utters a single pregnant syllable: *'Trinch!'*

This is an important particular in which Rabelais differs from most Sceptical thinkers. Whereas they emphasize the fluidity and complexity of actual experience, the inadequacy of the formulations devised by human thought, for Rabelais life is gloriously, primitively simple, and all complex formulas are suspect. Occasionally (as in Gargantua's dilemma, quoted earlier) he may indeed be struck by the contradictions and complexities of life; but he refuses to remain in this state of suspended judgement. Drink and sex cut all the Gordian knots of experience.

Not entirely, though. Frère Jean is a valiant trencherman, nor is he indifferent to a wench, but this is hardly the full liberty afforded by the single rule of his Abbey of Thélème: 'Do what you will', *'Fay ce que vouldras'*. As Rabelais explains, 'people who are free, well-born, well-bred, and easy in honest company have a natural spur and instinct which drives them to virtuous deeds and deflects them from vice; and this they called honour' (I. 57: Cohen, p.159).[29] Rabelais believes in a higher libertinism which, while allowing full satisfaction to the physical appetites, fulfils the superior faculties of man. In fact, the very term 'higher' libertinism is misleading: apart from Panurge, the figure of the physically absorbed man, all Rabelais's other heroes combine physical appetites with high moral and intellectual motives. This is no less an element of the Gargantuan ideal.

At its basis lies a deep sense of the virtue innate in man, or at least present in potential. For Rabelais is part-Sceptic, but part-idealist too. His most radiant vision of man occurs in the praise of the 'herb Pantagruelion':

By means of this herb, invisible substances are visibly stopped, caught, detained and, as it were, imprisoned; . . . By its help nations which

Nature seemed to keep hidden, inaccessible, and unknown, have come
to us, and we to them . . . and as a result, those celestial intelligences,
the gods of the sea and land, have all taken fright. (III. 51: Cohen,
p. 428)[30]

The tone is equivocal, even ironical. 'Pantagruelion' is nothing
but hemp (which Rabelais identifies with linen). But its
functions are shown to cover the whole range of human
activity, and the passage becomes more and more a celebration
of man in serious and even lyrical vein. More chastened, but
equally clear in its import, is the priestess Bacbuc's farewell
discourse to the voyagers:

So, when you philosophers, with God's guidance and in the company of
some clear Lantern, give yourselves up to that careful study and investigation which is the proper duty of man—and it is for this reason that
men are called *alphestes*, that is to say searchers and discoverers . . . (V.
47: Cohen, p. 710, where it is ch. 48.)[31]

The search involves both God and man, *'guyde de Dieu et
compagnie d'homme'*.[32]

Rabelais does not deny that man can achieve knowledge,
though he derides almost the total stock so far acquired and
the established methods of acquiring it. His faith in man
grows out of a deep and pervasive Scepticism, like flowers on
a thorn-bush.

Most humanists would admit the 'amphibious' nature of
man, the union of higher and lower faculties in his nature.
The main body of humanists might try to overcome this
duality, foster the 'higher' man alone through intellectual
labour or spiritual discipline; the religious-minded may stress
the need for God's grace to accomplish this task. But the
more heterodox, such as Rabelais and Montaigne, would not
consider such a separation desirable. They delight in exercising the intellect, but they also have a sense of its very limited
efficacy. Learning is tested against real life—to a great extent,
against the physical appetites—and is accepted only if it
agrees with basic human nature.

Man's capacity for learning and achievement is seen as a
single minor element in the totality of his being—a totality in
which the brute is as much present as the god, and far more
assertive and enduring. Rabelais joyfully accepts this totality;
Montaigne more wistfully, but still with a not unwilling

resignation and an admission—ultimately a firm admission—of the possibility of virtue. To this classic instance of the Sceptical humanist I shall now turn.

3. *Montaigne*

The uncertainty of the age is best crystallized in the writings of Montaigne: above all in the elaborate Scepticism of the longest of his essays, the *Apologie de Raimond Sebond*. Some of his arguments had been proposed by Agrippa, whose *De . . . vanitate* was a formative influence on Montaigne's thought. But Montaigne treats many other points, raised briefly by Agrippa or not at all, and forms it all into a new and searching philosophy of man.

The first important point on which Montaigne lays special stress is the unreliability of the senses. In the *Apologie de Raimond Sebond*, he repeats the examples cited by Sextus Empiricus: the flat painting that appears to have three dimensions, the sweet wine that tastes bitter to the sick, the single musket-ball that appears to be two. He takes more examples from Lucretius.[33] Man can have no understanding of the real nature of an object. 'Is it our senses, I say, which . . . fashion these objects out of various qualities, or do they really have them so? And in the face of this doubt, what can we decide about their real essence?' (Frame, p. 453.)[34]

Further, Montaigne develops something like a nominalistic approach to experience. Every phenomenon is unique, so that it is impossible to formulate any general principles of knowledge: 'The inference that we try to draw from the resemblance of events is uncertain, because they are always dissimilar: there is no quality so universal in this aspect of things as diversity and variety' (III. 13, *De l'experience:* Frame, p. 815).[35] Over and over he describes the variety of human customs, to prove the impossibility of any absolute social or ethical code:

If nature enfolds within the bounds of her ordinary progress, like all other things, also the beliefs, judgments, and opinions of men; if they have their rotation, their season, their birth, their death, like cabbages; if heaven moves and rolls them at its will, what magisterial and permanent authority are we attributing to them? (II. 12, *Apologie:* Frame, p. 433)[36]

This may be matched from Agrippa's *De . . . vanitate*; but
Agrippa had nothing of Montaigne's profound sense of time,
change, and the fluidity of perception. The lack of organization in the *Essais* is itself the best demonstration of the
impossibility of all intellectual system. The mind passes from
point to point, subject to subject, heedless of logical relations.
Moreover, it is itself in a state of flux:

> My history needs to be adapted to the moment. I may presently change,
> not only by chance, but also by intention. This is a record of various
> and changeable occurrences, and of irresolute and, when it so befalls,
> contradictory ideas: whether I am different myself, or whether I take
> hold of my subjects in different circumstances and aspects. So, all in
> all, I may indeed contradict myself now and then; but truth, as Demades
> said, I do not contradict. (III. 2, *Du repentir*: Frame, p. 611)[37]

So much for inductive knowledge. Derived knowledge is
no more reliable. Here too Montaigne uses Agrippa's arguments and even his examples, but with a new force and
subtlety. Just as customs clash, so do authorities. Besides,
they prove unreliable even when considered singly. They
depend on a self-propagated structure of words, unrelated to
the truth of experience, surviving only through totemic sanctity or the promise of practical benefits:

> Our disputes are purely verbal. . . . We exchange one word for another
> word, often more unknown. I know better what is man than I know
> what is animal, or mortal, or rational. To satisfy one doubt, they give
> me three; it is the Hydra's head. (III. xiii, *De l'experience*: Frame,
> pp. 818–19)[38]

Occasionally Montaigne may appear to grant a value, even
a great value, to genuine learning: '. . . in its true use it is
man's most noble and powerful acquisition' (III. 8, *De l'art
de conferer*: Frame, p. 707).[39] But against every such assertion can be pitted a hundred supporting Socrates' declaration,
quoted in the *Apologie de Raimond Sebond*: 'he knew this
much, that he knew nothing' (Frame, p. 370).[40] On the
whole, Montaigne seems to subscribe to academic Pyrrhon-
ism, the complete denial of knowledge: 'For we are born to
quest after truth; to possess it belongs to a greater power'
(III. 8, *De l'art de conferer*: Frame, p. 708).[41]
Human and animal intelligence are compared at great

length in the *Apologie*, to the grave detriment of the former. (Agrippa had only a few sentences on the subject, in the course of praising the ass.) Such a comparison opens up the question of man's place in the universe. Montaigne deals a blow to that most cherished premiss of Renaissance idealism, that man was not confined to any fixed place in the chain of being.

> He feels and sees himself lodged here, amid the mire and dung of the world, nailed and riveted to the worst, the deadest, and the most stagnant part of the universe . . .; and in his imagination he goes planting himself above the circle of the moon, and bringing the sky down beneath his feet. It is by the vanity of this same imagination that he equals himself to God, attributes to himself divine characteristics . . . (II. 12, *Apologie*: Frame, pp. 330–1)[42]

There is in Montaigne a constant humbling sense of *little* man, dwarfed by the universe and wondering at its ways. Pride is as ludicrous as it is reprehensible:

> Philosophy seems to me never to have such an easy game as when she combats our presumption and vanity, when she honestly admits her uncertainty, weakness, and ignorance. It seems to me that the nursing mother of the falsest opinions, public and private, is the over-good opinion man has of himself. (II. 17, *De la praesumption*: Frame, pp. 480–1)[43]

Scepticism carries other consequences too. One of these we had met in Agrippa: a *docta ignorantia* in which we accept upon faith the mysteries of revealed religion.

> It is not by reasoning or by our understanding that we have received our religion; it is by external authority and command. The weakness of our judgment helps us more in this than its strength, and our blindness more than our clear-sightedness. It is by the mediation of our ignorance more than of our knowledge that we are learned with that divine learning. (II. 12, *Apologie*: Frame, p. 369)[44]

As not uncommonly, Sceptical thought leads Montaigne to subscribe to a long tradition of Fideism.

The same humility and self-subordination leads to the curious but established premiss that the Sceptic, far from being an anarchic disruptor of society and learning, is as a rule an entrenched conservative. Since he cannot arrive at absolute truth, or declare one man's values to be more valid than another's, he proposes an ideal of toleration. Also, a uniform social order is required to preserve peace in all this diversity. No one can be permitted to disturb the common weal by introducing dissent. More pragmatically, or cynically, custom is to be valued and preserved as being man's best working substitute for knowledge. It argues the emptiness of philosophic pretensions, but it also provides the best guarantee for intellectual as well as social stability. 'People are right to give the tightest possible barriers to the human mind . . . They bridle and bind it with religions, laws, customs, science, precepts, mortal and immortal punishments and rewards; . . .' (II. 12, *Apologie*: Frame, p. 419.)[45]

However, adherence to custom is only half Montaigne's philosophy; for, as he himself demonstrates at such length, customs differ so widely between communities that it is impossible to lay down any absolute canons. Each community should follow its own customs; but this must be balanced by permitting each man to follow his own inclinations to the extent commensurate with public peace. This is the 'libertine' ideal for which Montaigne is principally celebrated. It exists as an ironic contradiction beneath his advocacy of discipline and uniformity. It forms for him the ultimate, undeniable reality:

> This is the way men behave. We let laws and precepts go their own way, we take another; not only because our character is dissolute, but often also because our opinion and judgment oppose them . . .
> . . . the same workman publishes rules of temperance, and publishes at the same time amorous and licentious writings. And Xenophon, in the bosom of Clinias, wrote against Aristippic sensuality. (III. 9, *De la vanité*: Frame, p. 757)[46]

This passage may also serve to illustrate another important matter. It gives particularly clear expression to a notable view, already seen in Rabelais, of the relation of mind and body. The union of the two in man is, of course, probably as old a concept as any in European thought; but in the Platonic–Christian tradition the two had been represented as opposed and distinct principles, merely residing within the same being or entity. The one could thus be abnegated, largely or even totally, to allow full expression to the other: *feritas* had to be curbed to release *divinitas*, the body 'bruised to pleasure soul'. Body and soul, this world and the next, could be

synthesized in the total world-scheme, but in the individual
life or the path of spiritual ascent they could only be conceived in alternation and opposition.

In Montaigne, however, the two principles are in the
closest possible relation—chemically compounded, so to
speak. There is no question of denying the body to bring out
our highest and most essential humanity; this humanity
resides in the very combination of the two elements, creating
the total entity of man:

We seek other conditions because we do not understand the use of our
own, and go outside of ourselves because we do not know what it is like
inside. Yet there is no use our mounting on stilts, for on stilts we must
still walk on our own legs. And on the loftiest throne in the world we
are still sitting only on our own rump.
The most beautiful lives, to my mind, are those that conform to the
common human pattern, with order, but without miracle and without
eccentricity. (III. 13, *De l'experience*: Frame, p. 857)[47]

This new importance of the body might occasionally
create a lusty, near-pagan idealization of the natural man, as
in a brief, brilliant phase of Renaissance art. Rarely, it might
grant to the body participation in the glories awaiting the
soul, as in Erasmus' interpretation of the text of Paul (1
Corinthians 15: 42–50):

Paul [puts] two men in the same man, so conjoined that neither may be
divided from the other either in heaven or hell, but also so disparate
that the death of one is the life of the other. (*Enchiridion militis
Christiani*, Ch. 6: Himelick, p. 73)[48]

The hope of a celestial body thus runs counter to the general
reviling of the fleshly body, as later in this very section of the
Enchiridion. Most often in Renaissance thought, the importance accorded to the body appears to create an unheroic
humility—which may however be coupled, as in Montaigne,
with a pride in the honesty with which it is expressed. Man is
not so grand as he would be, could he become a creature of
pure spirit. He must carry about with him the grosser reality
of his physical existence; his only happiness lies in the satisfaction of his natural impulses. He can snatch only such
strength and grace as is compatible with that basic condition
of his being.

Therefore Montaigne proposes, in relatively moderate

form, the supreme validity of the natural, especially physical, impulses which had earlier found an extreme and flamboyant vindicator in Rabelais. There is nothing Gargantuan about Montaigne's cannibals. Rather, natural impulse readily coincides in them with the restraints of communal custom, for their laws are the laws of nature:

The laws of nature still rule them, very little corrupted by ours; and they are in such a state of purity that I am sometimes vexed that they were unknown earlier, in the days when there were men able to judge them better than we. (I. 31, *Des cannibales*: Frame, p. 153)[49]

It is at a deeper level that the cannibals share in the Rabelaisian ideal of life—the belief in the ultimate beneficence, and benevolence, of unrestrained natural impulse. Without understanding the order of nature, the cannibals participate in it. This ideal of natural virtue argues for an implicit sympathy between human impulse and the order of nature. But if such a sympathy exists, it is unfathomable; the natural order is assumed but not understood. Man may indeed serve nature, blend into her schemes; he cannot master her, either intellectually or technically. The libertine ideal works within human limits, deliberately excluding all thought of its possible metaphysical dimensions.

In fact, Montaigne proposes an ideal of human conduct and virtue not supported by any intelligible moral or cosmic order—or, at most, an order assumed by custom, necessary for a social or intellectual contract, but not authenticated by philosophic conviction. As Auerbach puts it:

. . . among all his contemporaries he had the clearest conception of the problem of man's self-orientation; that is, the task of making oneself at home in existence without fixed points of support. . . . (N)ow the tragic appears as the highly personal tragedy of the individual, and moreover, compared with antiquity, as far less restricted by traditional ideas of the limits of fate, the cosmos, natural forces, political forms, and man's inner being.[50]

Montaigne's libertinism is best defined in its obverse or negative aspect: each man has his own limited perception, which provides him with his personal stock of wisdom. He can only be true to his own perceptions and conclusions, follow his own bent, while admitting that these are valid for himself alone. This partial, uncertain view of truth is an

individual's only rightful concern, the only subject on which
he can fitly express himself—as Montaigne does in his *Essais*.
The basic spirit of Montaigne's writings is an interest in the
human state founded on the littleness of man: he must
express himself because he is not fit to express anything
greater than himself. This preoccupation with the self is the
very reverse of anthropocentric; rather, it implies the awesome
mystery of a *pluralité des mondes*:

> Your reason is never more plausible and on more solid ground than
> when it convinces you of the plurality of worlds: . . . Now if there are
> many worlds, . . . how do we know whether the principles and rules of
> this one apply similarly to the others? . . . (W)hy do we claim title to
> existence, on account of that instant that is only a flash in the infinite
> course of an eternal night . . .? (II. 12, *Apologie*: Frame, pp. 390-1)[51]

The basic significance of Montaigne's thought, as I conceive
it, may now be spelt out. Needless to say, he comes too late
to be a major source or influence; his unique importance is as
an epitome. He enunciates certain principles whose subter-
ranean presence in much Renaissance thought might otherwise
have been felt but never defined, still less worked out as a
connected development. The full sweep of Montaigne's
Scepticism incorporates two currents of thought: assertion of
human independence (quite a different proposition from his
importance, achievement, or perfectibility), and its subjugation to a superior principle, often one accepted on implicit
faith. An equivocal, often hesitant resort to humanity,
opposed by a deep and most unequivocal distrust of man:
this seems to constitute the double movement of most
Renaissance thought. It is important to note that both these
trends emanate from the same nucleus. Again and again in
humanist and Protestant thought, we find the two strands
mingling with an intricacy that suggests just this common
origin. Here in Montaigne we have this nucleus of concepts
clearly exposed — and its general nature is patently doubt-
ridden, humble, unheroic.

II. *Humanists and Reformers*

1. *Neoplatonism: Nicholas of Cusa, Ficino, Pico della Mirandola*

The ambivalent nature of humanist philosophy may be strikingly illustrated from a number of prominent Neoplatonists. This is particularly telling because these philosophers contributed greatly to the body of thought that gave a new importance to man in the Renaissance. One cannot deny the originality and, in some respects, the revolutionary optimism of their ideas; yet their equivocal nature may emerge from a closer examination.

In practically all orthodox Christian doctrine there is, to put it simply, a great gulf between God and man. Creation is not a process of spontaneous emanation from the Godhead but a voluntary and gratuitous exercise of benevolent divine power. There is thus a difference in kind between Creator and creature. The Good is immutable and necessary, but human existence—though governed by God's firm and preordained scheme—is in the last resort contingent. God is infinite and eternal; man is finite, mortal (or rather, deathless in his soul, but blinded and confined within a mortal body).

It is therefore impossible for man to approach to any true knowledge of God: 'natural theology' can only demonstrate God's existence, not his essence. God's will is immutable, omnipotent, and all-benevolent; man's will is wavering, subject after the Fall to the domination of passion, of the 'inferior self':

> Great art Thou, O Lord, and greatly to be praised; great is Thy power, and Thy wisdom infinite. And Thee would man praise; man, but a particle of Thy creation; man, that bears about him his mortality, the witness of his sin, the witness, that Thou resistest the proud, yet would man praise Thee . . . (Augustine, *Confessions* I)

Platonism proper, and Neoplatonism in its Christian varieties, had tended to widen the gap between divine and human; but in the fifteenth century, we find a new Platonism that bids fair to close it. This new development finds its first notable exponent in Nicholas of Cusa (1401–64).

In his epistemology, Cusanus is a fairly orthodox late Scholastic. We may, he says, acquire knowledge by analogy, by comparing an object of inquiry with 'an object presupposed certain' and measuring the distance between the two (*De docta ignorantia*, I. i). But no two things are exactly similar (ibid., I. iii and II. i), and moreover, all matter is in a state of flux (I. ix). Therefore we cannot attain to perfect knowledge even of finite and material things.

This obviously precludes all knowledge of divine or infinite matters, between which and finite entities there is no proportion or comparison. 'Therefore a finite intellect cannot precisely arrive at the truth of things by means of comparison' (I. iii).[1] Our knowledge of these matters does not pass beyond 'conjectures':

As a result, every positive assertion of truth made by man is conjecture; for increase in our understanding of truth cannot reach completion. Thus, while in practice our understanding does not bear any comparative relation to the greatest knowledge of all, unattainable by man, the undetermined state of our feeble understanding introduces conjectures into our statements of what is true, removing them from the purity of truth. (*De coniecturis*, Prologue)[2]

In this Sceptical gloom, the only light is that of revelation and enlightened nescience. To attain to a knowledge of the infinite we must not simply go beyond empirical knowledge but systematically reverse its premises, attain to knowledge by paradox. The line will become a triangle, circle, and sphere; accident will be substance, body spirit, movement rest (*De docta ignorantia*, I. x). Cusanus revives the concept of 'negative theology' given currency by the Pseudo-Dionysius in the sixth century: 'It cannot be otherwise known than as being higher than all knowledge and thus unknowable, inexpressible by any speech, incomprehensible by any intellect, immeasurable by any measure, illimitable by any limits . . .' (*Idiota: de sapientia*).[3]

So far, Cusanus seems to be following the usual path of the Sceptic and Fideist in describing the ascent of the soul to God. This may be conceived in terms of Platonist mysticism, as in the first dialogue of *De sapientia*. But he has a simultaneous and equally Platonist concept of the descent of God into the created universe—not only in the voluntary and exclusive act of Incarnation, but in a constant and all-pervasive emanation that is almost pantheistically conceived: 'Creation is seen to be nothing else but the existence of God in all things' (*De docta ignorantia*, II. ii).[4]

The essence of all finite things is infinite (ibid., I. xvii). The plurality of things is derived, in a manner the reason cannot grasp, from the unity of God:

> It is as though there were a face in its own image, which is then reproduced from itself—in distant and close forms, as the images multiply. (I do not speak of distance in space but an increasing departure from the truth of the face, for multiplication is not possible without this happening.) (Ibid., II. iii)[5]

Thus the universe becomes a likeness of the absolute, '*similitudo absoluti*'. Further, this 'likeness' is wrought in the medium of finite being that (though finite) is itself a manifestation of the absolute and has no existence apart from it; like the reflection in a mirror, postulating that the mirror has no independent existence before or after the reflection (ibid., II. ii).

The material world is of its nature contingent, imperfect, of no positive or independent reality; yet it partakes of reality and of Being itself. Cusanus refuses to admit a dichotomy between the worlds of matter and idea. Instead he interprets the usual Platonist terms of this dichotomy so as to grant the two aspects equal validity, as two phases of the same existence:

> [It is] one and the same thing in different modes of being, by its nature existing in the intelligence earlier than in matter: not earlier in time, but in the sense in which the reason behind an object naturally precedes the object itself. (Ibid., II. ix)[6]

In other words, all matter is inherently spiritual. The divine is present in the human, not by an external infusion of grace, but as an essential condition of material being. Man can thus approximate to the divine by a holy principle within him. This is the basis of the concept of man as 'the contracted maximum': 'God and creature, the absolute and the limited' (ibid., III. ii)[7]—finite, but perfect in the realization of his finite nature, and thus touching infinity.

Man occupies a particular position on the scale of being; but because this position is an intermediate one, bridging or comprehending all categories of existence, he also has a unique capacity for ranging freely along the scale. The potential of the entire created universe can be realized and perfected in him, united with the absolute or maximum. To put it another way, in whatever scale of finite being the infinite may wish to realize its own perfection, human nature can serve as a medium, 'so that in this humanity itself all things would achieve their highest grade' (ibid., III. iii).[8]

But Cusanus grants man this freedom *within the limits of his manhood*. He can embody any order of being, realize any element of his potential, in the microcosm of his own existence, but he cannot affect the order of the macrocosm:

The realm of humanity embraces God and the universe within its own human power. Man can therefore be a human God and, as God, can, in a manner appropriate to human nature, be a human angel, a human animal, a human lion or bear or anything else. For within the limits of human power, all things exist after their own fashion. (*De coniecturis*, II. xiv)[9]

Within his mind, in terms of his own humanity, man re-enacts the divine roles of creator, controller, and preserver (*creator, rector, conservator*). Just as on the universal plane, all things seek their end in the absolute, so the *activae creationes humanitatis* have no end save to enhance the human state, to reflect the universe in the mind of man as in a contracted absolute: 'But man directs all this back towards himself, so that he can understand, rule and preserve himself. Thus man comes near to the condition of the divine, where all things rest in eternal peace' (*De coniecturis*, II. xiv).[10]

But when Cusanus first explains this, in the very first chapter of *De coniecturis*, it follows close upon his initial premiss that these creations of the human mind are ultimately invalid. They are, after all, 'conjectures', a mere reflection of divine realities (ibid., I. i). Here indeed is a paradoxical coupling of divine power and human limitation, divine power manifesting itself in the necessarily imperfect medium of humanity, thereby negating its divine nature.

Every individual, or group of individuals, belonging to finite humanity is equally removed from the unattainable infinite. In a more positive aspect, every individual or group is equally permeated by that infinite. Christ alone can resolve this contradiction and achieve the full perfection of humanity. Faith in man and reliance upon God are strangely blended in this doctrine.

This is not a mere transitional phase. Renaissance humanism is essentially ambivalent. Even at its brightest, it habitually admits the limits of human potential; and at any moment, these sober reflections might come to predominate, reviving and even surpassing the medieval *contemptus mundi*. This shows in the work of the most celebrated school of Renaissance Neoplatonists: the Florentine Academy.

Perhaps no other Renaissance polymath has fired our imagination so much as Giovanni Pico della Mirandola. His learning and brilliance, even the flamboyant challenge of his nine hundred *Conclusiones*, his early death—all this combines to present him as the flower of Renaissance scholarship. His work may be thought to constitute one of the most daring and hopeful assaults of the human intellect on the universe.

Such energy and optimism is indeed announced in his classic *Oration on the Dignity of Man*, composed as the introduction to a projected debate on the *Conclusiones*. Pico's premises resemble those with which Cusanus upheld man's power and importance. As Trinkaus demonstrates, they are also anticipated by Ficino in his *Theologia Platonica*.[11]

Man is the most fortunate and wonderful of creatures, *felicissimum proindeque dignum omni admiratione*, precisely because he is not of the highest, angelic order. Even the angels are confined to their single grade of being. Man, on the contrary, has no fixed position on the Great Chain, but can range up and down the scale. After his creation, God tells him:

. . . to the end that according to thy longing and according to thy judgment thou mayest have and possess what abode, what form, and what functions thou thyself shalt desire . . . Thou, constrained by no limits, in accordance with thine own free will, in whose hand We have placed thee, shalt ordain for thyself the limits of thy nature. (*De hominis dignitate*: Forbes, pp. 224–5)[12]

Thus for Pico as for Cusanus, man can re-create the nature of the universe within himself, in terms of his humanity: he can sink to a brute or rise to be 'an angel and the son of God' (Forbes, p. 225).[13] He can even progress beyond all orders of created beings into the centre of his own unity where he is made one with God. And this he achieves by his own will, 'as though the maker and moulder of thyself' (Forbes, p. 225).[14]

It seems impossible to celebrate humanity in more rhapsodic terms. Yet the pristine idealism of such passages is circumscribed even in the *Oratio*, and still more so in other works. The actual process by which man attains divinity argues quite a different approach to his prowess and virtue.

Pico grants the faculty of natural reason a strictly defined and limited role to play. Even in so far as he admits knowledge as an instrument of spiritual progress, he very largely identifies it with 'authority' and revelation. We cannot attain to cherubic wisdom by our own powers: '. . . we who are but flesh and know of the things of earth, let us go to the ancient fathers who, inasmuch as they were familiar and conversant with these matters, can give sure and altogether trustworthy testimony' (ibid.: Forbes, p. 228).[15]

Even such wisdom, the way of the cherubim, is no more than a *medius* to the love of God in the seraphs, and the judgement and active power of the thrones. This gradation of spiritual achievement is related to a gradation of faculties with the disciplines appropriate to each. Moral science and dialectic are followed by the successive stages of *naturalis philosophia*, the knowledge of natural things achieved by man's own powers. This leads us to the crowning happiness of theology (*theologica felicitate consummabimur*).[16] Man now abandons his natural powers for revelation through grace: 'Let us be driven, Fathers, let us be driven by the frenzies of Socrates, that they may so throw us into ecstasy as to put our mind and ourselves in God. Let us be driven by them, if we have first done what is in our power' (ibid.: Forbes, p. 234).[17]

Thus in *De ente et uno*, Pico can decry all categories of knowledge: sensible, rational, even the 'intellectual' cognition of the angels. He quotes the Pseudo-Dionysius to advocate a 'negative theology' as Cusanus had done. Knowledge as the human intellect conceives it, is light; God dwells beyond, in a darkness beyond comprehension:

. . . blinded by the darkness of divine splendour let us cry out with the Prophet, 'I have become weak in thy courts, O Lord,'[18] finally saying only this about God, that he is unintelligibly and ineffably above everything most perfect which we can either speak or conceive of him. (*De ente et uno*, ch. 5: Miller, p. 50)[19]

Pico's frequent praise of man's angelic powers breaks down in the detailed system of the *Heptaplus*, an esoteric sevenfold interpretation of Genesis. Here too, man's unique status is ascribed to his 'microcosmic' nature, his union of all the orders of existence (*Heptaplus*, V. 6). He is *caelestium et terrestrium vinculus et nodus*, 'the bond and link between heaven and earth' (ibid., V. 7).[20] But this makes him no less subservient to the divine law, with peculiar punishment if by his free will he abuses his privileged station.

By his own philosophy man can only attain to natural felicity, the fulfilment of his own nature with its limited participation in the divine. True and eternal felicity requires the help of grace. To make his point, Pico invokes the Platonic doctrine of circular motion: grace is the power that draws the highest created beings, men and angels, to return to their divine source. They cannot ascend there by their own effort (ibid., VIII, Proem).

Pico goes further. In his Cabalistic parallel between the six days of creation and the six thousand years of human history, the initially 'void and empty' earth is likened to the corrupt, sinful nature of man after the Fall (ibid., VII. 1). Over this waste, however, the Spirit of the Lord brooded still, and gradually carried out its creative process of human redemption. Here, man is not master over his own fate; the crucial element in his salvation is the creation of the sun and the moon—that is, the coming of Christ and the foundation of the Church (ibid., VII. 4).

In Christ alone does man realize his full divine potential (ibid., I. 7). Once more we find ourselves very close to Cusanus. Again, in VI. 7, in his account of the Sacrament, Pico asserts that man cannot be united to God except through Christ. There is no great gulf between God and man here— indeed, the gulf is bridged by man's divine potential. But this potential was destroyed by the Fall, and could thenceforth only be realized in Christ. Other men can partake of that perfection only through Christ, entering by baptism into the life of the Holy Spirit (ibid., VII. 7): in other words, through faith in revealed doctrine and surrender to a 'humanity' superior to their own.

The extreme importance of the theory of love in Renaissance Neoplatonism carries its own implicit surrender of human values. The creature always tends to find its goal and perfection in the Creator, the emanation to return to its origin: such is the fundamental principle of Platonic love. But this is only the latter half of a circular movement commencing in the Creator, in God.

This Divine Beauty creates in everything love, that is, desire for itself . . . (T)here is one continuous attraction, beginning with God, going to the world and ending at last in God, an attraction which returns to the same place whence it began as though in a kind of circle. (Ficino, Commentary on Plato's *Symposium*: the second speech, Ch. 2)[21]

Translated into Christian terms, this means that the movement towards salvation commences in the will of God, the gift of grace.[22] Man's free will (which Pico had so stressed in *De hominis dignitate*) is ultimately controlled by the disposition of the universe. Earlier, Lorenzo Valla had taken the same stand in his dialogue *On Free Will* (*De libero arbitrio*). So had Salutati, on Trinkaus's evidence.[23] In fact, this was a standard humanist solution to the problem of fate and free will—to conceive of man as 'the alert and conscious agent of the divine will'.[24]

Obviously, such a solution rests on a very fine balance between fate and free will. The effort of love which raises man to the divine is similarly ambiguous. The ultimate surrender of the soul to God becomes a voluntary death, a loss of one's wordly identity:

. . . whoever lives for love, first dies to everything else. And if love has in it a certain perfection, . . . it is impossible to arrive at that perfection without first dying with regard to the more imperfect things. (Lorenzo de' Medici, Commentary on his own sonnet sequence)[25]

It is true that in Ficino, the lover does not lose his personality by the act of surrender: he 'lives again in God and there finds his true self, and knows himself as he is known . . . The two lives, God's and man's, are made one while yet remaining two.'[26] But this distinction of entity does not dispense with the lover's need to discard his 'less perfect' interests, to deny every element in his composite personality except the divine seed. The assertion of the divine principle in man—a spiritual-ization, even deification, in Platonic terms—amounts at the same time to a loss of individuality, a death.

Only such death can revive the divine light within us and enable the intellect to achieve its true end, the knowledge of God and the attainment of its own perfection. The mind in its essential nature is capable of grasping universal truth and being, of recreating the universe in terms of its own exis-tence: '. . . the intellect, which is, as it were, the lowest of all supernatural things and the highest of natural things, can take on the spiritual forms of all things and become all' (*Quaes-tiones quinque de mente*: Burroughs, p. 200).[27] This is still reminiscent of Cusanus, and, as we have seen, it is repeated in Pico.

The universe is entirely infinite, *'penitus infinitum'*. The soul can conceive of the highest perfection only because of a certain affinity with it. Infinity is the origin and end of the soul:

Certainly, the effect nearest to the cause becomes most similar to the cause. Consequently, the rational soul in a certain manner possesses the excellence of infinity and eternity. If this were not the case, it would never characteristically incline toward the infinite. (Ibid.: Burroughs, p. 202)[28]

But here on earth this quest for infinity involves the soul in an eternal conflict. It has two lights. One is the divine, turning the soul towards God and illuminating it with its rays:

But this first light, when it is received in the substance of the soul, which was formerly naturally shapeless, becomes darker, and, being attracted to the suitability of the soul, becomes natural and proper to it, and therefore, through this light, as being on an equal plane with itself, the soul sees itself, and things below it, that is, all bodies. (Com-mentary on the *Symposium*: Fourth speech, Ch. 4)[29]

Hence man becomes for Ficino the eternal Prometheus,

striving for the heavenly fire of wisdom which we cannot attain as long as we are 'weighted down by the burden of a most troublesome body'. Behind this eternal ambivalence lies the Fall:

Indeed, we have been placed outside the order of first nature, and—O sorrow!—live and suffer contrary to the order of nature. The more easily the first man was able to receive happiness when in the beginning he was entirely devoted to God, the more easily he has lost ease itself when thereafter he turned against God. (*Quaestiones quinque*: Burroughs, p. 209)[30]

This recognizes the reality of the human will, but also the corruption of that will. Salvation lies once more in a completion of the circle, a return to God: Promethean man will suffer 'until the time comes when he is carried back to that same place from which he received the fire, so that, just as he is now urged on to seek the whole by that one beam of celestial light, he will then be entirely filled with the whole light' (ibid.: Burroughs, p. 208).[31]

Ficino concludes the *Five Questions* with a promise of immortality, when the soul shall be 'either free from the body or in a temperate immortal celestial body' (Burroughs, p. 211).[32] This obviously harks back to 1 Corinthians 15. Meanwhile, our earthly life is a ceaseless frustration, permitting neither sensual nor spiritual satisfaction.

Truly, reason is always uncertain, vacillating and distressed; and since it is nowhere at rest while thus affected, it certainly never gains possession of its desired end or permits sense to take possession of its proper end which is already present. (Ibid.: Burroughs, p. 208)[33]

I have dealt with Ficino after Pico, although he was the elder of the two, because the *Five Questions* seems to epitomize the Renaissance concept of human limitation. Like other Renaissance philosophers of man, the Neoplatonists appear to have a choice between an ordered universe with a circumscribed role for man, and a boundless aspiration that strains this ordered universe. When the leaders of the Reformation set out to demonstrate man's restricted role in an ordered, even inflexible, divine scheme, they did not have to destroy humanistic thought. They had merely to adapt to their requirements a not uncongenial frame of ideas.

2. Sin and Fall: Erasmus and other Humanists

We have seen how Montaigne ascribes man's unavailing quest for wisdom to pride, which makes him overstep the ordained limits to his faculties. The inevitable corollary to this idea is expressed several times in the *Apologie de Raimond Sebond*: 'The urge to increase in wisdom and knowledge was the first downfall of the human race; it was the way by which man hurled himself into eternal damnation' (Frame, p. 368).[34] Interesting too is the way Montaigne uses the story of Babel, one of the most significant Old Testament antitypes of the Fall itself.

It was for the chastisement of our pride and the instruction of our wretchedness and incapacity that God produced the disorder and confusion of the ancient tower of Babel . . .

The diversity of idioms and languages with which he troubled that work, what else is it but that infinite and perpetual altercation and discordance of opinions and reasons, which accompanies and embroils the vain construction of human knowledge? (Ibid.: Frame, pp. 414-15)[35]

Surrender to faith, to the gifts of revelation, now appears in its full accustomed implications as a spiritual necessity as well as an intellectual one. Montaigne writes: '. . . whoever will see man without flattering him, will see in him neither efficacy nor any faculty that savours of anything but death and earth. The more we give, and owe, and render to God, the more like Christians we act' (ibid.: Frame, p. 415).[36] The moral and intellectual indictments run *pari passu*: sin and folly merge into each other.

The association of man's innate ignorance with the Fall was, of course, traditional to Christianity:

. . . the whole human race has been condemned in its first origin . . . Is not this proved by the profound and dreadful ignorance which produces all the errors that enfold the children of Adam, and from which no man can be delivered without toil, pain and fear? (Augustine, *The City of God*, XXII. 22)

A thousand years later we find a close echo, though somewhat more moderately expressed, in Thomas à Kempis:

For the little strength which remaineth is but as a little spark hidden under ashes.

This is the selfsame natural reason encompassed with much darkness, having yet the judgment of good and evil, and the discernment of truth and falsehood, though it be unable to fulfil all that it approves; neither doth it now enjoy the full light of truth, nor the former healthfulness of its affections. (*The Imitation of Christ*, III. lv. 2)

Aquinas defines the concept in more detail in *Summa Theologica*, Ia. 94. The first man did not know all things; but he had knowledge of all natural things, 'which it is natural for man to be instructed in', and such supernatural things as were 'needed for the direction of human life in that state'.[37] Also, he would have gained more knowledge—both of supernatural things by further revelation, and of natural things, as experience confirmed what he first knew speculatively. For primitive man was created in grace, and hence lived in a state of rationality—that is to say, his passions were controlled by his reason. Hence he could not be deceived: the fact that woman was deceived was owing to her having already sinned in interior pride.

One of the commonest methods of referring to the Fall was in terms of its fundamental effect, the overthrow of reason by the passions—that is, the domination of *feritas* in man's composite nature, whereas the original purpose of God was to have developed the *intellectus*, the angelic element. 'For since', says Erasmus,

wisdom is no other than to be governed by reason, while folly is to be moved at the whim of the passions, Jupiter, to the end, obviously, that the life of mankind should not be sad and harsh, put in—how much more of passions than of reason? Well, the proportions run about one pound to half an ounce. (*The Praise of Folly*: Hudson, pp. 22–3)[38]

A few sentences later, the Fall-theme is reinforced by a discussion of woman, the instrument of the Fall, alleged to be bestial rather than rational in character.

Pride made man aspire to a knowledge beyond his condition. The resulting punishment deranged his faculties and destroyed even his earlier rational powers, so that every attempt at knowledge now re-enacts the Fall, ending in frustration and a damning exhibition of pride. By extending the concept, Erasmus associates folly also with the original Fall of the Angels, in its thin classical disguise of the Giants' attack on Heaven.

One of the finest fables of Renaissance humanism is the

parable of Cain told by Erasmus at an Oxford supper-table on his first English visit. Cain heard of the splendid wheat crops of Paradise, and went to beg some grains from the angel at the gate. God was not particular about such small matters, he argued; besides, was not the angel tired of his dull, fruitless vigil? Even fallen man was better off, for he could at least enjoy the bounty of the earth.

We are free to wander here and there, wherever our heart desires . . . so that if we were allowed to live here eternally, we would not greatly yearn for this paradise of yours. We are afflicted by diseases, but a remedy for these will be found by human diligence . . . There is nothing that tenacious industry cannot overcome.[39]

Thus the angel was seduced, and Cain got good harvests of the paradisial wheat. But God, angered at his audacity, sent storms and vermin to destroy the grain: 'The guarding angel was transformed and, because he was befriending man, confined within a human body. When Cain tried to placate God with a burnt-offering of fruit, and the smoke would not rise, he realised that His wrath was implacable, and despaired' (Letter to John Sixtin, 1499).[40]

Beneath the light Erasmian elegance of touch, this is in all essentials the view of Marsilio Ficino. Man is capable, in an almost tragic way, of attaining to a height that he cannot maintain, a perfection that cannot be fitly embodied in his nature.

If you had not been given a body, you would be part of Godhead; if you had not been endowed with this mind of yours, you would be a beast.

These two natures, so dissimilar to each other, the Supreme Artist once had united in felicitous harmony; but the serpent, enemy of peace, alienated them with jarring discord, so that now they can neither be separated without the utmost torment nor live together without continuous warfare. (*Enchiridion militis Christiani*, Ch. 4: Himelick, p. 63)[41]

Such rationality as man does possess is for Erasmus a purely ethical force. For both physical and metaphysical enquiries he has nothing but scorn, and theological speculation is given very narrow limits to play in. How well this conforms to the consciousness of the age may be seen from the credo of Barbatius the Protestant, agreeing in all important respects with that of Aulus the Catholic, in the colloquy *Inquisitio de fide*:

> Thus it is that, not trusting my own strength, I depend entirely on him who can do all things. When I consider his wisdom, I attribute nothing to my own, but I believe all things are done by him perfectly righteously and perfectly justly, even though by human judgment they may seem unreasonable or unjust.[42]

Erasmus therefore distrusts dogma as the exercise of empty human ingenuity, unrelated to the divine reality, which is unknowable:

> There are innumerable questions about this sacrament: how transubstantiation takes place, how accidents subsist without a subject; . . . and a great many others, which it befits those with trained faculties to consider rationally among themselves. For the common people it is enough to believe . . . (Letter to the Bishop of Hildesheim: 15 March 1530)[43]

Most questions in theology are what may be called 'open questions', on which scripture yields no dogma. Each man may therefore decide them by the light of his own reason—which will ideally, of its free will, acknowledge its own weakness and entrust man's salvation to God's grace and the premisses of the established faith. This is the substance of Erasmus' *De libero arbitrio*.

The faculty of reason is thus placed by Erasmus in *opposition* to the pseudo-rationalism which creates the complexities of speculation posing as dogma. Reason, by contrast, is a simple and natural force, which does not probe too far or presume to supply absolute knowledge, but only a working interpretation of the truths of revelation. The pinnacle of knowledge is the gift of revelation, to be accepted, not understood.

The same humility shows also in Erasmus' view of man's moral nature and salvation. There is no doubt that Erasmus 'believes in free will', as a most important safeguard to human dignity. What is less often noted is that the function he ascribes to free will is all the same a very limited one: 'Nor in the meanwhile does our will achieve nothing, although it does not attain the things that it seeks without the help of grace. But since our own efforts are so puny, the whole is ascribed to God' (*De libero arbitrio*: Rupp, p. 79).[44] Man cannot be set on the path to salvation except by the power of grace, nor can he be finally saved without it. By his free will he can merely open his spirit to the action of grace. These are Thomist premises: the difference is only one of emphasis.

One must not understate this difference, of course. Erasmus asserts the basic goodness of man in a way notably different from the standard Christian view. Christ effected the 'restoration of human nature originally well formed' (*Paraclesis*),[45] and not totally destroyed even by the Fall. But in a general way, the optimistic spirit breathing through his ethical writings is belied by all his explicit statements of doctrine. He admits the ambivalence of human nature, the weight of *feritas* which prevents man from realizing his spiritual power on his own:

> Because the body is itself visible, it takes pleasure in visible objects; because it is mortal, it pursues temporal objects; because it has weight and substance, its tendency is downward. The soul, on the other hand, mindful of its celestial quality, yearns mightily to ascend, and struggles against its earthly encumbrance; . . . (S)in has evilly corrupted what was happily created, injecting the venom of discord into things once well attuned. (*Enchiridion*, Ch. 4: Himelick, p. 64)[46]

Such peace can be restored only through grace.

I have no wish to deny the humanistic spirit of Erasmus' writings, his cultivation of learning and his very considerable faith in the power of reason. I am only suggesting that these should be viewed in the total context of his thought. If this is done, the optimistic emphases are seen to belie the over-all perspective. In fact, these emphases may as often be supplied by the modern reader as by the author himself. Certain tenets fostering a sense of human power and dignity are varyingly stressed within a world-view traditional, and even Sceptical, in most or all respects.

The same is true of other Christian humanists. John Colet takes up a complex stand, but hardly indulges in any simple faith in human powers. His Commentary on Paul's Epistle to the Romans may be used to explain his position.

To Colet the mind was weak in itself, and weakened further by being 'depressed into this heavy and gloomy body' (*Enarratio in Epistolam . . . ad Romanos*, Ch. IX; Lupton, p. 41).[47] Man may *learn* of God's purpose, but cannot presume to scrutinize it: it lies too far beyond human reason. Colet brings in Sceptical premisses to illustrate this. Sick men cannot taste the goodness in food, tinted glass falsifies colours, noisome vessels befoul their contents: 'everything ultimately becomes similar to its receptacle' (ibid.: Lupton, pp. 42-3).[48] The human vessel is therefore a very weak vessel to hold divine truths. Colet advocates a 'wise foolishness' in the accustomed manner of Christian Scepticism.

Man's moral powers are equally degenerate. Since the Fall of man, reason has been a slave to the senses and passion:

... this animal part of man ... has borne sway in man's estate ...

From its violence and tyranny the soul, that is, the poor inner man, being weak and powerless by reason of Adam's unhappy fall, has been incapable, with all its efforts, of releasing and liberating itself. (Ibid., Ch. VI; Lupton, p. 17)[49]

Hence Mosaic law, though good in itself, was unable to redeem man. It relied on man's own efforts, and man did not have the strength to follow the law; it could only highlight his sinful state. Redemption was possible only through God's grace and the vicarious sacrifice of Christ.[50]

Colet thus forces upon us a sense of man's utter folly and sinfulness, throws him entirely upon the mercy of God. The doctrine of predestination follows naturally from this.

His treatment of predestination is strangely equivocal. It does not appear to dismiss the function of the human will; in fact, the godliness of the elect may be described in strongly active and voluntarist terms: 'These are they who . . . have chased away all the wavering affections of the body; who have rendered the body a light burden, and obedient to reason; who persevere in a firm and steadfast hope . . .; who suffer all things, even the most bitter . . .' (Ibid., Ch. VIII; Lupton, p. 25).[51] There is even a curious suggestion that this election is not conclusive, that it is valid only 'whilst they (the chosen) retain God as their helper' (Ibid., Ch. VIII; Lupton, p. 25):[52] they may subsequently sin and fall from grace. But this is immediately followed by renewed emphasis on the divine purpose and the operation of the Holy Spirit.

Colet glorifies the 'spiritual man', reborn in Christ. Those reborn in this way are themselves so many Christs[53]—and this even though the body remains in conjunction with the soul.

But this ideal is robbed of pure humanity by the vital presence of a third and highest element—the 'embracing spirit', *spiritus complectens* (Lupton, pp. 28, 154), a gift of the Holy Ghost, a power external to ourselves. In the ideal man, the truly human elements are subordinate and the human faculties are disowned: 'Now the *intellect* of the spirit is faith in God; and its *will* is charity and the love of God' (Ibid., Ch. IX: Lupton, p. 46).[54]

These matters must be borne in mind when we consider the happier Platonic aspiration of Colet's Treatises on the Pseudo-Dionysius. Here man may ascend through the stages of the angelic hierarchy to an apprehension of God;[55] he may himself be called 'angel' or 'god'.[56] It is as well to remember that there is little or nothing in this incompatible with the Commentary on Romans. The Platonic ascent, as we saw in connection with the Florentines, argues an abdication of weak human powers and a surrender of personality in the divine. Colet is clearly conscious of the affinities of Christian and Platonic doctrine. In his Commentary on Romans, he brings in the Platonic concept of the 'cycle of love' at a crucial point, and quotes Ficino at length to prove that love transcends knowledge.[57]

Sir Thomas More is an even clearer advocate of faith and humility, increasingly with the years. True, in *Utopia* he declared the potential existence of a universal reason and benevolence in mankind; but as readers have noted, and as indeed the first book (on the state of England at the time) makes clear, he was equally impressed by the impediments in human nature, as well as the near-immovable debris of discredited but extant systems that had to be cleared before reform could be brought about. Thus, in Mason's words, 'what makes the discussion worth having is the *tension* it creates . . . between what reason demands to be done and nature permits to be done.'[58] Thus too, as Mason observes, More stresses the need for discipline to regulate the good life, whereas Rabelais had abjured it in the 'libertine' ideals of the Abbey of Thélème.

More holds to tradition by faith, not reason: concerning the celibacy of the stricter Utopian *religiosi*, for instance, and their preference for hard and unpleasant labour, 'if herein they grounded upon reason they [the other Utopians] would mock them. But now forasmuch as they say they be led to it by religion, they honour and worship them' (Book II).[59] In *A Dialogue of Comfort*, too, the only foundation for comfort is faith—the gift of God's grace (I. ii). The distrust of individual opinion—'false spiritual liberty', the doctrine of the devil —finds its strongest expression in the fable of the Fox, the Ass, and the Wolf (II. xiv). And this distrust of the intellect is expressed with restraint compared to the *contemptus mundi* and the sense of man's spiritual weakness and need for grace. The elaborate metaphor in Book III, of earthly life being an imprisonment, is surely one of the strongest counter-blasts to human ambition ever composed—and from the heart of the first flowering of the Northern Renaissance.

We are dealing not so much with an opposition as an ambivalence in the spirit of the times. Humanism contains within itself elements that can be turned into a contradiction of its own professed spirit. Ultimately, mature Christian humanism, particularly in the North, proves to foster not so much spiritual independence as a sense of humility and need for reliance either on scriptural authority, or on illumination by the direct grace of God. It thus comes close to the premises of Reformation theology.

3. *The Theologians: Scholastic and Protestant*

To consider Protestant doctrine in relation to the humanist spirit, one must first look briefly at the theology of the late Middle Ages. Thirteenth-century scholasticism, particularly at its finest point in St. Thomas Aquinas, raised a noble intellectual system on a harmony of faith and reason. In Aquinas the faculty of reason probably attains the greatest importance it ever reaches in Christian theology. This is not to deny the clear limits placed upon rational apprehension. Within the supra-rational province of revelation, Aquinas yields total obeisance to doctrine and 'authority'. (See *Summa Theologica*, Ia. 1. 2, Ia. 1. 8; *Summa contra Gentiles*, IV. 1.) But the distinctive feature of this supra-rationalism appears in his celebrated and oft-repeated principle that the truth of Christian doctrine may surpass, but it does not oppose, the truth of reason. (See *Sum. Theol.*, IIa. IIae. 8. 2; *Sum. con. Gen.*, I. 7, IV. 1.)

In fact, revelation embraces not merely the *revelata*, or truths inaccessible except by revelation, but equally the *revelabilia*, truths attainable by reason but divulged by revelation as being indispensable to salvation.[60] The doctrine of the *revelabilia* is one strong prop of St. Thomas's celebration of natural reason. Another is the concept of the ladder of being, by which sense-perception may ultimately lead to a real, though inadequate, apprehension of the divine. (See *Sum. Theol.*, Ia. 1. 9; *Sum. con. Gen.*, IV. 1.) And in any case, the truths taught by revelation can then be subjected to rational processes. In brief, the intellect is conceived as an instrument of worship, and theology the dedication to God of a glorious human faculty.

By and large, the Thomist treatment of reason is turned inside-out by the most influential of the later Scholastics. Instead of harmonizing revelation and natural theology, the Scotist doctrine of 'double truth' separates the two. Reason is given great potential power within its proper sphere, for it must be emphasized that Duns Scotus is no Sceptic. On the contrary, he specifically asserts the possibility of certain categories of knowledge by natural means (*Opus Oxonienses*, I D.III Q. iv), even the 'natural' knowledge of certain concepts about God though not of his essence (*Opus Ox.*, D.III Q.i). But in dogmatic and doctrinal issues we are led to a profound distrust of reason. Ockham carries on this trend of thought. Strict *scientia*—obtained by a syllogistic deduction from necessary truths, independent of the contingent world— is indeed possible for a few statements about God; but most of our knowledge of the divine is the gift of faith, to be held without reference to reason. We may contrast the position of Aquinas.

For Duns Scotus, the immortality of the soul and the necessity of the resurrection cannot be proved by reason, but is held upon faith (*Opus Ox.*, IV D.XLIII Q.ii). For Ockham, reason breaks down in proving that there is one God: 'This we hold only by faith', '*hoc fide tantum tenemus*' (*Quodlibeta*, I Q.1). So too with God's foreknowledge (*Ordinatio*, D.XXXVIII Q. *unica*) and the existence of an intellective

soul (*Quodlibeta*, I Q.x). There can be no clear demonstration of God's infinity, his omnipotence, his knowledge of
things outside himself, his freedom to produce creatures.[61]
Probable or persuasive arguments may be produced for all
these premisses, but no conclusive demonstration is possible.

But when we leave the intellectual sphere for the moral
and doctrinal, Aquinas takes a humbler stand and Ockham
proves the optimist. Admittedly, Thomas's admission of
man's sinfulness seems more doctrinal than emotional, especially in his treatment of predestination (*Sum. Theol.*, Ia.
23), based on a philosophic demonstration of God's power
and goodness rather than an actual sense of human weakness
and sin. In fact, man's capacity for good works has not
entirely disappeared even since the Fall (*Sum. Theol.*, IaIIae.
109. 2). But such merit, and the free will by which man
achieves it, are granted by God, so that 'by his work and
action man is to obtain from God as a sort of reward that for
which God has allotted him a power of action'[62] (*Sum. Theol.*,
IaIIae. 114. 1). The necessity of grace forms the subject of
Sum. Theol., IaIIae. 109. 1, and occurs like a refrain in the
section on merit (IaIIae. 114). It is grace, too, which grants
the 'gift of understanding' that supplements our natural
reason in the realm of divine knowledge (*Sum. Theol.*, IIaIIae.
8. 5).

Aquinas' belief in predestination is total, Augustinian; but
as I have said before, this is to illustrate his divine scheme,
not to express any deep sense of sin. Predestination is shown
to control the human will only by a logical distinction
between the first cause and a secondary cause (*Sum. Theol.*,
Ia. 23. 5). Harnack would say that in Aquinas there is actually
a conflict between the doctrine of grace and the doctrine of
merit.[63]

Oddly enough, the fideistic Modernists further emphasize
this tendency. If they stress the impenetrability of God's will
and grace, this latter is defined only as the first grace which
raises man above the level of the spiritually dead. Thence-
forward he can, as it were, guide himself towards salvation
by attracting the *gratia cooperans*, which accompanies the
action of his own liberated will. The process of grace is thus
linked to merit. And man's merit can indeed avail him to

some purpose, for by Duns's revision of tradition, original sin is mere deprivation of the 'supernatural good' of the *gratia gratum faciens*, leaving unimpaired the natural goodness (*justitia originalis*) of man.[64]

Ockham carries this idea further. Man can not only acquire merit to an extent (*de congruo*) where he qualifies by acquired faith or natural habit for the action of saving grace; he can even attain to a natural experience of the theological virtues of faith, hope, and charity. It is only by God's ordained power—determined by him in his absolute freedom of arbitration—that this natural experience of virtue is deemed insufficient for salvation, and the same virtues supernaturally infused through grace required to obtain merit *de condigno*, which alone can save man. Thus the power to save remains entirely with God, for he alone can accept and reward man's merit of his free and unbounded goodness. This clears Ockham from the charge of Pelagianism; but it does not negate the fact that man is credited with an unprecedented capacity for right reason and virtue.[65]

Moreover, the will is considered to be totally free in its choice of good and evil, though God alone can validate that choice into an act of merit. For Henry of Ghent, Duns Scotus, and Ockham, the will preserves its liberty of choice even in the presence of the universal good:

They look upon liberty as the primordial and essential attribute of volition, and ascribe to the will an absolute power of self-determination; the spontaneity of the act involves its liberty. In none of its volitions is the will *necessitated* by the good presented by the intellect: even in the presence of the universal good the will preserves its freedom both of exercise and of specification, for, says Scotus, it has the power of turning aside from the intellectual presentation.[66]

In the sixteenth century, school-philosophy must have appeared as a rather uncertain chess-board of human effort and devout surrender. This seems to have been particularly the case with Gabriel Biel's version of Ockham, 'the extremely inconsistent construction . . . which made now the divine and then the human element the deciding factor in salvation'.[67] This was the version most familiar to the young Luther, and may have served to form his own theology in vehement reaction.

Besides the mainstream of scholasticism, there were other important movements that profoundly influenced Luther. At least one of them deserves serious consideration: a highly personal, individual devotion originating in mysticism and always tending to pass into it. Meister Eckhart challenged the basis of Thomism by denying all possibility of apprehending God through sense-based natural reason:

> The soul has two eyes—one looking inwards and the other outwards. . . . The soul's outward eye is directed toward creatures and perceives their external forms but when a person turns inwards and knows God in terms of his own awareness of him, in the roots of his being, he is then freed from all creation and is secure in the castle of truth. (Sermon: on the text *In diebus suis placuit deo* . . .)

Ruysbroek agreed: 'as we pass away from ourselves and from all things, then we live in God' (*The Book of the Sparkling Stone*, Pt. 2). From Ruysbroek through Gerhard Groote, this mysticism based on the denial of rational knowledge became the doctrine of the Brethren of the Common Life, and found its definitive expression in *The Imitation of Christ*. This was the influential *devotio moderna*.[68]

Yet needless to say, Luther also imbibed his Christian scepticism more directly from the works of the German mystics.[69] An easy source lay in the fideistic and mystical interludes in the works of Johann von Staupitz. Staupitz saw man as elected to salvation by divine grace; he had power of neither will nor intellect, but could attain to a saving love of God, 'born out of the revelation of God's love for us' as revealed in the life of Christ. Beyond this very direct influence, Luther discovered Tauler's sermons at Erfurt in 1516, and the *Theologia Germanica* by an unknown priest of the Teutonic order, in the same year. Here again was the call to an absolute annihilation of personality in God. No doubt Luther interpreted these works in his own spirit, for even the humility of the mystics contained an element of volition; this clashed with Luther's sense of man's extreme weakness and complete reliance on grace. But the mystics provided him with at least a starting-point for a 'wisdom of experience' (*sapientia experimentalis*) rather than a 'wisdom of theology'.

The significant point is that Luther's own theology may be said to combine the various elements of humility and surrender separately present in all the earlier systems. The Ockhamist scepticism about reason is combined with an Augustinian preoccupation with sin and the need for grace. The result is an image, beyond most medieval ones, of the weakness and foulness of man. Eugene F. Rice gives a good summary of the position adopted by most Protestant reformers, 'attributing as much as possible to God and as little as possible to man': 'It is an ascetic rejection of *humanitas* and the world. The result is a depreciation of the powers of natural reason, a denial of the freedom of the will, and a forcible insistence on man's inability to cooperate in his own salvation'.[70]

Yet Luther may sometimes celebrate man's fortitude and even his power. No external force can either induce or destroy the liberty of the soul; the spiritual power of the true Christian

rules in the midst of enemies and is powerful in the midst of oppression. This means nothing else than that 'power is made perfect in weakness'[71] . . . so that the cross and death itself are compelled to serve me . . . This is a splendid privilege and hard to attain, a truly omnipotent power, a spiritual dominion . . . (Luther, *The Freedom of a Christian*; Lambert, p. 355)[72]

Moreover, 'not only are we the freest of kings, we are also priests forever, which is far more excellent than being kings . . .' (ibid., p. 355).[73]

For all the disparate elements in the compound, Luther is laying the foundations for a Christian Stoicism, just as the humanists expounded a Stoicism of a more pagan variety. Calvinism yields a stranger phenomenon: that paradoxical consequence of the doctrine of predestination, the hierarchy of the elect. This strange revaluation of predestination, from a proof of man's weakness to a proof of some men's power, was held justified by the general corruption of man, the human will being vitiated at the root. This premiss—central indeed to all Christian doctrine—was specially stressed by the Protestant reformers. There can be no question of justification by works, by the fulfilment of the commandments. As Luther says,

Although the commandments teach things that are good, the things taught are not done as soon as they are taught, for the commandments show us what we ought to do but do not give us the power to do it. They are intended to teach man to know himself, that through them he may recognize his inability to do good and may despair of his own ability. (Ibid., p. 348) [74]

The only justification, by faith, was regulated by God's will and his gift of grace:

Grace properly signifies freely given mercy, or freely granted acceptance on account of Christ. For when it is said that we obtain remission [of sins] through grace, if you understand it to mean that we obtain remission through the virtues given to us, you clearly destroy Paul's whole standpoint, and deprive our consciences of their true solace. (Melanchthon, *Loci Communes*: '*De argumentis adversariorum*', V) [75]

Once the role of the divine will is so strongly admitted, predestination is a natural corollary, even to its culmination in Calvinism. (It had already been proposed by Wyclif, and more strongly by Hus, against the general tendency of Ockhamist doctrine.) The Thomists, and after them Christian humanists such as Erasmus, had postulated an essentially rational moral order, though human reason in its present debased state may not be able to grasp it. Calvin, however, contends that not only is the divine will beyond human understanding, but that human standards of good and evil, of rational morality, do not apply to the divine will.

We assert that, with respect to the elect, this plan was founded upon his freely given mercy, without regard to human worth; but by his just and irreprehensible but incomprehensible judgment he has barred the door of life to those whom he has given over to damnation. (*Institutes*, III. xxi. 7) [76]

We may detect in this, altered beyond recognition, the vestiges of the long-established concept of Fortune; [77] but the arbitrariness of this goddess is replaced in Calvinism by the preconceived, immutable, but still arbitrary will of God—determinism in place of secular fatalism.

It is being increasingly granted that the most oppressive, authoritarian, and self-righteous features attributed to Calvinism either misrepresent Calvinist doctrine or allude to features introduced by later Calvinists, perhaps contrary to their master's own teachings. [78] We may dismiss the mythical monstrosity of the Calvinist Church; but the changes and additions to Calvin's own doctrines cannot be dismissed. As a historical force, the two must be associated. We find in Calvin's thought the seed of later development.

Calvin forgoes the impulse of most theologians to rational-ize the doctrines of predestination and salvation through grace: he will not compromise with their nature as articles of pure faith. He thereby runs the danger that this arbitrary dis-pensation may be too repugnant to man's moral sense. It may not be accepted as compatible with divine benevolence.

In a sense, this is an invalid objection. Calvin does not dis-miss the connection between salvation or election on the one hand and, on the other, the external signs or concomitants of goodness: faith, perseverance, and godly living. His distinction is to postulate the former as the cause of the latter—not the other way about as (to varying degrees) in systems inclining towards the doctrine of merit. Given man's utterly weak and sinful state, his apparent goodness cannot indicate any effort on his part *meriting* salvation; they are signs or consequences of an election freely bestowed by God.

The apparent presence of these signs should not induce pride or confidence, as they may later disappear, or in fact exist without grace (*Institutes*, III. xxiv. 7). Nor should the absence of the signs lead to despair, as the action of grace may be manifested at a later stage of life (Ibid., III xxiv. 10, 11). In this way Calvin reconciles predestination with the need to dwell in steadfast faith and godly living. The will and strength to accomplish this is indeed the free gift of God; but at least Calvinist man recognizes the need to foster such will and strength. He thereby assumes a sort of secondary moral responsibility or at least a vigilant regard for his moral state.

For it is, of course, a truism of history that Calvinism did not induce a passive fatalism of spirit. On the contrary, it inspired a new ethic of work and material achievement, total dedication to a communal ideal that would provide an earthly version of the reign of the elect. The sense of the individual's weakness and insignificance readily produced this dedication to the community. At the same time, the most reliable assurance of election lay in unfailing exhibition of the signs thereof: the faithful would dedicate their utmost powers to ensure this happy continuity. There was moreover the con-trolling concept of the 'illumination of the spirit', whereby implicit authority could be commanded by the rulers or elders, whose own election must be taken as a more or less unquestioned hypothesis. The Calvinist Church was the symbol and instrument of the divine will on earth. This is said to be the point on which later Calvinism most departed from Calvin's own doctrine; but at least the concept of 'illumination' is derived from the *Institutes*.

Here then we have the most paradoxical assertion of the human spirit in the age. Historically it is perhaps the most influential. The whole system, theological and ecclesiastic, is the *caput mortuum* of the medieval order. The Calvinist ideal is exclusive, not assimilative; authoritarian, not rational or persuasive. It denies many aspects of existence which, though rejected at the spectacular ascetic fringe of medieval life and thought, had then found their place in an ordering of man's entire being. Medieval authoritarianism based its legitimacy on a graded scheme of all existence, a vast structure of correspondences and hierarchies that the reason could explore.

Calvinist man, on the contrary, abdicated his own faculties —only to recover them under a new sanction. They could henceforth be exercised inviolably, as part of a dispensation directly ordered by God. It is all too easy to lapse into irony when describing such a system, to attack it with the rational premises it deliberately rejects. But considered as an historical phenomenon, it affords an astonishing instance of the unlikely and contradictory motives behind the growth of the human spirit in the sixteenth century.

Thus from the early to the late Renaissance, there appears to be a basic homogeneity. Doctrines and systems may change; they may appear directly hostile or entirely unrelated to each other. But beneath the surface, they all contain certain recurring, or at least related, conceptions of the nature of man and his place in the universe.

These conceptions all reflect the same constriction of man's powers, the same supra-human bias of physical, moral, and social systems, that have been considered to be general features of medieval thought. Humanist and Reformer are forever attempting to break free from their medieval moorings; but for all their individualism and intellectual inquiry, they seldom dismiss, or even wish to dismiss, the entire substance of the orthodoxies they combat. The quest for new wisdom may foster classicism, the free exercise of the faculties and even a cult of paganism; but in the central currents of thought, these tendencies are moderated and disciplined within a framework of traditional beliefs. Thus in fact, the exercise of intellect and moral virtue leads Renaissance man to Biblical study, faith in revelation, and a self-conducted yet self-critical analysis of man's sin and folly. In one form or other, nearly all Renaissance thought balances freedom against compromise and even surrender. The same doubts and limitations underlie the work of Scholastic, humanist, and Reformer. What shifts, wavers, and collapses is the delicate superstructure of a new optimism.

III. *The English Renaissance*

1. *The Condition of Humanity: Sidney and Some Other Writers*

Turning now to English authors, it seems appropriate to begin with Sidney. *The Defence of Poesie* places poetry in the context of all human learning, and also considers man's moral state. It explicitly mentions Cornelius Agrippa, and is deeply indebted to *De . . . vanitate*. In spite of this, it illustrates a remarkable optimism.

The optimism is far from complete: in fact, Sidney presents the state of man as basically fallen: '. . . that first accursed fall of Adam, since our erected wit maketh us know what perfection is, and yet our infected will keepeth us from reaching unto it' (MP, 79. 24-6). A few pages later, he talks of our 'degenerate souls'. Nature has fallen with man, for he was set by God 'beyond and over all the works of that second nature' (79. 20-1): nature's world is therefore 'brazen' (78. 34).

Man's predicament is pictured in traditional terms. The passage on 'our degenerate souls' needs to be quoted in full:

> This purifying wit—this enriching of memory, enabling of judgement, and enlarging of conceit—which commonly we call learning, under what name soever it come forth, or to what immediate end soever it be directed, the final end is to lead and draw us to as high a perfection as our degenerate souls, made worse by their clayey lodgings, can be capable of. (82. 11-16.)

This assumes two impediments to a full development of humanity: the intrinsic degeneration of the soul (the Fall, or some analogous but more subtly conceived spiritual loss)[1] and the further curb of our lower, physical natures. Christianity and Platonism are cast into a traditional compound: we can hardly distinguish the elements. In the very next paragraph we have a similar but more optimistic assertion: 'But all [pursuers of learning], one and other, having this scope: to know, and by knowledge to lift up the mind from the dungeon of the body to the enjoying of his own divine essence' (82. 25-7).

This does not quite agree with what goes before, for it seems to consider the body to be man's only impediment. But by and large, Sidney's basic assumption seems to be not so much of two natures united in man—body and soul, beast and angel —as of two successive states of the soul, the pristine and the fallen, in something like a temporal sequence. Knowledge brings the soul back to its pristine state.

This is not at all a simple business, for most branches of learning will not serve:

. . . by the balance of experience it was found that the astronomer, looking to the stars, might fall in a ditch, that the inquiring philosopher might be blind in himself, and the mathematician might draw forth a straight line with a crooked heart . . . (82. 28–32)

Here Sidney is following Agrippa and the Sceptics generally: like them, too, moving between intellectual and moral considerations. He therefore proposes self-knowledge, a moral regeneration that could apply the 'serving sciences' towards a genuine rehabilitation of man:

. . . directed to the highest end of the mistress-knowledge, by the Greeks called ἀρχιτεκτονική, which stands (as I think) in the knowledge of a man's self, in the ethic and politic consideration, with the end of well-doing and not of well-knowing only . . . (82. 35–83. 2)

Sidney is building upon the hope that runs fitfully beneath Agrippa's gloom; but he differs from Agrippa in his emphasis. Instead of the vanity of learning, his discourse treats of the branch of learning which he considers fruitful above all. The basic bent of his work is optimistic: it admits all the traditional shortcomings of the human state, but at the same time proposes something very like the infinite perfectibility of man.

This is shown by the fact that, of all the disciplines concerned with self-knowledge and morality, Sidney ranks law as the lowest, because it assumes of necessity the wickedness of man. The higher arts are those that 'plant goodness even in the secretest cabinet of our souls' (85. 4).

This is best achieved by poetry rather than philosophy or history. Interestingly enough, it is not because poetry appeals exclusively to the highest faculties: philosophy does that, and fails as a result. It aims too high, preaches only to the converted. By the paradox I am trying to trace through the

Renaissance, poetry is the highest and most successful of the arts because it best suits man's imperfect nature. It makes no extraordinary demands of virtue or intellect:

[The poet] cometh to you with words set in delightful proportion, either accompanied with, or prepared for, the well enchanting skill of music; and with a tale forsooth he cometh unto you, with a tale which holdeth children from play, and old men from the chimney corner. (92. 7-11)

Sidney bases himself on the Horatian formula that poetry must teach and delight. Man's teachability argues the intrinsic excellence of the soul; the need for delight indicates its imperfection. Poetry accommodates itself to man's total being.

Sidney's remarkable achievement is to combine such precepts, linking poetry with the mixed, imperfect nature of man, with the praise of poetry as the highest achievement of the human spirit, ranking *above* philosophy, raising man to an ideal plane of existence. This is no naïve rhetoric on the excellence of poetry but a balanced piece of humanist optimism, utilizing man's imperfect nature to consolidate his assault on perfection. It is a relatively simple but adequate foreshadowing of similar syntheses in later English authors.

It is reinforced by a second paradox, concerning the union of the real and the ideal in poetry. There is an incipient Neoplatonism running all through the *Defence*, giving rise to a dual conception of 'nature'. Poetry is mimesis, 'an art of imitation', a 'counterfeiting, or figuring forth' (79. 35, 80. 1). The original that it imitates is nature. But it relates to nature in a unique way. Other arts follow nature, are tied down to the world as it is. ('Nature', in this context, is obviously 'brazen' reality.) Even the moral philosopher 'standeth upon the natural virtues, vices, or passions of man; and follow nature (saith he) therein, and thou shalt not err' (78. 10-12). That is to say, he can understand human nature as it is, but cannot improve it. The poet alone transcends the actualities of nature *with a power born from within himself*: he,

disdaining to be tied to any such objection, lifted up with the vigour of his own invention, doth grow in effect another nature, in making things either better than nature bringeth forth, or, quite anew, forms such as never were in nature . . . so as he goeth hand in hand with nature, not enclosed within the narrow warrant of her gifts, but freely ranging only within the zodiac of his own wit. (78. 22-30)

Poetry releases human nature from natural necessity, discovers an ideal dimension within the entity of man. Considering the direct and emphatic rhetoric of Sidney's language at this point, and recalling his stock reputation as the 'ideal courtier', we may be tempted to dismiss this as the naïve radiance of textbook 'Renaissance optimism'. But my earlier points will indicate how Sidney understands the complex state of man and works that ambivalent material into the substance of strong faith.

The avowal of human independence through poetry carries a danger. It may release man from all moorings in reality, enable an achievement of no absolute meaning or value. In fact, Sidney contrasts the poet's function with the metaphysician's, who 'doth . . . indeed build upon the depth of nature' (78. 21-2). The poet, it may seem, needs no such foundation for his work. As we shall see, other writers—including Shakespeare in some plays—brilliantly advance such ideals of purely human validity. Sidney, however, does not explore so far. His view of the poet's function is solidly rooted in the orthodox world-order. Man can transcend nature because God made him in the divine image and placed him above nature: 'having made man to His own likeness, set him beyond and over all the works of that second nature: . . .' (79. 20-1). In man's fallen state, he can realize this divinely appointed power only through poetry. The ideal world he creates in poetry thus acquires a metaphysical sanction as well as a moral one.

Sidney does not actually presuppose a Platonic world of ideal entities; but he proposes such concepts to indicate the deepest reality beneath material appearances. The poet makes 'the too much loved earth more lovely' (78. 33-4). And further, if this world of ideal being had no previous existence —'nothing of what is, hath been, or shall be; but . . . what may be and should be' (81. 4-6)—yet the poetry itself may create such a being in reality: '. . . so far substantially it worketh, not only to make a Cyrus, which had been but a particular excellency as nature might have done, but to bestow a Cyrus upon the world to make many Cyruses . . .' (79. 12-15). Man's creative independence gives him a forming, mastering authority over nature. His creations do not have to conform to reality; reality is moulded in response to his creative urge. It is scarcely possible to conceive of greater power for man.

Through poetry man unites the two 'natures', actual and ideal. Sidney places great value on the specific and individual, castigating the abstractions of philosophy and stressing the need for examples and embodiments.

'If the poet do his part aright, he will show you in Tantalus, Atreus, and such like, nothing that is not to be shunned; in Cyrus, Aeneas, Ulysses, each thing to be followed; . . .' (88. 24-6). Hence Sidney's contrast between describing an elephant and, more effectively, showing a picture of the animal (85. 30). Unlike the Sceptics, he emphasizes the educative function of the senses, not their errors and deceptions.

But the sensory, individual, and 'real' are valuable only in so far as they reflect the ideal. Sidney explains this so many times that I hardly need to quote. This is what distinguishes the purely individual examples of history from the representative, 'philosophical' examples of poetry. Poetry links the real world of disparate and imperfect beings with the ideal world of co-ordinate and perfect forms. Thus man brings order to the universe.

There is probably no comparable work of the English Renaissance which affirms man's capacities in such exalted form. We may indeed wonder how seriously to take the work. It has the structure of an oration,[2] and is undoubtedly conceived as a rhetorical exercise. It seems to marshal its designedly elaborate style with a certain self-correcting irony, an occasional piece of open flamboyance that suggests something less than deathly earnest. In this way, Sidney shows that he is not carried away by his rhetoric, and also frees the reader from any such obligation. But this merely gives the work a certain sanity, ensures that the simple rhetorical appeal does not prevent a deeper conviction in the more discerning reader. It surely does not invalidate the arguments; rather, the 'happy valiancy' of the style arouses an enthusiasm that helps to carry them through.

It may appear a pitiful anticlimax to descend from this remarkable work to certain stock versified discourses on the human state. But they indicate the philosophy of man that prevails at the general level and colours the literature of the times. They may usefully supplement an account based upon the greatest writers and perhaps untypical for that very reason. As examples of these pedestrian discourses I have taken John Davies's *Nosce Teipsum* (1599) and Phineas Fletcher's *The Purple Island* (published in 1633, but probably composed over the preceding twenty years). I have deliberately chosen examples that stress the power and dignity of man. This makes more notable the contrary elements that emerge none the less, and form the bias in the work of more important authors.

Though later in date than Sidney's *Defence*, these poems present a less demanding and sophisticated philosophy: intellectually they are more primitive. And as at this level there seem to be few variations and revisions, we may consider the two poems together, ignoring chronology.

In that curious poem *The Purple Island*, the 'island' of man is ruled by the Intellect, a faculty 'more then celestiall' (VI. 28: Boas, p. 75). The human virtues too are a heavenly race, offspring of Spiritto and Urania (IX. 6 ff.: Boas, p. 120). John Davies's more direct account differs in detail but tends to the same end. At several points, man's soul is declared to be angelic in nature, though corrupted by the Fall. The Delphic maxim of Davies's title was often applied by Socrates; but Davies uses it to inspire an un-Socratic simplism of faith in man.

All the same, Davies holds that feeble man regains his powers only through the mediation of Christ:

> Oh what a livelie life! what heavenly power!
> What spreading vertue! what a sparkling Fire!
> How great, how plentifull, how rich a dowre,
> Do'st thou within this dying Flesh inspire!   (ll. 1261–4)

In Fletcher, the theme of *felix culpa* is less marked. A passage on the triumphant phoenix-rebirth of man is mingled—rather confusingly, in fact—with an account of man, even after Christ's sacrifice, as being in

> A baser state then what was first assign'd;
> Wherein (to curb the too aspiring minde)
> The better things were lost, the worse were left behind.
> (II. 2: Boas, p. 26)

In any case, the importance of the Redemption raises once
again the ambiguous equation of man and Christ, the proof
of man's spiritual potential by the power of God-made-man.
As we have seen, this often implied that man could realize his
potential only through divine aid or the mediation of Christ.
In Fletcher particularly, man's reliance on Christ is emphasized
time and again, with reference to *Christ's Victory and Triumph*, by the poet's brother Giles. In the psychomachia with
which *The Purple Island* concludes, Eclecta the soul, the
Bride of Christ, calls to Christ after all the knights of virtue
have been defeated; and it is through Christ's victory that she
is clad anew in sinless splendour.

The Fall is undone; but this restoration takes place within
a framework of traditional doctrine. There is no grand upward
revaluation of man's power or station: we have merely an
account of the traditional attributes of man, with a selective
emphasis upon certain superior elements and an optimism
founded on God's grace. Nor is it a consistent emphasis. The
psychomachia depicts the failure of the human faculties,
heroic as they are. Earlier, we are repeatedly given the
traditional reason for this failure: the Fall of Man. Thus, of
the faculties:

> Fit youth they seem'd to play in Princes hall,
> (But ah long since they thence were banisht all) . . .
> (IX. 9: Boas, p. 121)

The court of the Intellect and the Will, King and Queen of
the 'island', has lost its lustre with the Fall; the ruling faculties
themselves are now

> Prest down in captive chains, and pent in earthly mold.
> (VI. 65: Boas, p. 83)

Yet 'their darkest night outshines the brightest day' (VI. 60):
conscience and repentance may even repair the will 'trebling
her new born raies' (VI. 64). One is uncertain whether this
spiritual pattern redounds to man's glory or the reverse.

More detailed and illuminating, though of equally ambiguous import, is the account of the Fall in Davies's poem. His
oft-quoted description of the human state has the clarity,
even simplism, of a text-book account:

> *I know* my *Soule* hath power to know all things,
> Yet is she blind and ignorant in all;
> I *know* I'am one of *Natures* little kings,
> Yet to the least and vilest things am thrall.   (ll. 173-6)

Equally clear is the function of the Fall in bringing about this state. Davies does not consider man's quest for divine knowledge to be sinful. Rather, our first parents fell by pursuing the knowledge of lower things, *scientia* rather than *sapientia*:

> For then their minds did first in passion see,
> Those wretched shapes of *Miserie*, and *Woe*,
> Of *Nakednesse*, of *Shame*, of *Povertie*,
> Which then their owne experience made them know . . .
>
> But we their wretched Ofspring, what do we?
> Do wee not still tast of the fruite forbid?
> Whiles with fond, fruitelesse curiositie,
> In books prophane, we seeke for knowledge hid?
>   (ll. 29-32, 37-40)

The profanity of such a quest does not preclude the search for spiritual enlightenment. We overcome the limitations imposed by original sin by rising higher, exercising the divine faculty implanted in us. The tone of Davies's poem contradicts his premises: it implies that original sin is a transgression of a purely formal or theological nature. And in any case, Davies celebrates the doctrine of *felix culpa*. All this, of course, is clean contrary to the Sceptical spirit.

The same use of Sceptical propositions and their subsequent reversal appears in another way. The quest for profane knowledge is thwarted by the error of the senses, and the failure of reason when it operates through the senses:

> What can we know? or what can we discerne?
> When *Error* chokes the windowes of the mind;
> The diverse formes of things how can we learne,
> That have bene ever from our birth-day blind?   (ll. 57-60)

Such vain knowledge breeds a variety of false and unverifiable opinions; and this babel, like Babel itself, is the outcome of the root sin of pride:

> *God onely wise*, to punish pride of Wit,
> Among mens wits hath this confusion wrought;
> As the proud *Towre*, whose points the clouds did hit,
> By Tongues confusion was to ruine brought.   (ll. 237-40)

These are Sceptical assumptions; but again, Davies parts company with the Sceptics when he ascribes man's error to the bodily faculties alone. In contrast to animals, man can correct sense-impressions by the exercise of reason. Davies is not afflicted with the deeper Sceptical doubts of the efficacy of rational processes. The pure soul is an immaterial substance; thus in supra-mundane matters, where she is not weighed down by the body or corrupted by sin, she is capable of correct and firm knowledge.

> Therefor no *Sense* the precious joyes conceives,
>   Which in her private Contemplations bee,
>   For then the ravisht spirit the *Senses* leaves,
>   Hath her owne powers, and proper actions free.   (ll. 373-6)

Davies admits the frustration of man's quest for knowledge in this world. Again we may be fitfully reminded of Ficino's Prometheus; but in fact, Davies argues from this the immortality of the soul and the fulfilment of its quest in the next world.

The spirit of the poem is strongly optimistic; its importance for us lies in the contrary elements it works into the pattern. We see how closely such optimism relies on traditional theology and ambivalent concepts of man. We see also the ease with which the same premises may be reshaped to present the human state in a darker and less flattering view.

The same ambivalence shows in a more celebrated thinker like Sir Walter Ralegh. Perhaps one should not lay too much stress on his brief essay, 'The Sceptic', which enumerates the common Pyrrhonist arguments: the fallacies of the senses; discrepancies between the senses; differences between man and the animals, and the often superior powers of the latter; divergence of custom and opinion between nations and between individuals. That Ralegh should have once summarized these arguments does not of itself imply that they are fundamental to his thought.

But some of the arguments are repeated in the Preface to the *History of the World* with less system but more eloquent conviction—the diversity of opinion, for instance, and their consequent weakness and uncertainty:

. . . every one hath received a several picture of face, and every one a diverse picture of mind; every one a form apart, every one a fancy and cogitation differing; there being nothing wherein nature so much triumpheth, as in dissimilitude. (*Works*, II. iii)

It is true that in the Preface, Ralegh castigates authority (specifically that of Aristotle) only in order to uphold the dignity of the unfettered reason. But ultimately reason bows down to faith. Ralegh does indeed hold that faith does not contradict reason. Reason may lead us to faith—for instance, by demonstrating the necessary existence of God. But it cannot probe the mysteries of the divine: the highest knowledge cannot strictly be known but only believed.

This cautious and perfectly orthodox approach, arguing at best for a deeply qualified reliance on human power, is basic to Ralegh. Book I of the *History* treats directly of the soul and the human state. This account can be supported by reference to *A Treatise of the Soul*.

Man is made in God's image—though this obviously applies to the soul alone and not to the body (*Works*, II. 46). The mind of man is thus above the influence of the stars. Their effect on the body may ultimately influence the mind, but even this can be countered by spiritual fortitude. The souls of other beasts are of earthly origin, generated from the seed. Man's soul was breathed into him by God: it is immortal and capable of 'things hidden, and secret, and heavenly' (*A Treatise*: *Works*, VIII. 572). There is indeed a native goodness in man, though it is merely a shadow of the goodness of God.

What is notable is that Ralegh attributes this goodness to a special faculty of the soul, distinguished from the rest. The soul (*anima physica*) he defines after Aristotle as the *forma vel natura hominis*, 'the form or nature of man' (II. 48). The truly divine element is the *mens* or intellectual mind, the purest faculty of the soul, devoted to the perpetual contemplation of the truth. It is 'the eye of the soul', as Augustine says (II. 49), and can have knowledge independent of sensory or contingent matters. The *anima physica* is natural to man; the *mens* is a 'faculty or gift of God' (II. 48). A little later, this *mens* seems to be identified with the 'habit of original righteousness' (II. 52) which alone preserves us in virtue.

Reason, understanding, and other faculties of the soul make us capable of receiving God's image in our beings (II.

52); but even the reason, if unassisted, would incline to earthly rather than heavenly things. What corrects this bias and truly makes us the image of God is the *mens*, an *infused* faculty, bestowed upon us 'not by nature, nor by her liberality . . . but from the bountiful grace of the Lord of all goodness' (II. 52). A little later, Ralegh talks again of the 'liberality of his mercy' (II. 53) for having granted us these eyes to our souls.

This results in a curious position. The highest element of the soul, in which the divine image inheres, does not really belong to man. It is not an organic part of his humanity but merely an addition made by God, testifying to his mercy rather than man's power. It enables man to guide and fulfil the potential of his own nature; but the motive force is God's free and arbitrary goodness. This is obviously a less than total idealization of man.

Given this imperfect state of man's own proper being, it is no wonder that he should be subject to sin and suffering. We are trapped within our base and frail bodies:

. . . our bodies are but the anvils of pain and diseases, and our minds the hives of unnumbered cares, sorrows and passions; and . . . (when we are most glorified) we are but those painted posts, against which envy and fortune direct their darts; . . . (II. 54)

This *contemptus mundi* suits Ralegh's moral tone, but it does raise some awkward problems for his moral scheme. He has, after all, denied the reality of Fortune in an earlier section (I. i. 15: *Works*, II. 37-42). And though 'mind' in the passage quoted above obviously does not mean the intellective *mens*, this *mens* has just been said to guide man's moral being and 'bring knowledge and object to the mind and soul' (II. 53). How can it permit such a sinful decline of man? There is some contradiction between Ralegh's rapture over the *mens* and the moral gloom of the rest of his account. He cannot present us with a concept like Ficino's, of the divine soul trapped in a mortal body. For Ralegh the divine soul, all too readily abandoning its divinity, grows sinfully absorbed in the mortal body.

Ralegh repeats many premises of Neoplatonic idealism, but always with this thwarting moral twist. Like Cusanus, he presents man as microcosm, matching in his human, moral being the 'lively image of other creatures' (II. 63) at all levels of existence from the highest to the lowest. But this concept is simplified into a mere allegory of copybook ethical states: '. . . as by serpents were signified deceivers; by lions, oppressors and cruel men; by swine, men given over to lust and sensuality; . . .' (II. 63). He quotes Pico's image of the 'seeds' in man, practically verbatim, to indicate man's free will and infinite potential. But in the next chapter, he negates this theoretical freedom by pointing out man's actual subjection after the Fall: 'For man having a free will and liberal choice, purchased by disobedience his own death and mortality; . . .' (II. 64). In Ralegh's moral, biblical outlook, the Fall limits man's potential once and for all.

In *A Treatise of the Soul*, man's soul is presented as being entirely in the hands of God: '. . . for God toucheth our souls, and is joined to them in the creation; is joined likewise to them in our regeneration; and most of all will become one spirit with us, or rather we with him, in our glorification' (VIII. 585). In the *History*, all human history is governed by stern divine power: '. . . God, who is the author of all our tragedies, hath written out for us and appointed us all the parts we are to play; and hath not, in their distribution, been partial to the most mighty princes of the world; . . .' (Preface: II. xlii). God's power dispenses reward and punishment in this world, but ultimately directs us to the next. The Preface to the *History* contains a long meditation on transience and earthly vanity. For all his notoriety as an 'atheist', Ralegh's vision is essentially other-worldly. And for all his idealizing of the truth-seeking *mens* and his discovery of God's image in man, he does not change the traditional view of the human condition. The very idealizing is carried out in traditional terms, and illustrates once again the ambiguous nature of such concepts.

We may consider one more author before moving on to other matters. Fulke Greville's *A Treatie of Humane Learning* covers somewhat the same ground as did Davies and Fletcher in the poems described above. We may also cite Greville's other works. The celebrated chorus in *Mustapha* on the 'wearisome condition of humanity' repeats the substance of Davies's introductory stanzas, partly quoted earlier. But Greville goes much further. In contrast to the textbook accounts of received learning in Davies and Fletcher, he presents tradition in a dynamic, individualized version. At once we note a difference: while Greville also ascribes the ruin of man's faculties to the Fall, he has no such notion as Davies's of man's pristine power.

Greville's stand emerges early in the poem (although the opening stanza is ambiguous). Knowledge itself is divine, but in man's present state the pursuit of knowledge is both sinful and futile. This raises a further question: is this unhappy state the cause or the effect of the Fall? Greville's conclusion, unlike Davies's, seems to be that owing to man's 'amphibious' state, he is *essentially* incapable of free and perfect knowledge:

> For Knowledge is of Powers eternity,
> And perfect Glory, the true image-taker;
> So as what doth the infinite containe,
> Must be as infinite as it againe.
>
> No maruell then, if proud desires reflexion,
> By gazing on this Sunne, doe make vs blinde,
> Nor if our Lust, our *Centaure*-like Affection,
> Instead of Nature, fadome clouds, and winde . . .
>
> (3. 3-4. 4)

There follows an account of all the standard premises of Scepticism. First comes the deceit of the senses, the 'feeble instruments' that vitiate the understanding. The imagination, which collects and classifies sense-data, is corrupted by both subjective distortions ('self-applications') and the influence of the passions or affections. The memory is also enfeebled. Above all, the understanding itself is corrupted by the Fall:

> . . . though it containe
> Some ruinous notions, which our Nature showes,
> Of generall truths, yet haue they such a staine
> From our corruption, as all light they lose; . . .
>
> (15 2-5)

Moreover, 'Change from without' (8. 1) also frustrates knowledge. Greville is filling in the other half of the Sceptic view: the object of cognition is as unstable as the intellect itself. God alone, 'eternall, infinite, all-seeing' (23. 1), can penetrate to 'the abstract essences of Creatures' (23. 2) to arrive at absolute and timeless truths. For man, in a material and contingent world, the knowledge of universals is impossible to attain.

With this nominalism goes a sense of the futility of words. What frustrates Greville above all else is the factitiousness of the arts, purely verbal systems with no bearing upon experience.

> *Life* is the *Wisdome*, *Art* is but the *letter*,
> Or *shell*, which oft men for the kernell take;
> In Moodes, and Figures moulding vp deceit,
> To make each Science rather hard, than great.
> (35. 3-6)

These brain-spun arts are but 'vain Idols of humanity'. They die away both by external accident and innate decay—mortal creations, not records of eternal truth. This inadequacy appears in theology, physic, logic, rhetoric: everywhere we find trafficking in words, neglectful of

> . . . precepts . . .
> As without words may be conceiu'd in minde. (106. 5-6)

Woven in with this account of the futility of learning are repeated reminders of man's fallen state. The two strands coincide in the declaration that this unavailing knowledge testifies to

> An Angel-pride, and in vs much more vaine
> Since what they could not, how should we attaine?
> (45. 5-6)
> *These Arts, moulds, workes can but expresse the sinne,*
> *Whence by mans follie, his fall did beginne.* (47. 5-6)

In other words, these arts serve to augment the very sin of which they are the outcome. They make the nobler faculties serve the baser, which was the result of the Fall itself (stanza 53).

In fact, the true end of knowledge should be the spiritual regeneration of man:

> Thus are true Learnings in the humble heart
> A *Spirituall worke*, raising Gods Image, rased
> By our transgression; . . . (150. 1-3)

Two important corollaries follow. One is that man should

confine his knowledge to human concerns, and particularly to self-improvement:

> ... that we doe not ouerbuild our states ...
> But measure first our own Humanity; ...   (146. 1, 4)

The other is that even this knowledge is unattainable except by

> ... gifts of Grace, and Faith ...
> For without these, the minde of man growes numbe,
> The body darknesse, to the soule a tombe.   (149. 4-6)

Greville's stand is very close to the classic premisses of Scepticism. Yet as I remarked before, he does not differ radically from the more optimistic poets. This may illustrate the remarkable persistence of certain basic doubts and reservations beneath a great variety of Renaissance philosophies of man.

2. *Francis Bacon*

Remarkably too, these doubts persist even when the traditional attitudes are radically altered. Greville is supposed to have composed his *Treatie* in reply to the optimistic spirit of Bacon's *Advancement of Learning*. It may appear all the stranger that the two works should have so much in common, particularly in their use of the concepts of Scepticism. There is indeed a difference in orientation, but by no means as radical as may be supposed.

At first sight it seems perverse to associate Bacon with the doubt and gloom of the English Renaissance. The apostle of science, the 'instaurator' of learning and the human intellect, he appears rather to rescue us from the pessimism and exhaustion of the old order. For Bacon, the mind of man is greater than the totality of the works he contemplates (*Advancement*, I. i. 3); and 'the just and lawful sovereignty over men's understanding, by force of truth rightly interpreted, is that which approacheth nearest to the similitude of the divine rule' (*Advancement*, I. viii. 3: Johnston, p. 57).

Further, knowledge is declared to give 'law to the will itself', and thus act simultaneously as an intellectual and a moral good. '*Veritas* and *Bonitas* differ but as the seal and the print' (*Advancement*, I. viii. 2: Johnston, p. 56). The pursuit of knowledge thus implies spiritual development as well: 'Certainly it is heaven upon earth to have a man's mind move in charity, rest in providence, and turn upon the poles of truth' (*Essays*, 'Of Truth': Abbott, I. 3. 58–60).

We find in Bacon an interesting reversal of the common Sceptic interpretation of the Fall. He ascribes it not to the pursuit of knowledge itself—which is man's legitimate activity —but to proud knowledge, lacking in charity: 'to the end to make a total defection from God and to depend wholly upon himself' (*Advancement*, I. vi. 6: Johnston, p. 38). True knowledge induces the proper understanding of man's place in the divine order. Neither this subservience to a greater order, nor the admission of incomprehensible 'first causes', nor the demarcation of the province of 'divinity', revelation, and faith, can be said to offset the trust in human capacities. It is customary to note the purely formal nature of Bacon's devoirs to the Great Unknown.

It may not, however, be entirely formal. We must take stock of some suggestive points in Bacon's treatment of natural and supernatural wisdom. There is in particular the seminal distinction between two sorts of 'natural light': one, simple natural reason and virtue, the other a higher *implanted* power, present in man but not to be explained in terms of the human faculties (*Advancement*, II. xxv. 3: Johnston, p. 201). This distinction should be borne in mind when considering any glorification of man in this period: it may frequently serve to expose a deeper humility, a circumscription of the truly human faculties.

We may also proceed by a different route, to conclude that Bacon's faith in man is very cautiously defined. It is based on a profound sense of human limitation, at times echoing the premisses of pure Scepticism. It makes the operation of man's powers contingent upon external factors, indeed governed by them. Moreover, it is tempered with a cynicism about human nature that almost vitiates the idealistic spirit of his work.

One soon discovers that Bacon's faith in the intellect is far from absolute. In fact, he is repeatedly struck by the near-impossibility of knowledge: '. . . that all things are hidden away from us, that we know nothing, that we discern nothing, that truth is drowned in deep wells, that the true and the false are strangely joined and twisted together . . .' (*De sapientia veterum*, Ch. 26: ES, VI. 749).[3] The reasons for such pessimism are much the same as the Sceptics'. On the value of sense-impressions, Bacon's stand is indeed ambiguous. At times, he argues that by and large, the senses register data correctly (*non fallunt magnopere*), but these are misinterpreted by the intellect (*Novum Organum*, I. 16). In fact, his whole method of induction, proceeding from the record of phenomena in a 'history' of the subject, relies entirely on sense-data for the natural sciences at any rate. But elsewhere he seems aware that 'all perceptions as well of the sense as of the mind are according to the measure of the individual and not according to the measure of the universe' (*Novum Organum*, I. 41: ES, IV. 54).[4] He therefore finds it imperative to propose many aids to the senses.

More pervasive is Bacon's distrust of all accepted intellectual methods, based on the discovery of follies and biases endemic in man. In the doctrine of Idols, one must particularly note the way in which the Idols of the Tribe are balanced by those of the Cave. The former are akin to the universal blindness of intellect admitted by the formal Sceptics; but unlike Montaigne and his followers, Bacon does not seek refuge in individualism, assuming or creating an order as a personal support for the intellect. This would be to surrender to the Idols of the Cave. One must beware also of the Idols of the Market and the Theatre—words and concepts, brain-spun figments which conceal or distort reality. Here we come very close to Sceptical conceptions.

This total demolition of man's intellectual equipment exceeds the thoroughness with which many Sceptics expound their views. Bacon also exceeds the Sceptics in the desire to come to grips with actual experience, the face of things. He is no less concerned with the protean nature of experience:

Our notions of less general species [than physical principles and philosophical notions] . . . and of the immediate perceptions of the sense . . . do not materially mislead us; yet even these are sometimes confused by the flux and alteration of matter and the mixing of one thing with another. (*Novum Organum*, I. 16: ES, IV. 49)[5]

At the very outset of his work of 'instauration', Bacon presents us with this stark, apparently hopeless confrontation between an intractable universe and man's inadequate powers. The constant denunciation of authority, of the worthlessness of the knowledge acquired so far, is a mere corollary, scarcely needing illustration. The primary truth is the tenuousness of all such engagement between nature and the intellect.

> But the universe to the eye of the human understanding is framed like a labyrinth; presenting as it does on every side so many ambiguities of way, such deceitful resemblances of objects and signs, natures so irregular in their lines, and so knotted and entangled. And then the way is still to be made by the uncertain light of the sense, sometimes shining out, sometimes clouded over, through the woods of experience and particulars; while those who offer themselves for guides are (as was said) themselves also puzzled, and increase the number of errors and wanderers. In circumstances so difficult neither the natural force of man's judgment nor even any accidental felicity offers any chance of success. (Preface to the *Instauratio magna*: ES, IV. 18)[6]

Bacon knows how closely he approaches the Sceptics. Of course, he at once points out how radically he differs from them too:

> For the holders of that doctrine [Scepticism] assert simply that nothing can be known; I also assert that not much can be known in nature by the way which is now in use. But then they go on to destroy the authority of the senses and understanding; whereas I proceed to devise and supply helps for the same. (*Novum Organum*, I. 37: ES, IV. 53; cf. *N. O.*, I. 75)[7]

But this distinction does not invalidate what I have pointed out before. In fact, a true assessment of Bacon's principles shows how the Great Instaurator weaves all his distrust of man's powers into his plans for the advancement of learning. It is a strange case of fostering achievement by abdicating the faculties and suppressing their action.

Briefly, Bacon proposes that knowledge should be acquired not by encouraging the productions of the mind but by stalling or neutralizing them, rendering them subordinate to external reality. The operative centre of the process of knowledge passes out of the human intellect into the object of cognition. We record, absorb, learn; at most we arrange and summarize, but even that with caution and humility, taking care to impose no artificial order upon the data. We cannot recast, extend, or qualify.

The proper function of the intellect according to Bacon is indicated by a phrase that recurs significantly in his writings: 'trained experience', *literata experientia*. This seems to mean the intelligent recording and ordering of experience. The intellect is kept absorbed in the object, its course guided by the latter's form. True, there is another stage beyond this, the establishment of axioms or first principles. But the model discourse on heat in Book II of the *Novum Organum* —however preposterous it appears to the student of physics—illustrates how even at this final stage, the axiom is born out of the data without resort to extended interpretation, let alone speculation. All that the intellect permits itself is to arrange and rearrange the data in, ideally, a statistically exhaustive series of permutations and combinations, until it yields a sequence that supports itself by its own inner logic.

Obviously we do not have here a simple vindication of human powers. Rather, we find distrust and discipline of the faculties: humility, a purging of the mind, almost an intellectual asceticism. 'Nature to be commanded must be obeyed' (*Novum Organum*, I. 3: ES. IV. 47).[8] It is another version of the paradox we find in so much Renaissance thought. Man prepares himself for fulfilment through sacrifice, self-castigation, even a complete suppression of the ego. His power appears mysteriously out of a sense of weakness. He surrenders himself to a higher principle—in this case, a truth exceeding all human formulations—and only in this way realizes the noblest potential of his own nature. We may even feel that he comes to transcend the principle to which he nominally owes submission. After obeying nature, he comes to command her.

Bacon expresses this essentially moral pattern in intellectual terms. In fact, for him the moral and intellectual principles coalesce: '. . . the truth of being and the truth of knowing are one, differing no more than the direct beam and the beam reflected' (*Advancement*, I. iv. 8: Johnston, p. 29). One may recall here the discourse on knowledge and charity in *Advancement*, I. i. 3. The advancement of learning and the mastery of nature imply simultaneously the enlargement of the soul; but all this is made possible only by the initial admission of the limitations of man's being.

This impression is borne out by two related tendencies in Bacon's scientific writings. It has long been pointed out how, in his study of the physical sciences, Bacon dwells not on the mathematical laws governing objects but the material nature of the objects themselves. As Rudolf Metz says:

> . . . like Aristotle and the scholasticism and medieval alchemy which developed from him, he was acquainted only with things and their qualities. And if ancient science is governed essentially by the idea of substance, and modern science by the idea of mathematical function and law, then Bacon's outlook remains in the former category, and he was without any understanding of the latter. Bacon's thought was that of the medieval alchemist, not of the modern physicist.[9]

At times one feels like dubbing Bacon's standpoint animistic or even anthropomorphic. He attributes to the objects of nature almost human motives, impulses, and desires. He talks of 'sympathy and antipathy' in physical bodies; of a substance multiplying 'its own nature upon another body'; of how the nobler agent 'excites a motion dormant and latent in another'; and of the 'motion of *Royalty*, or restraint of other motions by the motion predominant' (*De augmentis scientiarum*, III. iv: ES, IV. 356).[10] In astronomy, he laments the emphasis upon the mathematical study of motions and distances, and advocates instead inquiries into the 'physical causes . . . of the substance of the heavens both stellar and interstellar'. This he terms '*Living Astronomy*, in distinction from that stuffed ox of Prometheus, which was an ox in figure only' (ibid.: ES, IV. 348-9).[11]

In plants and animals, Bacon attributes perception to all bodies—a point noted by Whitehead in *Science and the Modern World*.[12] In *Sylva sylvarum* and the *History of Life and Death*, not created beings alone but the very elements and spirits of which they are composed take on a quasi-human existence. Spirits (in the old physiological sense) are 'the agents and workmen that produce all the effects in the body' (*History of Life and Death*: ES, V. 268).[13] Even abstract conceptions like love and envy are endowed with motive and personality. In fact, Bacon does not consider them to be abstract, but entities generated by the operation of the spirit. 'They [love and envy] both have vehement wishes; they

frame themselves readily into imaginations and suggestions
. . .' (*Essays*, 'Of Envy': Abbott, I. 25. 2-4).

All this must not be dismissed as mere explanatory
rhetoric, a resort to personification to make a point vivid. Far
too many passages indicate that Bacon took these ascriptions
literally; he was living in the medieval universe, in which all
objects in the Chain of Being functioned and realized their
ends as graduated expressions of a divinely inspired life-force.

Through such vitalization, the simple goal of man's conquest of nature is exchanged for a much more complex
pattern in which man diverts and induces to his ends a senti-
ent, independent natural order. Science becomes at best the
interaction of mind and matter, a 'closer and purer league
between these two faculties, the experimental and the
rational', than has yet been attempted (*Novum Organum*, I.
95: ES, IV. 93).[14] This union may not even be on equal
terms: at times at least, Bacon declares his purpose to be
'that of rendering the human understanding a match for
things and nature' (*Novum Organum*, II. 19: ES, IV. 149).[15]

Man has to assert his power by pitting it against great
external forces. He cannot control these forces; he can merely
'divert' them, or perhaps, more honestly, simply ensure that
their working coincides with his interests to the greatest
possible extent. Even applied science thus appears to be a
sort of co-operation between man and nature: 'Towards the
effecting of works, all that man can do is to put together or
put asunder natural bodies. The rest is done by nature working within' (*Novum Organum*, I. 4: ES, IV. 47).[16]

All this affords a strikingly new angle on the way Bacon
relates man to the universe. Man is placed at the centre of an
inexhaustible play of forces. He may command this by an
effort and discipline that is basically moral in nature, though
intellectual in its sphere of operation. Such effort demands
that we reject nearly everything that a more expansive
humanity holds precious.

Truth may perhaps come to the price of a pearl, that sheweth best by
day; but it will not rise to the price of a diamond or carbuncle that
sheweth best in varied lights. A mixture of a lie doth ever add pleasure.
Doth any man doubt, that if there were taken out of men's minds vain
opinions, flattering hopes, false valuations, imaginations as one would,

and the like, but it would leave the minds of a number of men poor shrunken things, full of melancholy and indisposition, and unpleasing to themselves? (*Essays*, 'Of Truth': Abbott, I. 1. 20–2. 29)

To take all knowledge for our province is to shrink our own sensibilities, gazing instead on the range and mystery of the universe. 'There is a great difference between the Idols of the human mind and the Ideas of the divine' (*Novum Organum*, I. 23: ES, IV. 51).[17]

In another way too, and a particularly ironic one, Bacon limits his own humane ideal. The impersonal, immutable laws of greater nature—material necessity, one may almost say—are seen to act upon human nature itself. Bacon ascribes such laws, or set patterns of behaviour, to the human mind, and laments that they are not better known: '. . . this kind of observations wandereth in words, but is not fixed in inquiry' (*Advancement*, II. xxii. 4: Johnston, p. 162). By proposing the study of character-types and patterns of conduct, Bacon seems to deny the possibility of free and unlimited mental growth. Instead, such growth is brought within the fold of material phenomena: observable, predictable, almost (one may say) determined. More than once, Bacon explicitly compares mental with physical phenomena, as 'receipts and regiments compounded and described, as may serve to recover or preserve the health and good estate of the mind, as far as pertaineth to human medicine' (*Advancement*, II. xxii. 7: Johnston, p. 164).

This also means that instead of genuine development, Bacon often seems to advocate mere control of human nature. The fact that this includes self-control does not make it basically more ennobling for man. When Bacon leaves aside his scientific optimism and contemplates actual human nature, he seems to favour suppression rather than encouragement and growth. This is as plain from the relevant sections of the *Advancement* as from the essays on such subjects: 'Of Nature in Men', 'Of Custom and Education', even 'Of Love' and 'Of Goodness, and Goodness of Nature'. This is a paradox in Bacon's thought. While lifeless objects, or the material forces and elements, are endowed with a sort of life, human nature itself is reduced to a curiously mechanistic entity. Its operations can be observed and codified, though sadly neglected so far; they can then be changed or controlled by 'custom and education'. Such moral manipulation is in fact simply another form of applied science: the effective control of human nature as of any other aspect of nature.

Fortune, in Bacon, is not a mysterious power of fate; it consists in uncomprehended but perfectly concrete circumstances and attributes. There are 'a number of little and scarce discerned virtues, or rather faculties and customs, that make men fortunate' (*Essays*, 'Of Fortune': Abbott, II. 35. 24-6). To triumph over fortune is simply to study such factors and bring them to the light of day:

. . . to procure good informations of particulars touching persons, their natures, their desires and ends, their customs and fashions, their helps and advantages, and whereby they chiefly stand: so again their weaknesses and disadvantages, and where they lie most open and obnoxious; . . . (*Advancement*, II. xxiii. 14: Johnston, p. 181)

With this one must study means to suppress or alter these circumstances:

. . . points which are within our own command, and have force and operation upon the mind, to affect the will and appetite, and to alter manners: wherein (one should include) custom, exercise, habit, education, example, imitation, emulation, company, friends, praise, reproof, exhortation, fame, laws, books, studies: . . . (*Advancement*, II. xxii. 7: Johnston, p. 164)

All this is as different as could be from a genuine expansion of being. Instead of intensifying the challenge of man's circumstances, Bacon diffuses it, reducing it to comprehensible and controllable factors. Instead of encouraging a heroic persistence, he advocates adaptation and compromise. One finds here the clear influence of Machiavelli, but lacking the ideal of human aspiration enshrined beneath all the violence, cynicism, and ruthlessness in Machiavelli's concept of *virtù*. For Bacon, man might possess qualities to be developed, but he shows no intrinsic, unqualified urge to rise above his being. Rather, he advances by exploiting the circumstances, even the limitations, of his being. What is important is not self-realization or self-development, but external power and success.

Further, the human state within which such success must

be achieved is all too imperfect. 'What would men have? Do they think those they employ and deal with are Saints? Do they not think they will have their own ends, and be truer to themselves than to them?' (*Essays*, 'Of Suspicion': Abbott, II. 4. 18-5. 21.) The means of survival in this competitive world are also plain: 'The best composition and temperature is to have openness in fame and opinion; secrecy in habit; dissimulation in seasonable use; and a power to feign, if there be no remedy (*Essays*, 'Of Simulation and Dissimulation': Abbott, I. 19. 110-13). The 'unfallen' intellect of Bacon's scientific ideal is set at work, in the sphere of civil knowledge, to record a patently fallen state of man.

One may indeed collect a set of quotations, especially from the *Essays*, which present a more idealistic view of human nature. Whole essays may advocate forgiveness and self-sacrifice ('Of Revenge', 'Of Wisdom for a Man's Self'); and there are frequent expressions of genuine humanity. But I think every impartial reader must admit that, taking all in all, these values remain unrealizable or at best contingent. They are qualified by rivalry, self-interest, cynicism, and the simple frailty of the flesh. Admittedly desirable, they must generally give way in any possible dispensation that Bacon can envisage for man.

In fact, such goodness seems to be just one more factor that the man bent on success must reckon with: he may follow it or not as he chooses, provided only that it does not stand in his path. Bacon's ideal man exercises the human faculties to override values created by those very faculties. He studies nature and morality so that he may turn it to use, often by denying its value and dignity. Bacon's view of civil and even of moral knowledge cannot exactly be equated with human engineering, but the underlying philosophy seems much the same: a denial of the absolute nature of human values and a desire to manipulate human nature to some external end. When Bacon is lauded as the visionary philosopher of modern science, we forget the ethics of his science of man.

No less depressing are the intellectual implications of his stand. Whether Bacon turns the *radius directus* on to nature, or the *radius refractus* towards God, or the *radius reflexus* upon himself,[18] he makes the intellect circumscribe its own powers and question man's station. This cynicism about the self proves a strange binary to the brave new world of Baconian science. The promise held out by his ideal of material inquiry does not transform the nature of man.

Strangely, it is in the rearguard of the old learning that we find a more genuine vindication of man. These authors fully admit the limits of man's being; they are bound in by imperfect observation, fabulous lore, 'authority', and sheer superstition. But they have a greater respect for the state of man. In them we truly find the new, paradoxical humanity that admits and yet transcends the limits of man.

The best-known exemplar of this tendency is Sir Thomas Browne. I have chosen to deal instead with a less celebrated author, but one closer to the main period of my study. The work of Robert Burton provides one of the subtlest keys to the valuation of learning and morality in Jacobean England.

3. Burton's *Anatomy*

The first thing to note about Burton's *Anatomy of Melancholy* is the title of the work. According to McKerrow[19] the 'anatomy' of a subject is a general term for any investigation or inquiry into it. Perhaps a more exact definition is not possible if one considers the long line of 'anatomies' of various subjects that appeared all through the Renaissance. But Burton seems to have had one instance in mind above all others: 'Anthony Zara, . . . his Anatomy of Wit, in four sections, members, subsections, etc., to be read in our libraries' ('Democritus Junior to the Reader': EL, I. 20).

The *Anatomia ingeniorum et scientiarum* (1614) of Antonio Zara was indeed planned with a very careful division of material into four parts, a general section on the dignity and excellence of man followed by sections dealing with the sciences of the imagination, the intellect, and the memory. This was a common tool of Renaissance methodology, *partitio* or the systematic division and part-by-part treatment of a complex subject. Bacon uses this partitive structure in nearly all his major philosophic and scientific writings. The same *partitio* may be seen in such varied works as Puttenham's

Arte of English Poesie, Hooker's *Laws of Ecclesiastical Politie*, and Browne's *Pseudodoxia Epidemica*; or, for that matter, in the basic scheme of *The Faerie Queene*. To go back in time, it can be found in works of medieval divinity from *The City of God* to the *Summa Theologica*, taking in many lesser works on the way. Still more to our purpose, *partitio* is, as one might have expected, the formal principle in encyclopaedic works from Pliny onwards, through the Middle Ages and the Renaissance.

Such *partitio* may be deduced from Burton's table of contents—the neat pattern of partition, section, member, and subsection: 'first general, then particular; and those according to their several species' (2. 1. 1: EL, II. 5). But this division relates to the topic of melancholy—which is only a part of Burton's subject-matter. The encyclopaedic range of his material is not confined within any systematic structure. The total effect is one of gothic confusion, masses of unsorted information scattered unevenly over the basic theme of melancholy. To quote Burton's own description, he deals in 'toys and fopperies confusedly tumbled out, without art, invention, judgment, wit, learning, harsh, raw, rude, phantastical, absurd, insolent . . .' ('Democritus': EL, I. 26). The elaborate structure is superimposed on this confusion in obvious futility. There is a constant tension between the content of the work and its formal arrangement. One loses sight of the titular subject for pages and whole chapters at a time. The partitive structure, an established and popular method of intellectual discourse, is strained, questioned—ultimately, almost flouted. It is rather like Agrippa's use of a partitive survey of learning to demonstrate the uselessness of all such surveys.

Partitio is only one of the intellectual methods which Burton discredits by the ironic flattery of over-use. Equally important is his wide-eyed reverence for all authorities—often disastrously for those authorities. He quotes conflicting sources and makes no attempt to choose between them.

If either Sextus Empiricus, Picus Mirandula, Sextus ab Heminga, Pererius, Erastus, Chambers, etc., have so far prevailed with any man, that he will attribute no virtue at all to the heavens . . . I refer him to

Bellantius, Pirovanus, Marascallerus, Goclenius, Sir Christopher Heydon, etc. (1. 2. 1. 4: EL, I. 206)

The celebrated chapter on bad diet (1. 2. 2. 1) ends up by forbidding every food known to man; in 2. 2. 1. 1, then, most of these reappear as desirable items of diet on other authority. In the 'Digression of the Air' (2. 2. 3), Burton discusses a huge variety of geographical and astronomical matters—either as reports which he doubts or as problems of which the solution is unknown. Ultimately, all astronomical theories are dismissed as makeshift explanations: '. . . our latter mathematicians . . . have invented new hypotheses, and fabricated new systems of the world, out of their own Daedalian heads' (EL, II. 56). In the process, the old system is discredited too: '. . . one saith the sun stands, another he moves; a third comes in, taking them all at rebound . . .' (EL, II. 57).

The sections on physic, 2. 4 and 2. 5, may be thought the most egregious instances of Burton's unquestioning use of authority. But let us look closer. Complex arguments, both pro and con, are quoted without solution—about the use of compounds, for instance, in 2. 4. 1. 5, or antimony (2. 4. 2. 1) or lapis lazuli (2. 4. 2. 2). A contrast is provided by a single paragraph amidst this gnarled erudition:

> Tobacco, divine, rare, superexcellent tobacco, which goes far beyond all the panaceas, potable gold, and philosophers' stones, a sovereign remedy to all diseases. A good vomit, I confess, a virtuous herb, if it be well qualified, opportunely taken, and medicinally used; but as it is commonly abused by most men, which take it as tinkers do ale, 'tis a plague, a mischief, a violent purger of goods, lands, health; hellish, devilish, and damned tobacco, the ruin and overthrow of body and soul. (2. 4. 2. 1: EL, II. 228)

The prose leaps suddenly into a more flowing movement; there is no citing of reference; the Gordian knot of authorities is cut by an obvious declaration of personal taste, a piece of sardonic lyricism. The author who so robustly rejoices in his spontaneous choices implies that he has no use for authority.

As we might expect, it is in the section on love-melancholy that Burton most ridicules authority by quoting it with ironic pedantry over the most common, spontaneous, unacademic experience of mankind. Here he also casts doubt on standard logical and rhetorical methods by applications so ridiculously malapropos that they cannot but be considered facetious parody. The whole edifice finally comes crashing down in 3. 2. 5. 5: 'The last refuge and surest remedy . . . is to let them go together, and enjoy one another: . . .' (EL, III. 228).

All these examples point to the same conclusion: the Protean nature of actual human experience. Burton may be said to foster a sort of nominalism of experience—each item of knowledge being cherished for its own sake, but not combining with the rest to form a coherent system. The whole work is so centrifugal in tendency that it demonstrates the impossibility of any system, and worse, the inadequacy of all our intellectual methods.

Burton can therefore weave a fantasy out of the stuff of knowledge. He orders his vast range of material by the laws of free association rather than scientific deduction. His prose reflects this gay disorder of method: the endless piling up of words and phrases, brief tentative observations in the 'Senecan' style slung out into the long, easy movements of irresponsible learned chatter. Morris Croll proposes the term libertine prose[20]—implying not merely a stylistic trait but a philosophic position, as go-as-you-please personal survey of the realm of knowledge, that differs both from Bacon's 'magistral' exposition of firm knowledge and his 'probative' method of cautious enquiry.

The obvious parallel is with Rabelais's work. Auerbach's remarks on Rabelais provide penetrating insight into both authors:

Almost all the elements which are united in Rabelais's style are known from the later Middle Ages . . . But . . . The way in which these elements are exaggerated and intertwined produces an entirely new picture . . . Late medieval works are confined within a definite frame, socially, geographically, cosmologically, religiously, and ethically . . . But Rabelais's entire effort is directed toward playing with things and with the multiplicity of their possible aspects; upon tempting the reader out of his customary and definite way of regarding things, by showing him phenomena in utter confusion; upon tempting him out into the great ocean of the world, in which he can swim freely, though it be at his own peril.[21]

Burton resembles Rabelais in a number of points: the vast unsystematic sweep of knowledge; satire of all social institutions, coupled with much love for the weak and foolish creatures who create them; the contrast between the intractable range of passions, appetites and experiences, and the narrow desiccated world of Latinate learning; ultimately, perhaps, the sense that all search for knowledge is futile, with the plea for a simpler and more heartfelt morality.

True, Burton's Scepticism is largely confined to a pattern of nuances playing about the margin of his work. Our sense of proportion must prevent us from suggesting that the entire *Anatomy* is primarily a satire of the common intellectual methods of the day. It would be a poor joke that barely emerges in a thousand pages. The *Anatomy* is a storehouse of serious knowledge, especially of melancholy in the medical sense. But I do suggest that while exploring the labyrinths into which his study of melancholy led him, Burton grows keenly conscious of the inadequacies and absurdities of his methods. Confirmed in his suspicions by the Sceptical tendencies of a doubt-torn age, he weaves these questionings into his work as a separate intellectual strand. And by mocking the meat he feeds on, he assails his readers with constant doubts of the truth of what they read. They are led to look elsewhere for his central purpose. The work takes on a new orientation. Let us examine what this might be.

Again and again, Burton proposes the traditional explanation for the impossibility of knowledge, the Fall of Man: ' . . . to know that secret which should not be known, to eat of the forbidden fruit . . . What is most of our philosophy but a labyrinth of opinions, idle questions, propositions, metaphysical terms?' (1. 2. 4. 7: EL, I. 366). All the world is mad, foolish, sick. This open declaration of universal folly is made most stridently in the 'Satirical Preface' of Democritus Junior, but piecemeal through the entire work. And this folly is but one aspect of 'melancholy'—a term that finally comes to embrace all physical, social, and spiritual ills known to man.

Melancholy was traditionally a psychiatric disorder as much as a physical one, a 'common infirmity of body and soul'. Burton carries this duality to its extreme. Again and again, anatomical or physical analysis of melancholy passes in the turn of a sentence into moral censure and homily. Particularly important is 1. 2. 5. 1, describing the interrelation of body and soul, and—most notable this—tracing the source of all physical maladies to sin: '. . . concupiscence and original sin, inclinations, and bad humours are radical in every one of us, causing these perturbations, affections, and several distempers, offering many times violence unto the soul' (EL I. 374). This indeed repeats the opening assertion in 1. 1. 1. 1, anticipated in the 'Satirical Preface', repeated throughout the *Anatomy*, that the cause of Melancholy is sin—and its cure moral discipline and exhortation. Even where the immediate cause of melancholy is choler adust, the ultimate cause is the devil (1. 2. 1. 2). And where 'melancholy' is neither sin nor folly, it is sorrow and suffering (e.g., in the 'Satirical Preface' *passim*, and in 1. 2. 3. 10).

Burton often describes melancholy as the overthrow of reason by passion—the standard account of the moral consequence of the Fall. Interesting also are passages like the following: 'They [the passions and perturbations of the mind] are born and bred with us, we have them from our parents by inheritance . . . ('T)is propagated from Adam; Cain was melancholy, as Austin hath it, and who is not?' (1. 2. 3. 1: EL, I. 251). The list of unruly passions, in the Preface and more extensively in 1. 2. 3. 7-14, is somewhat reminiscent of the Seven Deadly Sins—including as it does such items as Envy, Emulation, Anger, Ambition, Covetousness, Excessive Pleasure, and *Philautia* or Self-Love.

One is drawn every time to the conclusion that 'melancholy' is for Burton an allegory of the fallen state of man. Beneath the satire of society and academia there lies this deeper 'tragical satire' of the human state itself. Once we recognize the moral scheme of the work, the most digressive passages fall into place. The constant moral exhortations are justified—above all, the climactic rejection of human wisdom and the turning to God in the final section on religious melancholy. The satiric impulse has its obverse in the homiletic one.

The *Anatomy* begins with the 'Satirical Preface', which describes the sin and folly of fallen man; it is appropriately balanced by the homiletic sections of the close, the discourse on God's mercy and grace, salvation and election:

A true desire of mercy in the want of mercy, is mercy itself; a desire of grace in the want of grace, is grace itself; a constant and earnest desire to believe, repent, and to be reconciled to God, if it be in a touched heart, is an acceptation of God, a reconciliation, faith and repentance itself. (3. 4. 2. 6: EL, III. 415)

Burton's loose meandering sentences are here disciplined into the formal patterns of sermon rhetoric. It would be false to claim that this is Burton's usual style towards the end of his book; but it is significant that he could so curb his luxuriance, even for brief spells, at the climax of his spiritual theme.

Though Burton jumbles all his material in a bewildering way, his subject is obviously divided between two moral levels: the knowledge of earthly and human things (rendered suspect by the imperfection of all earthly means to knowledge), and the conviction of God's power and grace that is born from a confession of ignorance. The former ideal of learning is assessed in terms of the latter, *scientia* in terms of *sapientia*, the intellect by the canons of virtue.

Distrust of the human intellect makes the soul turn to God, to trust in faith when reason fails. Burton does not ostensibly clear the mind of all knowledge; instead he piles up more and more information—but in such luxuriance that the upshot is the same distrust and rejection. The soul comes to rest in faith in God.

I know that in true religion itself, many mysteries are so apprehended alone by faith, as that of the Trinity, which Turks especially deride, Christ's incarnation, resurrection of the body at the last day, *quod ideo credendum* (saith Tertullian) *quod incredibile* . . . (3. 4. 1. 3: EL, III. 351)

Yet even now we have not exhausted the complexity of Burton's design. It would be a mistake to imagine that Burton ends with a firm faith in the impersonal divine. Sceptical bewilderment drew another response from him, as from the age: a belief in the morality of natural, individual impulse. Such is the proposed cure for love-melancholy by 'letting them go together and enjoy one another'. In the section on 'Diet Rectified by Substance' (2. 2. 1. 1–2), the hectic confusion of authorities is quelled by a simple appeal to inclination: 'I conclude, our own experience is the best physician; that diet which is most propitious to one is often pernicious to another; such is the variety of palates, humours, and temperatures, let every man observe, and be a law unto himself' (2. 2. 1. 2: EL, II. 29).

Above all, it is in the section on religious melancholy, apparently preoccupied with doctrinal and homiletic authority, that careful reading reveals a constant call to the sensibility of the individual Christian. Burton discourses on election and on God's wrath; but the rigid divine scheme is mild enough to respond to the least unhardening of the heart. All through, Burton stresses the ease and beauty of service to God: '. . . it is a sole ease, an unspeakable comfort, a sweet reposal, *jugum suave, et leve*, a light yoke, an anchor, and an haven' (3. 4. 1. 1: EL, III. 320). Fasting, flagellation, and all excessive rigour are decried:

As in fasting, so in all other superstitious edicts, we crucify one another without a cause, barring ourselves of many good and lawful things, honest disports, pleasures and recreations; for wherefore did God create them but for our use? (3. 4. 1. 4: EL, III. 374)

The virtue of asceticism lies in its being voluntary and spontaneous. The whole of 3. 4. 1. 4 pleads for liberalism in this matter, and in the next subsection is a noble and learned exposition on religious tolerance. Its point is scarcely removed by the final admission that many of the eccentrics so tolerated might better be in Bedlam, or the advice that heterodoxy in 'the vulgar' should be forcibly suppressed in the interest of public order.

In fact, Burton may be said to take the standard position of the moderate Protestant. He realizes the relativity of all customs, practices, and secondary beliefs, and therefore allows a certain freedom of mind to the individual. But he welcomes a degree of uniformity in the interests of communal order, admits the ultimate weakness of man's faculties, both intellectual and moral, and finally comes to rest in revelation and the grace of God.

In the last analysis, however, this sober vindication of man emerges less from explicit declarations than from the constant evidence of Burton's use of language. I have talked about his 'libertine' style, and how it tests the validity of theory by the flux of actual experience. It does something else too: it submits nearly the entire spectrum of life and learning to the judgement of an uncommitted sensibility. Each particle of information is torn from the intellectual system to which it belongs and which might have deceived us into credence by a spurious self-contained neatness. Instead we find it naked, isolated, scrutinized by a sensitive and extremely risible intelligence. Each fragment of information or opinion emerges valid only as far as it stands up to this test. If it is in any way weak or false, the language in which it finds expression will at once expose it to laughter and rejection, without need for more direct censure. Burton's style is not ironic in itself; but it automatically generates irony when the subject-matter deserves it.

Where Burton's prose seems most like a deadpan catalogue of authorities, he is in fact reacting emotionally to every piece of material. To put it more exactly, he is expressing the components of all the various systems on which he draws through the common medium of his 'libertine' style—the style of a man pledged to no system, but with sharp faculties and wide human sympathies that respond with extreme subtlety to any stimulus that reading or experience might afford.

Thus beneath all the satire of intellectual methods, beneath the scathing exposure of sin and folly, Burton quietly vindicates man's right to think and observe. The obvious intellectual energy of his work counters any simple denial of the power of the human faculties; in fact, it is this energy which makes him give vent to his doubt and Scepticism. Through the subtle cross-currents of his thought, one may trace not only a genuine love of man but even a sense of his due dignity. His wide-ranging work is crowned with the 'humble humanity' of the age in one of its most touching and impressive forms.

4. *Cross-Purposes in Spenser's Poetry*

In the poetry of the Elizabethan and Jacobean age, we discover the same movement that we have traced in the dissertative prose. The optimism of the earlier phase is found to conceal tensions and contradictions and even fall prey to them. But gradually we find a new ideal that incorporates these contradictions, accepts the terms of existence instead of trying to transcend them, and yet glorifies the state of man.

The abortive brilliance of the earlier spirit is nowhere better seen than in Spenser's *The Faerie Queene*. Spenser goes far towards reconciling his ideals to the reality of material life. The medieval framework of allegorical romance supports a promise of new achievement that substantially anticipates the work of John Donne. But Spenser never quite carries out the synthesis: the framework is recast and extended, but it crushes the new spirit in the end.

This imperfect innovation is best introduced through a similar tension in the Platonic *Fowre Hymnes*. The opposite tendencies embodied in the Hymns are described by Spenser himself in the Dedication:

Hauing in the greener times of my youth, composed these former two Hymnes in the praise of Loue and beautie . . . I resolued at least to amend, and by way of retractation to reforme them, making in stead of those two Hymnes of earthly or naturall love and beautie, two others of heauenly and celestiall.

The matter of the Hymns comes from the newly revived 'mysteries' of the Renaissance; but the controlling spirit, as expressed in this Dedication, is that of the medieval palinode.

Admittedly, all four Hymns are philosophically consistent; but Spenser shifts his emphasis, focusing now on matter and now on spirit, contrasting the principles of immanence and transcendence. Love and beauty derive their nature from a heavenly prototype; but they operate in the created universe. Love it is

> Through which now all these things that are contained
> Within this goodly cope, both most and least
> Their being haue, and dayly are increast . . .
> ('Hymn of Love', 94-6)

In man, love is inspired by beauty, which too, though patterned from heaven, 'The duller earth it quickneth with delight' ('Hymn of Beauty', 51).

Yet the soul cannot rest in mortal beauty:

> He thereon feeds his hungrie fantasy,
> Still full, yet neuer satisfyde with it,
> Like *Tantale*, that in store doth sterued ly:
> So doth he pine in most satiety,
> For nought may quench his infinite desyre,
> Once kindled through that first conceiued fyre.
> ('Hymn of Love', 198-203)

We are reminded of Ficino's Prometheus: man is caught between finite powers and infinite aspiration. He is endowed with finer impulses, but imperfectly; and the very fineness of these impulses dooms them to frustration by the sense of their own imperfect presence. Release from this frustration comes only by rejecting the material state, rising upon the orthodox Platonic ladder of ascent: a path most clearly indicated in 'A Hymn of Heavenly Beauty'.

The pattern is complicated by a more clearly Christian note. The Neoplatonic concept of emanation, of heavenly love operating downwards into the material order, finds a peculiarly Christian application in the doctrine of the Incarnation:

> Out of the bosome of eternall blisse,
> In which he reigned with his glorious syre,
> He downe descended, like a most demisse
> And abiect thrall, in fleshes fraile attyre . . .
>
> ('Hymn of Heavenly Love', 134–7)

In Christian thought, the Incarnation has always provided a basis for the integration of flesh and spirit, a check to the complete rejection of material existence. But interestingly, Spenser does not exploit this potential here. Rather, he stresses the foulness of the flesh in which Christ immures himself, and exhorts us to repay this loving sacrifice by abjuring the flesh:

> Then rouze thy selfe, O earth, out of thy soyle,
> In which thou wallowest like to filthy swyne
> And doest thy mynd in durty pleasures moyle,
> Vnmindfull of that dearest Lord of thyne;
> Lift vp to him thy heauie clouded eyne: . . .
>
> ('Hymn of Heavenly Love', 218–22)

The exaltation of man's material being that Spenser elsewhere carries out in Neoplatonic terms is not permitted here in Christian ones. Instead, the soul is led out of the created universe towards 'the glory of that Maiestie diuine' ('Hymn of Heavenly Beauty', 124).

But it is not led out in any excess of gloom and *contemptus mundi*. The *Hymnes* breathe an air of spiritual optimism. This is perhaps the most important function served by Platonizing the Christian doctrine. The emanation of the soul from the divine and its return to its source—the common Platonic 'cycle of love'—is conceived of as a single harmonious movement, testifying to the basic nobility of the soul and its oneness with the spiritual order. The material impediments are purely incidental, and themselves rendered significant by the spirit immanent in them.

All these ideas recur in *The Faerie Queene*; but it is material of ambiguous import, and Spenser alters his emphases. In fact, he alters them several times from several angles, as may be expected in so complex a work; and the over-all pattern too is different from the *Hymnes*. We have a loftier ideal of human achievement; and to counter it, a stronger spirit of gloom and resignation.

Spenser's new ideal shows in a distinctive use of chivalric romance as his basic, continuous metaphor. It may appear entirely appropriate that the chivalric values of the knight-errant should act as an allegory for the spiritual values of the seeker after virtue. Medieval literature goes far to uphold this view. The knight's task itself was thought to require not merely physical strength or skill at arms, but lofty ideals:

> . . . fro the tyme that he first bigan
> To riden out, he loved chivalrie,
> Trouthe and honour, fredom and curteisie.
> (Chaucer, General Prologue to the *Canterbury Tales*, ll. 44-6)

Yet such knightly virtue proved inadequate by the highest spiritual standards of the Middle Ages. Most strongly expressed in the Grail romances, this idea seems to pervade much medieval literature, as Rosèmond Tuve shows. Lancelot's unchastity stands for all sin: it is not the root cause but only a symbol of the corruption in Arthur's court.[22] The ultimate cause lies in the inadequacy of a chivalric code that finds its end in feats of arms, favours of women and, at most, a stable and evil-free social order in this imperfect world. Opposed to this stands 'celestial chivalry', chaste and unworldly. Sir Galahad can fight a bloody battle on occasion, but he submits to supernatural guidance with a curious passivity, and his gaze is constantly beyond this world: '. . . Now, my Blyssed Lorde, I wold nat lyve in this wrecched worlde no lenger, if hit myght please The, Lorde' (Malory, *The Tale of the Sankgreal*: Caxton, XVII: 22).

For all his divergence from his sources in French romance, Malory's work is still set in this other-worldly perspective. In the sixteenth century, the knights of God show a profound change of spirit. Tasso's Godfrey also professes to fight for God:

> Not hope of praise, nor thirst of worldly good,
> Enticed us to follow this emprise: . . .
>
> *(Jerusalem Delivered,* II. 83)

But in conduct of war he is no Galahad: his victories are won by 'earthly' martial prowess, and any aims beyond the capture of Jerusalem are left very vague indeed. Still less does Rinaldo embody any unusual spiritual power. In fact, *Jerusalem Delivered* so obviously takes the *Iliad* as its model that despite any possible motives of outdoing the pagan prototype, the action inevitably becomes oriented in a more temporal, human manner: sacred warfare is carried on by able, virtuous knightly conduct, not the extraordinary spiritual gifts of the Grail hero.

More radically, the medieval knight was turning into the Renaissance courtier, who could not only leap into the saddle with a *sprezzatura* worthy of Lancelot or Gawain, but aspire to letters and philosophy. His love of woman could lead him on to the 'main sea of the pure heavenly beauty.'[23] The spiritual world is no longer an alien, overpowering presence, demanding the rejection of courtly life and chivalry. There is no sense of sin in the court described by Castiglione; rather of full humanity come to flower. Philosophic perfection is passing from the sage to the courtier, and more and more being embodied in action. Spiritual perfection seems within the grasp of the 'earthly' knight, courtier, or gentleman. The medieval dichotomy is being bridged.

The Faerie Queene makes perhaps the most considerable attempt in this direction, by presenting spiritual progress in terms of chivalric action. This it does by raising the spiritual or moral impulse behind knightly deeds to the level of clear allegory. Once romantic chivalry is taken as a direct image of spiritual endeavour, the two cannot of course be contrasted. Rather, the chivalric feats—killing giants and dragons, succouring many damsels and wooing one—become identified with the higher chivalry searching for spiritual perfection and happiness in the next world.

As one might expect, this mode is clearest in the political allegory, especially where that allegory itself is clearest, in Book V. The Knight of Justice must engage in purely political warfare: a heavenly virtue is to be maintained by earthly chivalry. Tyranny and injustice are identified with Philip II and Mary Queen of Scots. Similar 'earthly' action is required in the case of Pollente and Munera, the Giant by the Sea, and all the other social menaces presented in Book V—and in the other books too. The knight who would quell an uproar must, quite simply, capture or drive away its instigators (II. iv). Defenders of chastity must rescue and escort maids in distress, as does Satyrane (I. vi, III. vii), or Timias (IV. vii), or Britomart herself with Amoret. Calidore's courtesy shows in his acts of conquest over such vile knights as Crudor, or the evil and villainy in human society, as signified by the Blatant Beast:

> Through all estates he found that he had past,
> In which he many massacres had left . . .   (VI. xii. 23)

The active role of all Spenser's knights contrasts with the passivity of Galahad that I noted earlier. We remember not what they are but what they do. Their external action cannot remain purely a metaphor for inner spiritual states.

The 'Mammon Canto' (II. vii) contains a notable exhortation to 'earthly' virtue. Mammon tempts Guyon with wealth and fame; his refusal is not as unworldly as it might have been:

> Regard of worldly mucke doth fowly blend,
> And low abase the high heroicke spright,
> That ioyes for crownes and kingdomes to contend;
> Faire shields, gay steedes, bright armes be my delight:
> Those be the riches fit for an aduent'rous knight.   (II. vii. 10)

It may of course be argued that this picture of chivalry is metaphorical for a purely spiritual effort. In fact, Guyon's temptations in this canto suggest the temptations of Christ. But if there is a spiritual allegory, vehicle and tenor are inseparably mingled.

By the very nature of his allegory, Spenser could make no

sharp distinction between the knight who fights battles to defeat the wicked, create a better society, and win fame and love, and the other class of knight who endeavours to form himself in Christian virtue to win reward in the next world. He had to show his knights as preserving the moral virtues and winning spiritual guerdon by victories over tyrants, giants, and monsters on a purely 'earthly' plane. The heavenly virtues appear accessible to any man determined on serious spiritual endeavour, without superhuman chastity or other gifts. It also appears possible to establish these virtues in this world by knightly warfare against evil.

Such reassessment of traditional judgements shows still more clearly in Spenser's treatment of love. In Chaucer's *Troilus and Criseyde* or Gower's *Confessio Amantis*, love had been associated with fortune and the mutability of a sinful world, and its ultimate futility brought out in the conclusion. A hundred years earlier, Jean de Meung's Genius had exhorted lovers to turn from the Garden of Mirth to the Heavenly Garden.[24] Even in Dante, where profane love is a pathway to the divine, the dichotomy never disappears—one must be rejected before the other can develop.

Yet at less exalted levels, medieval authors show much hesitation on the subject. Genius in *The Romance of the Rose* also advises the Barons to ensure their posterity, and aids Love's party in helping the Lover to a very physical 'deflowering'.[25] The world must be peopled, and human love and procreation form part of the rhythm of universal love. This association of sexual and cosmic love was a medieval commonplace.

The stock 'garden of love' shows bewildering similarities to the equally orthodox descriptions of the Earthly Paradise: eternal spring, birdsong, flowers, fruits, spices, and limpid streams, perhaps with a liberal sprinkling of jewels. It is beautiful and exhilarating, yet unmistakably voluptuous—typifying the ambiguity of medieval notions of love, Venus, Nature, sexual and procreative matters generally. At most, the garden might be divided into the provinces of 'Nature' and 'Venus', as in *The Parliament of Fowls*. But almost invariably, such gardens lay under the cloud of what might be called the 'palinodic spirit', a rejection of love.

In *The Faerie Queene* we find not one but several gardens
and palaces of love, radiating in different moral directions
from the central, traditional image. Spenser is trying to un-
ravel the different moral strands of the medieval tangle, so as
to separate the uplifting elements of love and establish them
at a purely human level, without any further movement on to
divine love.

Human love can be evil. The Bower of Bliss, Castle Joyous,
and the Hall of Busirane testify to that. Yet the sexual force
is basically a power for good, cosmic in range. Exactly mid-
way between the corrupt domains of Malecasta and Busirane,
Spenser has set the mighty force of life itself, in the Garden
of Adonis. All ephemeral perversions of human love are set
against the force of universal life, and corrected *sub specie
aeternitatis*.

It is only in a corner, as playfellow of the mighty life-god,
that Cupid finds a place—and that, too, stripped of his darts.
He is now the agent of the chaste or right love which serves
the purposes of Nature. The *'carpe diem'* theme of Acrasia's
island is countered by showing how the power of life defeats
time:

> All be he subiect to mortalitie,
> Yet is eterne in mutabilitie,
> And by succession made perpetuall . . .   (III. vi. 47)

Spenser was to give this doctrine a different turn later on,
but here it is a vindication of cosmic vitality.

Yet this vital force cannot by itself provide the emotional
compound of love; it can only yield its basis. Amoret must be
transferred to the narrower but more human and satisfying
Temple of Venus. Venus's connexions with universal fertility
are clear enough:

> Then doth the daedale earth throw forth to thee
> Out of her fruitfull lap aboundant flowres . . .   (IV. x. 45)

Within this sphere, human love appears to be her special
province, as indeed was only traditional. We may consider the
relation between Nature and Venus in *The Romance of the
Rose*, or the two gardens in *The Parliament of Fowls*. But
unlike these medieval precedents, *The Faerie Queene* does
not show the Temple of Venus as morally inferior to the

Garden of Adonis, only more restricted. Venus's court is adorned with 'thousand pairs of lovers', and the chaster 'lovers' of male friendship (though Spenser pays but lip-service to this Renaissance ideal).

The creative force has been reduced to the level of human emotion. Between the purely procreative energy and the sterile emotional preoccupation, a human compromise has been reached at last. It is a perfect but purely human love.

The same synthesis is embodied in Britomart. Her chastity is as inviolable as Belphoebe's, but does not preclude a delicate affection. Yet this young woman of tender love is a spirited warrior in the cause of right. She is a true combination of Diana and Venus, Belphoebe and Amoret. She appears as the object of a love that can provide a perfectly satisfying spiritual experience without transcending its human, erotic character. Sacred and profane love meet in Spenser's chastity.

In every way, then, Spenser sees humanity bodying forth order, beauty, love. Human love, human chivalry, and ordered earthly society lose their stigma of sin and moral inadequacy and become lofty spiritual goals. His 'this-worldly' approach makes for a strikingly new treatment of traditional themes and images.

But that is only one half of the story. Spenser could not sustain his experiment. The synthesis of 'earthly' and 'celestial' chivalry, erotic and divine love, strains the potential of the medieval material to the utmost. Almost from the outset, there is a tension in *The Faerie Queene* between the 'earthly chivalry' I have so far outlined, and a renunciatory, 'palinodic' spirit. The most elaborate expression of the latter in the early books comes in the discourse of Contemplation in I. x:

> But when thou famous victorie hast wonne,
> And high emongst all knights hast hong thy shield,
> Thenceforth the suit of earthly conquest shonne,
> And wash thy hands from guilt of bloudy field:
> For bloud can nought but sin, and wars but sorrowes yield.
>
> Then seeke this path, that I to thee presage,
> Which after all to heauen shall thee send;
> Then peaceably thy painefull pilgrimage
> To yonder same *Hierusalem* do bend ...   (I. x. 60–1)

For once this is very similar to the orthodox medieval views on 'earthly chivalry'. It might be part of some hermit's discourse in the Grail legend. In a less conspicuous way, the first four books contain many more references to fortune, mutability, and general world-weariness. Such observations form a sombre comment on the radiant vision of love and chivalry.

Book V opens on this note:

> Me seemes the world is runne quite out of square,
> From the first point of his appointed sourse,
> And being once amisse growes daily wourse and wourse.
>
> (V. Proem 1)

The 'tickleness' of mortal things grows more and more apparent in the chaos and iniquity lurking beneath the ordered vision of punitive justice and the higher loving concord of mercy.

Spenser's increasing world-weariness takes a more positive aspect in Book VI. Here, the heart of the allegory surely lies in the dance of the Graces. The vision of order is at its most fleeting and uncapturable in these shy figures of a delicately pure nakedness, fleeing at human approach. And there is, I believe, a further meaning.

The three Graces were a favourite Neoplatonic symbol, signifying 'giving, accepting and returning', and thus, Platonically, God's gifts to us, our appreciation of these gifts, and (out of the resultant love) our return to God. Ultimately, the symbol suggests the Platonic cycle of love: 'turning away from the world in which we are, so as to rejoin the spirit beckoning from the Beyond'.[26] In a larger context like that of Botticelli's *Primavera*, the Graces signify the turning to the infinite, balancing the earthly *emanatio* from the infinite in the group of Zephyrus, Chloris, and Flora. Venus presides in the centre.

Is not this the structure of *The Faerie Queene* as well—or of the four *Hymnes* taken as a group? On the one hand, Spenser prizes the earthly embodiments of Platonic beauty, as objects of love. On the other hand, he seeks the source of this beauty in a movement away from this world. In the dance of the Graces, Spenser is using a standard Neoplatonic image for worldly renunciation in search of the ideal or infinite.

This gives a distinctive quality to Spenser's pastoralism. There is nothing unusual in the poet's celebrating rustic life

above court manners, even in the middle of his book on
Courtesy. The Renaissance habitually uses pastoral in this
way. The standard pastoral drama or romance moves its leading figures from a corrupt court to a pure pastoral world on
the model of the Golden Age. Here the tangles of court
intrigue are sorted out in a regenerative, even magical, atmosphere; and finally, the revivified group of courtiers return to
court in new, pure strength. Even the shepherd maiden who
embodies the best qualities of the pastoral world turns out to
be a lost or disguised princess.

Superficially, this is the pattern of Spenser's pastoral
too; but the addition of the dancing Graces makes for a
striking difference in the design. The highest pastoral values
come to be embodied not in Pastorella but in the Graces
and their queen, the Venus-like 'fourth Grace', Colin Clout's
beloved. The setting is another variation of the Earthly
Paradise:

> It was an hill plaste in an open plaine,
> That round about was bordered with a wood
> Of matchlesse hight, that seem'd th'earth to disdaine,
> In which all trees of honour stately stood,
> And did all winter as in sommer bud ...   (VI. x. 6)

But this time, the paradisial garden is beyond human reach,
and its denizens flee at the hero's approach. Calidore wins the
shepherd-princess and returns to chivalric life; but back
on the hill there are still those evanescent dancing figures,
drawing one on to regions of the spirit far beyond the
reach of Calidore in a world haunted by the Blatant Beast.
The action moves on, but spiritually we are left with the
Graces, led away from court—not back to it, as in pastoral
generally.

The ultimate unworldliness comes in the Mutability Cantos.
I would perhaps be right in saying that there is nothing
radically new in 'Book VII'. Spenser had admitted the presence
of mutability as far back as in the Garden of Adonis. But the
power of death had there been swept away in the surge of
life. Similarly, Artegall had explained to the Giant by the Sea
the cosmic justice and concord behind the flux of nature
(V. ii. 39–43). In the Mutability Cantos too, the ultimate
permanence of the shifting universe is admitted:

> ... being rightly wayd
> They are not changed from their first estate;
> But by their change their being doe dilate:
> And turning to themselues at length againe,
> Doe worke their owne perfection so by fate: ...
>
> (VII. vii. 58)

'Eternity in Mutability' was a favourite Neoplatonic concept. It had strong medieval roots too, as may be seen from Genius's speech on procreation in *The Romance of the Rose* (11. 19505-906).

The difference in 'Book VII' from these and Spenser's own earlier passages is one of emphasis. The spectacle of change and decay had never been presented so vividly before, and never with so little of the balancing assertion of permanence. We should consider also the exalted role of Nature. Contrary to tradition, she had not appeared at all in the Garden of Adonis, and now Mutability, not Nature, appears as goddess of the sublunary world. Nature herself is left immutable, a sort of Platonic idea behind the 'dying generations':

> Still moouing, yet vnmoued from her sted;
> Vnseene of any, yet of all beheld; ...   (VII. vii. 13)

We are reminded of the 'Hymn of Heavenly Beauty':

> Vnmouing, vncorrupt, and spotlesse bright ...   (1. 68)

The poet's vision turns to the unchanging essence of created things. Contemplation of mutable nature leads the mind beyond it, and things below the moon seem a contemptible decline from that absolute perfection.

Moreover, the Masque of Mutability crowns the mounting world-weariness and longing for the beyond in Books V and VI. As it is, Spenser's last two heroes already play somewhat tragic roles, acting their parts in a world that has sunk too low to profit by their efforts. Artegall has to leave Irena, his task still unfinished; the Blatant Beast breaks out again. The enemy of eternity is no longer 'wicked *Time*' with his scythe and 'flaggy wings' (III. vi. 39), but a proud, defiant creature whose might seems to overrule the judgement of Nature. The poet himself ignores this judgement completely in his own conclusion:

> . . . yet very sooth to say,
> In all things else she beares the greatest sway.
> Which makes me loath this state of life so tickle,
> And loue of things so vaine to cast away; . . .   (VII. viii. 1)

The ending might be an actual medieval palinode.

Thus other-worldly sentiment negates a powerful attempt to rework the allegorical tradition in the light of changed attitudes. With his deepening sense of human transgression and universal mutability, Spenser could hardly write six more books of moral virtues, with the glowing vision of humanity they would imply. Perhaps I am wrong in seeing one tendency prevailing over the other, instead of the two being held in tension as in the *Primavera*, and indeed in Neoplatonism generally. But when the spatial composition of the *Primavera* is translated into the temporal sequence of a poem, the attitude expressed finally must, to a certain extent, supersede the earlier one. We pass from one to the other.

This gradual change of purpose might explain why the poem was left unfinished—or perhaps we should rather say, the original design was left incomplete. Spenser could not sustain the subtle reinterpretation of allegory. Yet, in another sense the poem is complete, in that we can trace in it the full 'palinodic' structure of the medieval romance. Chaucer's *Troilus and Criseyde* would provide a good parallel for the ultimate rejection of love after a magnificent elaboration of its rich beauty. *The Faerie Queene* is so subdued and orthodox in its conclusion that one hardly suspects the novel purpose with which it began.

5. *Greville and Donne: the Experience of Love*

Against Spenser we may place John Donne, who achieves a more successful synthesis. The imperfections of the human state are not transcended but incorporated in his ideal. Hence it is a mobile, dramatic ideal; it does not triumph once and for all, but continually reasserts itself as it explores the range of human experience. At any moment, life may present a new aspect, and Donne's ideal of love will have to adapt itself to meet its terms. It may appear a precarious victory; but from another viewpoint, perhaps the surer because of the opposition it has met and absorbed.

This conflict has been expressed by other poets of the age, though never so finely resolved. To show the extent of Donne's achievement, it may be just as well first to present the problem in its unresolved state. This is best illustrated from Fulke Greville's *Caelica*.

In the later part of *Caelica*, Greville treats directly of knowledge and ignorance, sin and redemption. Here he repeats the main theme of *A Treatie of Humane Learning*: man's incapacity to attain knowledge is matched by the sinfulness of the search. But earlier in the sequence, the poet has worked out a more intricate design. The same view of the human state there forms a paradoxical background to the rewarding experience of poetic love and its philosophic ramifications. He thus holds out a sober promise of human fulfilment—initially in love, but ultimately a richer contemplative fulfilment—while admitting the evil in man.

The latter, of course, is the newer and more memorable element in a sequence of love-poems. Greville repeatedly equates love with the fallen state and the consequent derangement of reason by the passions.

> *Loue*, of mans wandring thoughts the restlesse being, . . .
> What Angells pride, or what selfe-disagreeing,
> What dazling brightnesse hath your beames benighted,
>   That fall'n thus from those ioyes which you aspired,
>   Downe to my darkened minde you are retired?
>
> Within which minde since you from thence ascended,
> Truth clouds it selfe, Wit serues but to resemble, . . .
> Passion to ruin passion is intended,
> My reason is but power to dissemble; . . .   (X. 1, 5-10, 13-14)

The allurements of the senses are associated with the Sceptical distrust of the faculties:

> Sense is a spie, made to doe phansie treason,
>   Loue goe I vnder.
> Since then eyes pleasure to my thoughts betray me,
> And my thoughts reasons-leuell haue defaced . . .   (VI. 7-10)

This sense of fall and misery is associated largely, but by no means exclusively, with unrequited love. The most

extended account comes in poem LXXXIII, full of standard
themes and images of frustration:

> My Winter is within which withereth my ioy;
> My Knowledge, seate of Ciuill warre, where friends and foes
>   destroy,
> And my Desires are Wheeles, whereon my heart is borne,
> With endlesse turning of themselues, still liuing to be torne.
> My Thoughts are Eagles food, ordayned to be a prey
> To worth; and being still consum'd, yet neuer to decay. . . .
> In Paradise I once did liue; and taste the tree,
> Which shadowed was from all the world, in ioy to shadow me.
> The tree hath lost his fruit, or I have lost my seate,
> My soule both blacke with shadow is, and ouer-burnt with
>   heat: . . .   (ll. 31-6, 41-4)

We have here the standard images of Ixion and Prometheus
and a clear reference to the Fall. We find also the close inter-
mingling of emotional disturbance, intellectual derangement,
and moral fall:

> . . . ignorance and disobedience fight,
> In hell and sinne, which shall haue greatest part: . . .
>   (XCVII. 3-4)

Sometimes the beloved is a source of grace; elsewhere, she
herself partakes of the Fall. Sonnet XXXVIII presents the act
of love as the loss of paradise, aggravated by the beloved's
faithlessness:

> . . . that fine soyle, which all these ioyes did yeeld,
> By broken fence is prou'd a common field.   (ll. 13-14)

One is reminded at such points of Shakespeare's Dark Lady
sonnets, though of course there is little of Shakespeare's
tempering of 'fallen' lust with human fulfilment.

Where Greville does suggest fulfilment, it is kept locally
free from guilt and gloom. The sequence contains much
Petrarchan worship of the beloved. It may indeed be said that
this ideal love is cast out by the final world-weariness. In fact,
Greville quite abandons the theme of love in the end. But it
hardly seems possible to ignore this theme when determining
how the sequence works out. Everything else apart, the title
and the formal character of a 'sonnet'-sequence ensure that
the theme of love remains as an inwoven strand in the pattern.

And if Caelica, Myra, or Cynthia are close to being disembodied nymphs of contemplation, the link between the love-poems and the later philosophic pieces becomes the stronger.

Everything is related in *Caelica*, though nothing is worked out. Greville's achievement is to associate a rich human experience with the essential evil in man. But the fragmentary nature of a lyric-sequence, with the consequent emphasis now of one aspect and now another, prevents him from synthesizing love and sin into a heroic compound. Greville's subtle, cogitative pieces present a conflicting tangle of emotional states and their traditional interpretations. To resolve this into order and fulfilment was to be the work of greater poets. The greatest was Shakespeare; but as an introduction to his achievement one should consider the work of John Donne.

An adequate study of Donne's role in these movements of thought would demand a book to itself. In many ways, this demand is met by Murray Roston's *The Soul of Wit*;[27] but I trust my material will not prove merely repetitious. At whatever distance, Donne provides the nearest analogue to the development I shall try to trace in Shakespeare. For brevity's sake, I shall confine myself to the *Songs and Sonets* and the two 'Anniversarie' poems in memory of Elizabeth Drury.

The 'Anniversaries' illustrate Donne's profound participation in the gloom and *contemptus mundi* of his times, even to the fear of the physical disintegration of the world. But there is an obvious paradox. Against the background of gloom, Donne celebrates the celestial potential of man, as expressed in the figure of Elizabeth Drury. She is described in quasi-Platonic terms as the soul of the world, and in quasi-Hermetic ones as its balm and vital essence. In fact, she rises to a supra-mundane spiritual existence (granted to man alone of all earthly creatures) to which material existence is as the body to the soul. Even after Elizabeth has left the world,

> yet in this last long night,
> Her Ghost doth walke; . . .　　　　　('I Ann.', 69–70)

This 'twilight of her memory' suffices to create a new world, 'from the carcass of the old world, free':

> . . . all assum'd unto this Dignitee,
> So many weedlesse Paradises bee,
> Which of themselves produce no venemous sinne,
> Except some forraine Serpent bring it in . . .
>
> ('I Ann.', 81–4)

It is a world of prelapsarian innocence, conceived immacu-
lately, free from original sin. Elsewhere there is the suggestion
of Elizabeth's own immaculate birth: she is a figure of the
Virgin Mary. She undoes the effects of the Fall, revives an
'unvext Paradise' ('I Ann.', 175–82, 359–64).

This seems to be an image of man's spiritual potential
much like the Christ-image of man found in Cusanus. But
much more patently than in Cusanus, this ideal is divided
from the evil reality. The fact that even Elizabeth had to die
underscores the futility of virtue, the inevitability of corruption and death. If Elizabeth had undone the evil effects of
the Fall, her death is like a re-enactment of that Fall. The
'new world' generated by her spirit is soon forgotten. The
only abiding sign of her spiritual influence seems to be a
sense of sin and *contemptus mundi*.

Hence there is a tension, seen often enough in that age,
between spiritual insight and the weakness revealed by that
insight. The contemplation of Elizabeth's life and death
inspires not triumph but humility. The potential perfection
of man, thwarted by the basic circumstances of his being,
casts his actual corruption into deeper gloom.

The contrast is strongest in 'The Second Anniversarie',
where the next world is kept more constantly in view as the
final end of the 'progress of the soul'. A sense of sin and a
sense of ignorance combine to turn the soul towards heavenly
knowledge, 'conversation' with patriarchs, prophets, apostles,
and martyrs ('II Ann.', 345 ff.). Obviously related to this is
the reliance on revelation:

> And that except thou feed (not banquet) on
> The supernaturall food, Religion,
> Thy better Grouth growes withered, and scant; . . .
>
> ('I Ann.', 187–9)

This is based on the common Sceptical arguments for the
impossibility of knowledge. Only in heaven will we be free
from the limitations of the senses:

> When wilt thou shake off this Pedantery,
> Of being taught by sense, and Fantasy?
> Thou look'st through spectacles; small things seeme great
> Below; But up unto the watch-towre get,
> And see all things despoyld of fallacies: . . .   ('II Ann.', 291-5)

Elizabeth's body, it is true, was free of these limitations, endowed with angelic faculties of instant apprehension:

> . . . one might almost say, her bodie thought . . .
> > ('II Ann.', 246)

But as part of the general contrast between Elizabeth and the rest of mankind, this idealization of her 'spiritual body' is marked by a corresponding vilification of the natural body of man.

Yet it is not merely man's imperfect faculties that prevent knowledge. A deeper cause is the corruption of the very subject-matter of knowledge:

> For, before God had made up all the rest,
> Corruption entred, and deprav'd the best:
> It seis'd the Angels, and then first of all
> The world did in her Cradle take a fall,
> And turn'd her braines, and took a generall maime,
> Wronging each joynt of th'universall frame.
> > ('I Ann.', 193-8)

The celebrated passage on the New Philosophy makes a common Sceptical point: the contradictions between various systems of thought. So does the slightly later passage ('I Ann.', 251 ff.) on the disproportions recently discovered in the universe, with consequent revisions of scientific theory. The obvious parallel is with Burton's 'Digression of the Air'.

But Donne is going further than Burton. He is questioning the stability, the very reality, not only of the human conceptions of things but of things themselves. The world itself is disjoint, in a state of flux: the imbalance of the human mind is only a concomitant of this. The actual parallel is with Montaigne's meditations on the flux of things.

> Poore couse'ned cose'nor, that she, and that thou,
> Which did begin to love, are neither now.
> You are both fluid, chang'd since yesterday;
> Next day repaires, (but ill) last daies decay.

Nor are, (although the river keep the name)
Yesterdaies waters, and todaies the same.
So flowes her face, and thine eies, neither now
That Saint, nor Pilgrime, which your loving vow
Concernd, remaines; but whil'st you thinke you bee
Constant, you are howrely in inconstancee.
('II Ann.', 391–400)

Material knowledge thus proves both impossible and un-
rewarding. Over and over in 'The Second Anniversarie',
Donne draws the common Renaissance contrast between
material *scientia* and spiritual *sapientia*. We are turned again
towards heaven and the gifts of revelation, with the spirit of
Elizabeth Drury as intercessor on our behalf.

The theme of universal decline carries some interesting
implications, however. It means that man is not the only
alien member in a happy and harmonious world, doomed to
frustration by this contrast with his environment. Instead,
the disordered universe provides a potentially tragic challenge
for man, a stimulus for the growth of his sensibility. In the
'Anniversaries', this growth consists entirely in a movement
away from the world; there is no true engagement with the
conditions of man's earthly being. The *Songs and Sonets*
depict such an engagement, with striking results.

I am aware that the *Songs and Sonets* almost certainly
preceded the 'Anniversaries' and most of the Divine Poems.
Indeed, this argues for a striking decline in Donne's optimism.
But one can hardly say that the later poems supersede in any
absolute sense the brilliant synthesis of experience in the
Songs and Sonets. This remains permanently valid.

A proper consideration of the *Songs and Sonets* will require
a new approach to poetic form. In the 'Anniversaries', the
themes were presented clearly and directly. In the *Songs and
Sonets*, there is little such explicitness. Even the apparently
explicit passages are riddled with counter-statement and
irony. Here we have to consider the form of each poem, the
placing of elements in a unique composition, utilizing material
from sources foreign to itself for ends peculiarly its own.

The presence of such material is too obvious to need
detailed description. Donne's images and allusions range
across the whole field of contemporary learning. Often he

darts from science to science with swift agility. Sometimes he may adhere to a single basic image right through a poem, but even this is modified and extended by a battery of subsidiary references. These elements are unified, not by any conception belonging to their original context, but by the theme of love to which they are related in the poem. To satisfy their new function as contributors to this theme, they are torn from their first affinities; or perhaps just as much of their source-contexts as suits Donne's purpose is brought over with them, like a clod of turf around the roots.

"'Tis all in pieces, all cohaerence gone' ('I. Ann.', 213.) Perhaps I exaggerate. The images and allusions assume the existence of an intricate network of sympathies and correspondences. But I wonder if one can build up from these even a tentative 'world picture'. They seem to lack not only absolute validity but all genuine metaphysical relevance. They imitate, with varying exactitude and uncertain causal connections, a truth of emotion, a system and a reality that exist within the mind.

This is best illustrated from 'A Valediction: of the Booke'. Here, all knowledge and experience is synthesized in the experience of love, summed up in the annals culled from love-letters where

> Should againe the ravenous
> Vandals and Goths inundate us,
> Learning were safe; in this our Universe
> Schooles might learn Sciences, Spheares Musick, Angels Verse.
>
> (ll. 24-7)

This relates to that vitally important conception in the *Songs and Sonets*: a 'microcosm' of love superior to the macrocosm. But to what extent is the synthesis valid in *this* poem? How seriously is love said to contain or combine these various experiences? Are they evoked simply, with a hyperbole more remarkable for its energy than its tact, to provide images for a love that may be ordinarily moving or enjoyable, but that scarcely rises to sublimity? Certainly the poem will not support any very profound synthesis; at one point, Donne is openly sceptical about the possibility:

> In this thy booke, such will their nothing see,
> As in the Bible some can finde out Alchimy.   (ll. 53-4)

In other words, there is a possible levity about the imagery, reflecting on the one hand upon love itself, and on the other hand upon the learning which can be deflected to serve as the love-poet's tools. Yet it is only a *possible* levity, of whose actual degree (or even the very presence) we are in constant doubt. And no less important, it is not a basic levity of approach, but a levity arising from a serious sense of the inadequacy of these spheres of experience. Donne responds lightly to divinity, law, and statesmanship, and perhaps to love, because he has thought deeply about life itself.

I have referred to this second-ranking poem at unusual length because it seems to illustrate particularly well two contrary tendencies in the *Songs and Sonets* which, between them, define Donne's approach to experience. First, he breaks up the various disciplines and categories of experience and reorganizes them around a new centre of relevance, love: or, more generally, the irrational, indefinable sensibility of the individual man, the new unity of personal response. But then secondly, Donne appears uncertain of the nature and value of these new principles as well. Moreover, by being constantly related to far-flung fields of experience, they take on a centrifugal tendency that impedes all attempts to define them. On the one hand, the attempt at a radical redefinition of experience; on the other, a sense of the impossibility of definition: between the two, there emerges a subtle vindication of human experience. Certain values and tendencies, endlessly evolving and fluctuating, survive and even triumph over a sense of flux.

Let us first consider this sense of flux. There is in the *Songs and Sonets* a constant presentation of the mystery and complexity of experience, a deliberate blurring of stereotyped patterns. 'The Legacie', for instance, uses the convention of the 'exchange of hearts'. Technically a paradox or an emblem of disorder, this has grown so conventional that as a rule it scarcely disturbs our sense of order. But Donne heightens the intricacy of the paradox, framing it in by several minor ones:

> When I dyed last, and, Deare, I die
> As often as from thee I goe,
> Though it be but an houre agoe,
> And Lovers houres be full eternity,

> I can remember yet, that I
>   Something did say, and something did bestow;
>   Though I be dead, which sent mee, I should be
>   Mine owne executor and Legacie.   (ll. 1-8)

There is also the deliberate evasion of a firm moral evaluation of the mistress's heart:

> Yet I found something like a heart,
>   But colours it, and corners had,
>   It was not good, it was not bad,
>   It was intire to none, and few had part.   (ll. 17-20)

This is not one of Donne's most serious poems; but in a minor way, Donne does succeed in taking a conventional, categorized, 'placed' experience and displacing it from its moorings in poetic convention. The 'exchange of hearts', that had degenerated into a mechanical poetic ritual, becomes once again an intractable and mysterious experience, a cause not merely of pain or surprise but of genuine intellectual puzzlement.

Again, in 'A Valediction: my Name in the Window', Donne concludes his speculations on his mistress's possible infidelity with an abrupt recantation:

> But glasse, and lines must bee,
>   No meanes our firme substantiall love to keepe;
>   Neere death inflicts this lethargie,
>   And this I murmure in my sleepe;
> Impute this idle talke, to that I goe,
>   For dying men talke often so.   (ll. 61-6)

How far does this counter what goes before? How serious was the earlier admission of a possible break of faith, a latent imperfection in their love? We are led from this to poems like 'The Apparition', where the cynicism of the subject-matter is belied by a tone of jesting intimacy, a confident audacity that argues for a secure and long-standing love—and yet admits the possibility of cessation, perhaps by indifference or betrayal.

These instances point to that constant phenomenon in Donne's poetry: the happy celebration, even the genuine idealization, of a love compounded of many moral imperfections—sometimes actual, always eminently possible in a variety of ways.

No less notable is the way Donne admits the physical
element in love. I pointed out earlier, in continental authors
like Rabelais and Montaigne, the conception of man as *essentially* a dual entity, body and soul, whose basic humanity has
to express itself through both these vehicles simultaneously.
If he goes to heaven, he must take his body with him; and it
will be a body somehow purged of corruption and grossness,
a thing of joy, without losing a jot of its physicality. This is
not the same as St. Paul's conception of a celestial body,
which too Donne upholds elsewhere. In the *Songs and Sonets*,
he can sometimes celebrate a purely spiritual love; but most
often, he proves kin to Rabelais and Montaigne—earthly, all-
inclusive. Here, man soars not by negating the physical
elements in his nature in favour of the spiritual, but by a
development of his total being. This is most finely developed
in 'The Exstasie', but the idea occurs in various keys through
most poems in the *Songs and Sonets*.

This union of opposites is rendered still more complex by
the constant ambiguity of tone. How important are these
baser strains and imperfections? How seriously does Donne
subscribe to the standards by which they are judged to be
base or imperfect? It is impossible to reach any conclusions
on such a love, to deem it viable once and for all. It has to
revalidate itself continually by its actual existence, its influence on two lives. It is true because it successfully survives
the test of experience.

One or two low-keyed, playful poems illustrate this clearly
if somewhat simplistically: 'Womans Constancy' or 'Communitie', for instance. These poems are based on logical
exercises; but in the first, the various arguments for incon-
stancy are patently playful, and in the second the logical
structure leads the poet to confess the impossibility of logical
conclusions or moral appraisal:

> Good wee must love, and must hate ill,
> For ill is ill, and good good still,
>   But there are things indifferent,
> Which wee may neither hate, nor love,
> But one, and then another prove,
>   As wee shall finde our fancy bent.   (ll. 1–6)

The truth of these poems is an emotional truth: in

'Communitie', no more than sensory pleasure. These poems may seem too light to uphold any weighty conclusions. The same may be said of 'The Will', which also plays off emotional against logical truth, holding the former valid while the latter is not. But when we come to 'The Prohibition' or 'Loves Infiniteness', the paradoxes are obviously born of profounder experience. Strictly speaking, these may not be paradoxes at all. In 'Loves Infiniteness' especially, logic is not the serious antagonist of the emotions, but merely their plaything: an instrument used, for what its feeble strength is worth, to reinforce the truth of emotion:

> Yet I would not have all yet,
> Hee that hath all can have no more, . . .
> Thou canst not every day give me thy heart,
> If thou canst give it, then thou never gav'st it:
> Loves riddles are, that though thy heart depart,
> It stayes at home, and thou with losing sav'st it: . . .
> (ll. 23-4, 27-30)

Similarly in 'The Dissolution', an intricate logical structure supports a simple emotional truth: the truth hyperbolically expressed in the theme of the poem, that the beloved's death will kill the lover too. The very application of fine logic to so trite a hyperbole undermines the dignity of reason.

Considering the common belief in the severe logical structures of Donne's poetry, it seems worth pointing out that what the *Songs and Sonets* yields, as often as not, is an emotional pattern concealed by quasi-logic or even mock-logic. Or to put it more accurately, Donne is upholding emotional states whose complexity admits of rational ordering to greatly varying extents, and never completely. This intractability is Donne's constant concern, and often leads him to play off experience against logic and method. The gap between the two fluctuates from poem to poem; but Donne's primary loyalty is always to the intricate experience, never to its rational ordering. He may *define* the experience with a subtle precision that the indolent reader calls obscurity. But he will not artificially order or assess the experience by simplifying it in terms of standard categories, methods, and values.

Donne's imagery, too, never confines an experience within

the limits of certain parallels, extensive though these may be. 'A Jeat Ring Sent' provides a fine instance of an image that does not merely define or illustrate a point: such definition could only be at the cost of the total experience. Rather, the image of the ring *becomes*, through its ramifications, the exact reflection of a complete emotional state in all its intricacy. The image sets out by providing exact logical comparisons:

> Thou art not so black, as my heart,
> Nor halfe so brittle, as her heart, thou art;... (ll. 1-2)

But though logical in themselves, they combine to produce a paradox, if a fairly superficial one:

> What would'st thou say? shall both our properties by thee
>   bee spoke,
> Nothing more endlesse, nothing sooner broke? (ll. 3-4)

The conventionality of such treatment is transcended in the next lines:

> Marriage rings are not of this stuffe;
> Oh, why should ought lesse precious, or lesse tough
> Figure our loves? (ll. 5-7)

The power of this love does not preclude doubt and resentment (ll. 8, 12); yet in between comes a delicate touch of affection:

> Yet stay with mee since thou art come,
> Circle this fingers top, which did'st her thombe. (ll. 9-10)

The image grows as the experience itself is explored.

Elsewhere, Donne works in a different way. Instead of a single all-encompassing image, he applies image after image, each avowedly incomplete, but defining one aspect or limit of a complex emotional state. Such are the successive images in 'A Valediction: forbidding Mourning': a virtuous man's death, cosmic disturbances, the elementing of bodies, 'gold to ayery thinnesse beate', a compass. None of these images is comprehensive; but they provide lightning-points of contact with the central experience of love, so that it is defined or at least delimited by the end of the poem. (Perhaps the discomfiture many readers feel over the compass image is that, by its length and position, it assumes a spurious finality, raises expectations that it cannot fulfil, and thus appears to be specially inadequate.)

With both these types of images, the comprehensive and the tentative, the chief point of interest is the central emotional reality. It is this that authenticates the images, lends them life. It is also the source of the poem's intricacy. The images may or may not mirror this intricacy, but they do not generate it: 'For, he tames [grief], that fetters it in verse.' Yet the aim is always to mirror, or at least to suggest, the full complexity of the experience, never to reduce its significance to the clear boundaries of a structure of words.

It seems particularly necessary to make these points in view of the current scholarly reaction to the earlier praise of the Metaphysical 'unity of sensibility'. The scholars largely base themselves on the work of Rosemond Tuve. Tuve, indeed, is very careful to define her terms: she distinguishes between the logical use of imagery, and the application of such imagery to themes which express 'distrust and disillusionment concerning man's ability to come at a sufficient working knowledge of this order [of values in the universe], and discontent with orthodox ideas of the moral order.'[28] Yet it cannot be denied that Tuve's own work, and still more that of her followers, induces the reader to conceive of Donne as the apostle of order, assessment, and practical application, like (it appears) all other Elizabethan and Jacobean poets. 'It ['the great Renaissance master-art of rhetoric'] inclined them to see all discourse as approximating to the oratorical; that is, as disposed to dispute, to prove, to persuade, to teach.'[29]

Such assertions leave out of account Donne's profound sense of human experience as a dynamic balance of elements, requiring a constant alertness of response, a constant readjustment of one's judgement and ethical stand, an eagerness to imbibe rather than to impart. As an exponent of the philosophy of experience, Donne must be ranked with Montaigne.

Even as Donne denies the validity of external systems, he asserts the truth of emotion and of human values. In different ways, and with varying degrees of seriousness, at least three poems even assert that physical existence is regulated—in fact, generated—by emotional states. These poems are 'Witch-craft by a Picture', 'A Valediction: of Weeping', and 'A Noc-turnall upon S. Lucies Day'.

> For I am every dead thing,
> In whom love wrought new Alchimie.
>   For his art did expresse
> A quintessence even from nothingnesse,
> From dull privations, and leane emptinesse:
> He ruin'd mee, and I am re-begot
> Of absence, darknesse, death; things which are not.
>
> ('Nocturnall', ll. 12–18)

Donne can idealize the human condition by reorienting the very premises of Scepticism. The Sceptics had exposed the fallibility of the senses; for Donne, this symbolizes man's spiritual power over the elements:

> Thy beames, so reverend, and strong
>   Why shouldst thou thinke?
> I could eclipse and cloud them with a winke . . .
>
> ('The Sunne Rising', ll. 11–13)

In 'The Good-morrow', the lovers' eyes build up a sphere that is superior to the great earth itself:

> Where can we finde two better hemisphears
> Without sharpe North, without declining West?   (ll. 17–18)

In 'The Flea', there is a Gulliverian inversion of scale by which the little insect grows gigantic in its power:

> This flea is you and I, and this
> Our mariage bed, and mariage temple is;
>   Though parents grudge, and you, w'are met,
> And cloysterd in these living walls of Jet.   (ll. 11–15)

What happens in all these cases is that an imaginative en-largement of physical scale provides a metaphor for the great importance of an apparently feeble or insignificant object. Donne applies a novel scale of values: all experience is internal-ized, judged according to its bearing upon the inner being of man, not the external or material order. In the extreme cases cited here, he even suggests that the material order is literally overruled. The senses gain as expressions of human emotion precisely as they fail to be instruments of knowledge. Sense-data can be falsified in the interests of emotion and personality, just as a logical sequence may be distorted to give the lyrics the logic of emotion.

By according this primary importance to the inner life of man, making it the central truth and the ultimate standard for the assessment of experience, Donne paves the way for an image—one may almost say a philosophical conception—of great importance in the *Songs and Sonets*. He conceives of a self-created, self-contained little world, inhabited by the lovers alone, superior to the macrocosm. This is obviously a variation on the traditional concept of man as microcosm. In Donne, two persons unite in love to form between them a single entity, a single microcosm.

So prominent is this concept—in 'The Good-morrow', 'The Sunne Rising', 'The Anniversarie'—that it scarcely seems necessary to dilate upon it; but it is profoundly important. Occasionally, Donne works still more audacious variations on the central theme. In 'The Canonization', the lovers provide a quasi-Platonic ideal ('Who did the whole world's soul contract') of which 'countries, towns, courts' are the antitype. In 'The Sunne Rising', the decline of the great world, so lamented in 'The First Anniversarie', is more than compensated by the birth of the lovers' world of the emotions:

> Thou sunne art halfe as happy'as wee,
> In that the world's contracted thus;
> Thine age askes ease, and since they duties bee
> To warme the world, that's done in warming us.
> Shine here to us, and thou art every where; . . . (ll. 25-9)

As commonly in the Renaissance, Donne breaks up the relation between human existence and a greater order:

> What Artist now dares boast that he can bring
> Heaven hither, or constellate any thing . . .
> The art is lost, and correspondence too.
> For heaven gives little, and the earth takes lesse,
> And man least knowes their trade, and purposes.
> ('I Ann.', 391-2, 396-8)

But in the *Songs and Sonets*, human life is given an independent and even superior validity. In contrast to Burton's quiet humanity (or Sir Thomas Browne's, even later) we here find positive exuberance; but this exuberance, far from being superficial or immature, arises from a greater synthesis of elements, a greater exercise of intellectual energy. In the midst of a dissolving world-order, the accompanying fragmentation of knowledge, and the grossness, corruption and debility of man's state, Donne asserts human power and dignity. His work provides the most fitting approach to Shakespeare's vindication of man.

IV. Marlowe and Shakespeare

1. Marlowe and the Problem of the Tragic Hero

The first notable expression of heroic idealism in English drama is in the work of Christopher Marlowe. So at least runs the traditional interpretation of his plays, and only a gross distortion of their themes could deny such a concern. But it would be as naïve a misreading to regard this treatment as a simple celebration of Renaissance man's quest for infinity. This quest is described in most equivocal terms; and furthermore, it is questioned and set in perspective by the total action of the plays.

On a first reading of *Tamburlaine*, our attention may be wholly captured by the hero's energy and ambition. It has been said that the only limitation to Tamburlaine's power is mortality itself, which claims first Zenocrate and then Tamburlaine in person. There is indeed the well-recognized irony of 'my servant death' assuming dominance over his self-styled lord. But Marlowe's critique of heroism does not rest upon such obvious and external oppositions. Nor is it based upon the ultimate frustration of

> One thought, one grace, one woonder at the least,
> Which into words no vertue can digest: . . .
>
> (*1 Tam.*, V. i. 172-3)

This, after all, is only the obverse of infinite perfectibility; and death itself, at least by a rhetorical turn, can appear as a transcendence of one's previous imperfect being:

> . . . this subject not of force enough,
> To hold the fiery spirit it containes,
> Must part . . .   (*2 Tam.*, V. iii. 168-70)

But there are deeper oppositions in the play, unresolved because their full implications are not recognized by the protagonist, and therefore not met by the terms of his action and rhetoric. Rather, this action and rhetoric take on unsuspected dimensions, raising wider issues that undermine Tamburlaine's conscious motives and aspirations.

At several points of the play, Tamburlaine asserts that his power is born out of struggle, that the universal order is itself an endless struggle and interchange of elements:

> Nature that fram'd us of foure Elements,
> Warring within our breasts for regiment,
> Doth teach us all to have aspyring minds: . . .
>
> (*1 Tam.*, II. vii. 18-20)

Properly speaking, this is no order at all. The traditional system of the universe has dissolved; in its place we have a fragmented and consequently predatory view of society and the cosmos. Every element, every individual is pitted against every other, and gains ascendancy in an indeterminate succession. They are not graded or regulated by any order, and no order evolves out of their interaction. In fact, this interaction may be said to be mere opposition, as the parts are mutually hostile, each trying to subjugate or eliminate the others rather than to harmonize with them to build up a genuine order.

This also implies that any triumph or success consists in a sort of metaphysical balancing feat: a momentary union of conflicting elements or suppression of opposing forces, soon to be overthrown in the constant revolutions of power:

> . . . the shepheards issue, at whose byrth
> Heaven did affoord a gratious aspect,
> And join'd those stars that shall be opposite,
> Even till the dissolution of the world . . .
>
> (*2 Tam.*, III. v. 79-82)

Tamburlaine's distinction lies in that for him, this balance is indefinitely sustained; but its character remains the same. He can assert his individual power *only because of the absence of a set world-order*; nor can he consolidate or justify his success in terms of such an order. He can enjoy only the precarious justification of success itself.

Tamburlaine's rhetoric creates the same dissatisfaction. His vaunts cannot be dismissed as *mere* rhetoric, as they convince Tamburlaine himself and inspire a genuine and successful urge for achievement. At the same time, these vaunts merely emanate from his imagination: there is no sense that they indicate the actual status of man in the universe. The rhetoric is intrinsically insubstantial, though it helps to inspire the military achievement that lends it a meretricious substance.[1]

There were two principal versions of the medieval concept of Fortune. By one, Fortune dealt reward and punishment—especially punishment—in fairly direct proportion to a man's deserts. By the other, the workings of Fortune were more inexplicable, consisting of irrational turns and catastrophes. The metaphysic of *Tamburlaine* is obviously closer to the latter. Tamburlaine may deserve his success because of his innate *virtù*, but hardly in terms of moral desert. Yet Fortune's wheel does not turn to punish him.

The power of man is seen to assert itself beyond traditional categories of good and evil. The action bears some resemblance to the medieval stories of 'Falls of Princes', but Marlowe reverses the traditional morality-pattern of such tales. The very concept of a moral order is negated. As so often in Renaissance thought, the expression of man's power implies the total disintegration of any sense of greater order. By realizing his latent energies, man cannot influence the universe outside him in any meaningful way: self-expression becomes an unavailing expense of spirit. To put it in a different way, his achievement appears admirable only in the context of the moment. In its actual impact upon the working of the universe through time, it is insignificant and futile.

Though there is no moral order in *Tamburlaine*, we may detect a not too faint assertion of moral values at a purely human level. From one perspective, Marlowe seems to present Tamburlaine's career as an amoral barbaric triumph that provides its own justification. But with this he juxtaposes moral concepts whose relevance must at least be examined even if not ultimately granted. The play is full of little counter-currents of action that may well be thought to provide implicit criticism of the deeds of Tamburlaine. Such are the fates of Agydas, of the Captain and Olympia, above all of Bajazeth and Zabina. The speeches of Bajazeth and Zabina, or of the captive kings with their apparently futile curses, provide a sort of chorus to the play—a prophetic chorus, we realize, when we hear the imagery of darkness in Bajazeth's last speech repeated at the deaths of Zenocrate and Tamburlaine himself.

Marlowe accomplishes much simply by juxtaposing action in different keys. The last act of Part I provides a fine instance. The virgins of Damascus die after a truly moving lament; Tamburlaine boasts, yet mourns the loss of 'one thought, one grace, one wonder'; Bajazeth and Zabina brain themselves; and Zenocrate comes on to mourn their death and bewail the course of her husband's career:

> Ah myghty *Jove* and holy *Mahomet*,
> Pardon my Love, oh pardon his contempt,
> Of earthly fortune, and respect of pitie, . . .
> And pardon me that was not moov'd with ruthe,
> To see them live so long in misery: . . .
>
>   (*1 Tam.*, V. i. 363–6, 369–70)

Zenocrate is surely a character with whom we may sympathize; and her appeal to Jove, coming after our emotional reaction to the deaths of the virgins, Bajazeth and Zabina, ensures that we cannot remain in a consistently amoral frame of mind.

In Part II a harder and more bitter Tamburlaine emerges. His earlier philosophic humanism, the unsated quest for beauty and virtue, disappear altogether. The fire and splendour is now quite earthly, based on power

> I will with Engines, never exercisde,
> Conquer, sacke, and utterly consume
> Your cities and your golden pallaces . . .
>
>   (*2 Tam.*, IV. i. 191–3)

and egotism

> Ile ride in golden armour like the Sun . . .
>
>   (*2 Tam.*, IV. iii. 115)

His sensibility contracts, and in the light of this decline, his speeches in Part I, reaching out to infinity, seem profoundly ironical—a dream whose pursuit leads him deeper and deeper into inhumanity. Zenocrate's death foreshadows his own fall—but the thoughts of afterlife that this arouses make him defy providence further. Indeed, the most striking change in Tamburlaine is that whereas he earlier thought himself favoured by fate, he now defies it. The cosmic images he uses often describe catastrophes (*2 Tam.*, I. iii. 168 ff., II. iv. 97 ff.,

IV. i. 194 ff.). There are repeated allusions to Phaethon (2 *Tam.*, IV. iii. 7 ff., IV. iii. 125 ff., V. iii. 228),[2] and his boast of ruling over fate becomes more and more ironical. 'Sicknes or death can never conquer me', he declares at the end of a scene (2 *Tam.*, V. i. 221); and on his next appearance, he dies.

These countering elements may be thought to destroy the heroic image; but the complexity of the play lies in the fact that actually this does not happen. We never quite lose the sense of Tamburlaine as a superman-hero placed outside the orbit of good and evil; yet good and evil remain current concepts. The norm and the heroic aberration are placed side by side without interacting. They are mutually exclusive patterns, yet neither can be rejected. Tamburlaine is a hero; yet his heroism must remain precarious and incomplete, as there are undeniable moral standards which it cannot meet. There is an immature and factitious quality about it. It is not based upon a full acceptance of man's moral nature. Yet it is this very lack of understanding that makes Tamburlaine's pristine heroic energy possible at all. This is in telling contrast to Shakespeare's tyrant-hero, Macbeth, whose sinful career fosters an ever-deeper moral perception.

Here once more is the common dichotomy of Renaissance thought: an aspiration that can flourish only in the absence of greater values, and a moral awareness that cannot but thwart the aspiration. The distinction of *Tamburlaine* is that it presents this duality within a single work, as equally valid responses to the same material.

The Jew of Malta and *Edward II* are the most obvious material for any account of Marlowe's unheroic vision; but they demand little analysis. In *The Jew*, the heroic image of man is clearly abandoned before he is depicted in his narrow villainy. In the latter part of the play, we meet the same predatory society as in *Tamburlaine*, but constricted and impoverished so that mere self-preservation counts above triumph in conflict or the realization of latent power. In *Edward II* the heroic image is absent altogether, replaced from the outset by a contraction of sensibility that at best reaches to pathos, and is more generally confined to a drab meanness that could scarcely fire the dramatist's imagination.

The pettiness of the milieu is more demoralizing than any sense of deep sin could have been.

In *Doctor Faustus* we return to the concept of sin, and once more it is necessary to analyse the play in some detail. I am proceeding on the now prevalent assumption that *Doctor Faustus* is indeed Marlowe's last major work.

While *Tamburlaine* can conceivably be read as a celebration of *libido dominandi*, it is obviously impossible to take *Faustus* as a straightforward account of *libido sciendi*. On a simple reading, it is a morality play where the protagonist is damned for his sinful lust after forbidden knowledge. A deeper and more complex interpretation seems possible, but it does not materially add to the heroic idealism of the play.

Faustus' heroism, unlike Tamburlaine's, is not realized in tangible achievement. The choruses make much of his feats of learning; but the action shows a pitiful collapse of ambition, a descent to the level of practical jokes and errand-mongering, making horns sprout on a knight's head or fetching grapes for a pampered Duchess. Such scenes may of course be dismissed as interpolations. But so well do they continue the use of comedy in medieval drama to represent vice and degeneration, and so inconceivable is the structure of the play if we leave them out, that we must consider them as integral to the drama at least in their basic conception. 'From a proud philosopher, master of all human knowledge, to a trickster, to a slave of phantoms, to a cowering wretch; that is a brief sketch of the progress of Dr. Faustus.'[3] His debasement is fittingly represented by scenes of folly, triviality, and low humour.

Yet Faustus does not cease to be a hero on this score, though his heroism must be even more cautiously defined than Tamburlaine's. The comic and magical episodes alternate with tragic scenes where a different Faustus emerges. Here, he does not indeed attain the heroic stature denied him in the comic scenes; rather, he is obsessed with the contemplation of the mean diabolism he has himself released. But in this contemplation, he reveals a moral intensity and subtlety that raise him far above the level to which his own actions consign him. He gauges his sinful and truly unheroic position with an admirable freedom from self-aggrandizing cant, an urge to reach the truth at whatever cost of suffering and humiliation.

Faustus' quest for material and philosophic knowledge is rudely frustrated:

> FAUSTUS. ... now tell me who made the world?
> MEPHOSTOPHILIS. I will not.   (ll. 618–19)

It is in the admission of moral realities that his humanity finds what fulfilment it achieves; but like his first father he has to damn himself to acquire this ironically unavailing knowledge of good and evil.

In *Tamburlaine* we saw human aspiration being countered by moral considerations. There the opposition emerged from the entire work; in *Faustus*, it is embodied in a single character, and the opposed elements are allowed to interact. In a sense, Faustus damns himself.

That this is in accord with a greater divine order is not placed beyond doubt. Several times in the play, Faustus turns to God, calling on Christ to save him.[4] There is no response such as had been promised by both the Good Angel and the Old Man. This does not conclusively prove an 'atheistic' purpose in the play. Faustus's calls to Christ seem to express yearning rather than genuine faith and hope or a movement of the will. He succumbs to despair immediately after, or surrenders to the devils' threats, whereas in ll. 1791 ff. the Old Man, steadfast in his faith, can successfully defy them.

Yet we may find enough indications to cast doubt on the inviolable working of a divine order. Particularly disturbing is the silence after Faustus' last agonized call for 'one drop ... half a drop' of Christ's blood. It appears at times as though the devil wields enough power to thwart the purpose of God:

> MEPHOSTOPHILIS. ...
> 'Twas I, that when thou wer't i' the way to heaven,
> Damb'd up thy passage; when thou took'st the booke,
> To view the Scriptures, then I turn'd the leaves
> And led thine eye.   (ll. 1886–9)

Faustus cannot repent before God, but he 'repents' readily enough after offending Lucifer. This points back to Faustus' own compulsions as the determining factor in his spiritual career.

I do not contend that Marlowe aspired to overthrow the Christian dispensation. Certainly the play as it stands yields no such purpose; no Elizabethan play with this explicit purpose could have been published or performed. But I do contend that the play does not clearly support such a dispensation either: its presence is equivocal, almost irrelevant. The moral concepts that guide the action emanate from Faustus' own mind. The inscription 'Homo, fuge' that appears on his arm as he signs the bond is obviously projected by his own conscience-stricken imagination, like Macbeth's bloody dagger. This sets the tone for all his later tussles with his conscience. He ascribes to God and the devil the governing impulses of his own nature.

The irony is that Faustus believes in an external and mechanistic moral order, governed by forces that he cannot influence or command. He commits a sin and must be damned for it, and hell is an external place of punishment to which he is consigned. This is what Wilbur Sanders fitly describes as 'the paradox of man's submission to the values which he helps to create, his unfree freedom', which follows upon 'Faustus's desperate attempt to defy a reality of his own nature'.[5] This is the reality of his deep moral sense.

For in truth, of course, hell is a mental state, as Mephostophilis knows: 'Why this is hell: nor am I out of it' (l. 303). It is in his own mind that Faustus regards himself as damned: he yields to despair, and it is this despair and not the initial sin that renders his state irredeemable. There is a strong moral sense in Faustus; his aspiration is a conscious rebellion against this moral sense; and (quite unlike Tamburlaine) he is then deeply haunted by his own outraged morality.

The complexity of the pattern may now be fully seen. Faustus's true heroic power rests in his superior moral sensibility; but this sensibility makes him regard himself as sinful and unheroic, and what is more, robs him of the power to alter his situation. The man of superior faculties thus succeeds only in reducing himself to frustration and despair. Tamburlaine's unsubtle aspiration is suspect in the total context of human values which he himself does not perceive. For the more profound 'overreacher' like Faustus, who can himself comprehend those values, his aspiration bears the seeds of its own destruction.

We may detect a gross imbalance in Faustus' stand. I have talked of the intensity and refinement of his moral sense, but not of its accuracy. It is warped by the obsessions of the self-condemned reprobate. Here I must differ from Wilbur Sanders, though his account of the play renders mine superfluous in some ways. It seems to me that Sanders makes too ready an identification of Faustus with Marlowe, and transfers from the hero to the dramatist himself the despair which is the pernicious obverse of a misconceived doctrine of predestination. On the contrary, I feel that Marlowe consciously refrains from assenting to a moral order, controlled by the implacable divine will, that would bear out Faustus' own conviction of his reprobate nature. Rather, man's aspiration is frustrated by the innate impediment of his own morality. There is the further irony that this moral sense should itself be a product of the superior human faculties, a proof of man's intellectual power and nobility of intent. His distinctive excellences also constitute his peculiar limitations; and these limitations, imposed by any normal judgement, are dramatically magnified in Faustus' obsession with his state of sin.

Granted the obsessive nature of Faustus' morality, one may discover between the lines of *Doctor Faustus* a solution that is not worked out in the play itself. One may argue for the need to expel the innate sense of sin that lies at the root of Faustus' self-condemnation. His ambition is 'still joined, by the umbilical cord of a terror-which-is-still-faith, to the theism it purports to reject.'[6] In a truly bright world of pristine humanity, the search for wisdom and fulfilment would not be obstructed by a repressive moral order that may in fact have no objective basis. But this raises the question whether *any* sense of moral order is compatible with such full and free self-expression. I believe we have to wait till William Blake to find such a synthesis; Marlowe certainly does not afford us one.

Rather, the sense of sin remains the most inescapable reality in the play. I consider Marlowe to have been free from the obsessive and despairing sense of sin that he depicts in his hero; but the fundamental concept of sin retains for him its full validity. The Christian moral categories provide the unvarying scale of judgement in the play. Faustus' stand is condemned in terms of sin and despair. If we must discuss the play with reference to Calvinism, we may read it as an assessment of Calvinism by the more moderate but essentially similar tenets of basic Christianity. Marlowe may condemn Faustus' despair, but he does not appear to celebrate his ambition either. They are both sinful; they are both rejected in terms of the Christian moral order.

In every way, we find in Marlowe's heroes a frustrating lack of balance. They are placed against a system of contrary considerations which can be ignored but not dismissed. Each side of the balance renders the other suspect, and we conclude in a state of moral bewilderment. It is in contrast to this unresolved tension that the achievement of Shakespeare appears in its full success. For Shakespeare admits both sides of the impasse and reconciles them. He accepts the full weight of human limitations as Christianity conceives of them, and evolves through his middle and later plays a humanity that asserts itself through these limitations. He takes stock of the disorder and intellectual confusion of the age, but creates out of this a sense of achievement if not, at the same time, of order. He is not to be placed outside the compass of Renaissance doubt and gloom. He fully incorporates its spirit in his work, but he is unique in offering something in excess.

2. *Falstaff and the King*

The growth of Shakespeare's distinctive view of man appears principally in *Hamlet*, the dark comedies, and the tragedies following them; but it is with his most brilliant comic creation that the story may be said to begin. Seldom even in Shakespeare are the human and the heroic thrown into sharper opposition than in the two parts of *Henry IV*. Critics tend to blur this opposition in one of two ways: either by proposing, with various degrees of erudite unsubtlety, that we should not waste sympathetic laughter on Falstaff; or else suggesting that such sympathy, while legitimately evoked by the play as it stands, represents a failure of Shakespeare's intentions. The former approach shows an insensitivity to dramatic texture that need hardly be taken seriously, in spite of its advocacy by eminent scholars; while the latter view demands that we should ignore the most striking elements of the play while assessing it. It seems safer to interpret the play by the full formal evidence, without reference to the insoluble problem of intentions. If this is honestly done, one may detect a subtle treatment of human values which should not be ironed out by critical simplification.

Formally, the play appears to present the traditional duality in man. The heroic king-figure is opposed by the gross and unheroic form of Falstaff; it is *feritas* against *divinitas*, temptation against triumph, even (if we like) sin against grace. The action of the play represents the rejection of the lower elements to vindicate the royal or heroic ideal. So far, the pattern is that of an orthodox allegory that we may interpret at the political, moral, or theological level; and some interpreters feel no need to go further.

But it is the most patent truth about the play that at point after point, our intuitive response to this opposition is quite the reverse. Shakespeare confuses our responses so that such a simple moral interpretation is impossible. Many elements in the balance are transferred to the unorthodox side, so that an ideal may be divorced from the power needed to realize it, or a vice compounded with an indispensable human faculty. This is much more complex than mere antinomianism or inversion of values; but it does mean that the simple royal ideal is rejected for good. The dramatic sympathy attaches in great measure to the gross, unheroic aspect of man.

Nor is this sympathy born of pity or humility. For who can deny that the figure of Falstaff is an embodiment of energy and vitality? Of imagination too, for Falstaff opens up a new poetic dimension in all he talks about, be it Diana's foresters, or the lantern in Bardolph's poop, or 'a fork'd radish, with a head fantastically carved upon it with a knife'. This is a dimension that the kingly ideal leaves out of account, or rather rejects consciously: but it is with no sense of distaste that Shakespeare incorporates it in the spirit of Falstaff. Rather, it whets new appetites, suggests new possibilities of experience that will not be denied. 'Banish plump Jack, and banish all the world.'

What Falstaff *achieves* with this comprehensive power is of

course a different question. But he shows an undeniable zest
and acumen that we feel must leaven any true achievement.
Neither gout, pox, nor white hairs can quite constitute an
ironic negation of this energy. Rather, it coexists with them.
In fact, it joyfully seizes upon them as matter through which
it may declare itself the more strongly: 'valiant Jack Falstaff
—and therefore more valiant, being, as he is, old Jack Falstaff
. . .' (Pt. I, II. iv. 459-61). A comprehensive and satisfying
humanity must incorporate many elements of the Falstaffian
image. It must be built up through a full admission of the
gross, the enfeebling, the intractable—even the sinful, because
the vital energy of man is seen to lie in indivisible compound
with these.

We are obviously approaching the Sceptical concept of
man that we had noted at the outset in Montaigne, and
the somewhat different Scepticism of Rabelais as well.
But this generic resemblance conceals a radical difference
between Shakespeare and the French authors, which may
best be summed up by saying that what provides Montaigne
and Rabelais with their crowning concepts of man are in
Shakespeare only Falstaff's views, a mere starting-point for
Shakespeare's own. Montaigne's celebration of humanity—
more correctly, his preoccupation with it—was based on a
sense of the littleness of man and the impossibility of a
broader apprehension of things. It conceived of man as essentially linked to his body and markedly affected by his
appetites: '. . . on the loftiest throne in the world we are still
sitting only on our own rump.' (*Essais*, III. 13, *De l'experience*:
Frame, p. 857).[7] This is a very Falstaffian sentiment. Indeed,
Falstaff would surely evince a far more vehement, though not
unenvious, contempt for elevated stations. Was not King
Henry like a singing-man of Windsor, and did not the Hostess's
eldest son resemble the Lord Chief Justice? 'God help the
while! a bad world, I say.' But as this very vehemence may
make us suspect, this Sceptical view of man is not the total
theme of the play. Rather, it is checked and corrected within
the total context in a way that I shall presently demonstrate.

The resemblance to Rabelais is a more immediate problem,
for 'Rabelaisian' and 'Falstaffian' are commonly taken as
synonyms. But I believe there is a notable difference between

the two authors. To appreciate this, however, we must begin further back and treat the whole question of Falstaff's Scepticism (by no means the same thing as Shakespeare's own). We can hardly expect a systematic negation of the fields of knowledge one by one; but many of man's cherished methods and ideals are exploded.

Falstaff's demolition of honour is indeed too well-known to need mention; but the passage is worth quoting for another reason:

> What is honour? A word. What is in that word? Honour. What is that honour? Air. A trim reckoning! Who hath it? He that died o' Wednesday. Doth he feel it? No. Doth he hear it? No. 'Tis insensible, then? Yea, to the dead. (Pt. I, V. i. 133-7)

It is not only honour that is negated here, but the method of instruction through catechism. Logical processes are similarly reduced to absurdity:

> PRINCE. Sir John stands to his word—the devil shall have his bargain; for he was never yet a breaker of proverbs; he will give the devil his due.
> POINS. Then art thou damn'd for keeping thy word with the devil.
> PRINCE. Else he had been damn'd for cozening the devil.
> (Pt. I, I. ii. 113-19)

Christian morals are parodied, more daringly, a little earlier:

> Why, Hal, 'tis my vocation, Hal; 'tis no sin for a man to labour in his vocation. (Pt. I, I. ii. 101-2)

and much later as well:

> Care I for the limb, the thews, the stature, bulk, and big assemblance of a man! Give me the spirit, Master Shallow. (Pt. II, III. ii. 251-3)

False figures of rhetoric are unblushingly exploited:

> PRINCE. Sirrah, do I owe you a thousand pound?
> FALSTAFF. A thousand pound, Hal! A million. Thy love is worth a million: thou owest me thy love. (Pt. I, III. iii. 135-7)

In a word, intellectual methods are totally exploded, reduced to jests and playthings. And it is because they are so reduced that Falstaff can utilize them to provide an ironic rationale for his own actions:

> Counterfeit? I lie, I am no counterfeit: to die is to be a counterfeit; for

> he is but the counterfeit of a man who hath not the life of a man; but
> to counterfeit dying, when a man thereby liveth, is to be no counter-
> feit, but the true and perfect image of life indeed. (Pt. I, V. iv. 114-19)

And again:

> I disprais'd him before the wicked—that the wicked might not fall in
> love with thee; in which doing, I have done the part of a careful friend
> and a true subject; . . . (Pt. II. II. iv. 308-10)

Needless to say, Falstaff is not convinced by his own logic,
nor does he expect anyone else to be. He is merely concerned
with self-preservation, indulgence of his appetites, and instinct-
ive defence of his misdoings. He does not see the need to
satisfy any higher ideal of conduct, as he is fully convinced of
the hollowness of all such values and ideals. And as a final
mock at these rejected values, he tosses fragments of them
into his speeches, as a dog trots about with a plaything that is
'dead'.

The same cynicism lies behind Falstaff's consciously overdone mendacity. Of course he does not expect to be believed;
and to many readers, his unblushing fictions are simply proof
of his exuberant imagination. But unless I am much mistaken,
they show also a cynical contempt for both fact and opinion
that must not be overlooked because of the gay abandon that
clothes it. As Bradley says, 'There is nothing serious in any of
them [the lies] except the refusal to take anything seriously.'[8]
Or, in Harbage's stronger indictment, 'His seems to be the
larger guilt of having no principles.'[9] If people do not believe
Falstaff, he does not care. They will at least know that he
insists on having his own way, without discipline or altruism.
This is the libertine spirit at its most sterile.

The Falstaffian spirit now begins to show in a new and
less flattering light. His pristine, irrational vitality hides an
essential cynicism, a sense of the futility of all values and the
impossibility of achievement. The Falstaffian energy may be
necessary leaven for all human activity; but in Falstaff himself, it remains frustrated for lack of any object or direction.
In a truer sense than he knows, 'pregnancy is made a tapster,
and his quick wit wasted in giving reckonings' (Pt. II, I. ii.
160-2).

Falstaff's buoyancy exists in curious combination with an
innate defeatism:

> If I become not a cart as well as another man, a plague on my bringing
> up! I hope I shall as soon be strangled with a halter as another.
> (Pt. I, II. iv. 479-81)

In the last analysis, Falstaff's picture of life is very bleak, and
he looks forward to no future at all. He can thus accept war
casually, as an exercise in killing the regulation number of men.

> ...food for powder, food for powder; they'll fill a pit as well as better:
> ... (Pt. I, IV. ii. 63-4)

His account of his own virtue merely reveals that it is impossible for him to be virtuous—perhaps impossible for any man:

> I was as virtuously given as a gentleman need to be; virtuous enough:
> swore little, dic'd not above seven times a week, went to a bawdy-
> house not above once in a quarter—of an hour, paid money that I
> borrowed—three or four times . . . (Pt. I, III. iii. 14-18)

In fact, he is resigned to an endemic sense of sin:

> Thou knowest in the state of innocency Adam fell; and what should
> poor Jack Falstaff do in the days of villainy? (Pt. I, III. iii. 164-6)

To know the world is to fall. For Falstaff, the ideal of a comprehensive life seems incompatible with virtue:

> Before I knew thee, Hal, I knew nothing; and now am I, if a man
> should speak truly, little better than one of the wicked.
> (Pt. I, I. ii. 90-2)

In a word, Falstaff is a sceptic not only in the technical or
philosophic sense but the popular one as well. He views the
world without apparent gloom, but with a degree of levity
and cynicism unthinkable for the contemplative philosopher
essaying to establish a tenable code of life in the absence of
absolute values. Unlike Falstaff, such a philosopher would
not be able to borrow ten pounds from the Hostess in full
assurance that he cannot repay an earlier hundred marks; nor
seize any man's horse to greet the young king at his coronation;
nor, of course, misuse the King's press damnably. Falstaff
does all this, and with aplomb too; but he has to pay for it
by consciously divorcing himself from all norms that might
have upheld his actions. There is nothing he can look to
beyond the pursuit of his immediate satisfaction.

Nowhere does Falstaff's defeatism show itself more clearly

than in his attitude to the flesh. Here at long last we may take up the question of his contrast with Gargantua and Pantagruel. In Rabelais, we have a celebration of the appetites; drink and sex provide a direct solution to Sceptical bewilderment. Of Rabelais indeed one may say that he takes the duality of soul and body, god and beast, and solves it simply by aggrandizing the latter element to heroic proportions. Shakespeare's solution is less simple.

For Falstaff the flesh is indeed both origin and receptacle of the joys of life; but at the same time, it is a burden and a weariness, a perpetual reminder of human frailty. His bulk enfeebles him in the most literal sense. Witness his trials on Gad's Hill when Poins hides his horse: 'Have you any levers to lift me up again, being down?' As for the moral impediment:

> POINS. . . . Jack, how agrees the devil and thee about thy soul, that thou soldest him on Good Friday last for a cup of Madeira and a cold capon's leg? (Pt. I, I. ii. 110–12)

'Thou seest I have more flesh than another man, and therefore more frailty.' The appetites are not taken as heroic. They are seen to be imperfections, and Falstaff gets a sort of resigned, indolent pleasure in contemplating this imperfection in himself. This is not to deny that he empties his cup of sack with the profoundest satisfaction to his throat; but this is compounded with a sense of his frailty in drinking it. Paradoxically, it is a comforting sense, indicating the frailty and futility of life generally, which justifies him in indulging his own weaknesses.

I wonder if this paradox cannot be substantiated by another: nowhere in the two parts of the play can we find a single speech where Falstaff directly states these motives for drinking. Rather, he argues more than once that 'If sack and sugar be a fault, God help the wicked!' Above all, he delivers in Part II his celebrated eulogy of the ennobling properties of sherris-sack (IV. iii. 103 ff.). It is, of course, the style and context of these speeches that turn the apparent praise of drink into ironic banter, the usual hollow reasons trotted out with easy cynicism to gloss over indefensible addiction. The first-quoted speech is part of an ironic display of one-sided rhetoric and a parody of contemporary literary style. The second speech parodies contemporary medical methods. They show less true faith in the virtuous powers of sack than mere lack of faith in an ideal of abstention.

I have tried to define the limits of the Falstaffian ideal from the basic premisses of the ideal itself, not the darker elements that are thought, with some justice, to overshadow it in Part II. In so far as Falstaff challenges the inadequacy of the orthodox order, his more comprehensive ethos seems feasible and attractive; but it achieves nothing, and its comprehensiveness finally proves to be sadly spurious. His topsy-turvydom holds meaning only as a temporary aberration from the norm.

The problem is that while Falstaff declines in stature, these normative values, as embodied in the royal ideal, do not acquire a compensating validity. This is what makes *Henry IV* —or the 'second tetralogy' of History Plays as a whole—so uncertain in dramatic effect. We are presented with two opposite, incompatible approaches to life: ethical alternatives that seem to cancel each other out.

The sense of a 'hollow crown' runs through *Henry IV*. For some time now, critics have seen the political world of *Henry IV* as entirely fragmented, even corrupt. Deprived of all absolute values, it can at most epitomize in Hal a sort of benevolent Machiavellism.[10] The case for this is easily over-stated; but indeed there is a case. Henry IV sees his reign as a bewildered and makeshift career, guided by no firm principles. His doubtful claim to the crown is an indication of this greater doubt of the justification of his rule.

> God knows, my son,
> By what by-paths and indirect crook'd ways
> I met this crown; and I myself know well
> How troublesome it sat upon my head: . . .
>
> (Part II, IV. v. 184-7)

There is not even a consistently evil purpose like Richard III's. 'By-paths and indirect crook'd ways' indicates a less assured course of deviation; 'crook'd' loses its moral connotations and becomes more of a descriptive metaphor. Whether or not a just account of Bolingbroke's usurpation, it certainly indicates the light in which he comes more and more to regard it. He has lost faith in his own ideal of royalty.

In this uncertainty of values, John of Lancaster fulfils his
limited objectives by simple treachery. The sordidness and
disloyalty pervasive in the rebellious state of the nation is
ironically—and hence ominously—quelled by directing those
very evils to a decisive climax. The evil is not cast out but
absorbed into the very fabric of the state.

Hal's conduct is far from parallel, however. In fact, one
may see him attempting to build up an ideal of kingship, a
consistent path of preparation for his role. In an uncertain
society, he is seeking some tenable if not absolute course to
follow. The early speech 'I know you all . . .' (Pt. I, I. ii.
188 ff.)—which has probably damned him in more readers'
eyes than the Rejection of Falstaff itself—should also be seen
in this more favourable light. Resorting with the Eastcheap
crew is indeed a strange preparation for kingship, a progress
through 'indirect crook'd ways'. But it shows Hal's consciousness of his purpose, his early assumption of the role of future
king. The royal ideal, which seems so doubtful in the play,
holds meaning for Hal. He fitfully recalls the ideal through all
his sowing of wild oats, and even tackles the problem of
relating the two worlds in which he moves.

> But indeed these humble considerations make me out of love with
> my greatness. What a disgrace is it to me to remember thy name, or
> to know thy face to-morrow . . . (Pt. II, II. ii. 11–14)

Such quizzical contemplation of his position argues a genuine
inclusiveness of spirit. So does the easy energy with which he
can pass in a moment from one world to the other. As he is
tormenting Falstaff before Doll Tearsheet, Peto enters with
an urgent summons. Hal responds at once to the new situation
and rushes out into the 'tempest of commotion' (Pt. II, II. iv.
350).

One may wonder which is the true Hal: the scheming
prince who sees his raffish companions as creatures to serve
his cynical ambition? or the maturing citizen of the world
who declares such a motive as an easy explanation for his
training in a rarer humanity? We must not too easily succumb
to the first explanation.

Yet we cannot readily accept the second either. Hal's sardonic regret of his taste for small beer shows how impossible

it is to reconcile the two worlds. In a sense, the attempt to include them both in his being makes Hal a stranger to both. His royalty sets him apart from his companions. He must turn it into a jesting paradox so that they can accept it.

> From a god to a bull? A heavy descension! It was Jove's case. From a prince to a prentice? A low transformation! That shall be mine; for in everything the purpose must weigh with the folly.
>
> (Pt. II, II. ii. 167–70)

The last words carry a double sense, of course: they are directed at himself, for he again feels the need to justify his conduct.

At court, on the other hand, his Eastcheap exploits cast a shadow upon him. When we first see him with his father, he is bitterly admonished for his 'inordinate and low desires' (Pt. I, III. ii. 12). His exploits at Shrewsbury indeed give his wildness some countenance, combine it with his valour and royal spirit into the paradox beloved of popular myth. Yet after his father's death, his brothers and courtiers are fearful where his wildness may lead him. 'I fear all will be overturn'd,' says the Chief Justice (Pt. II, V. ii. 19).

Hal is caught between two worlds. He cannot combine the two, but must reject one for the other: 'being awak'd I do despise my dream'. He cannot sustain his ideal of an inclusive, all-experienced royalty. The Rejection of Falstaff shows the very betrayal of humanity that Hal had moodily pondered in the 'small beer' speech. Yet the Rejection is necessary and indeed laudable in other terms, for Shakespeare does not overthrow the concept of order and royal authority. He merely notes the distance between such principles and those of a genuinely precious humanity.

The most elaborate treatments of the image of the king come in the other two plays of the tetralogy. At the opening of *Henry V*, the Archbishop of Canterbury describes the young king in terms of prelapsarian perfection:

> Consideration like an angel came
> And whipp'd th'offending Adam out of him,
> Leaving his body as a paradise
> T'envelop and contain celestial spirits.   (I. i. 28–31)

Once again, the pattern of action appears to bear out this

image; but the texture of the play tells a different tale. Nearly all through the work, Henry moves as one approximating to a preconceived, externally imposed image, rather than fulfilling the profound urges of his own nature. His ideal involves the necessary rejection of certain categories of experience. His speeches have a narrow range of imagery, and the syntax reflects the emphatic simplification of good rhetoric. In a sense, his is a comprehensive ideal, incorporating the range of accomplishments and sympathies that the good king must command; but by the very condition of his kingship, he cannot admit the full range of human experience. His ideal remains badly and even woodenly incomplete.

Richard II, in most other respects the antithesis to Henry V, provides the equally dissatisfying obverse to the problem. Richard makes a bad king; but he is unable to conceive of any role for himself other than that of king. Some readers discern in him a desire for personal happiness that impedes his success as a king. But in fact he never wishes for private peace until he is threatened with dethronement; and even then, his yearning for 'A little little grave, an obscure grave' is not a genuine desire for obscurity, but a consciously cultivated attempt at playing the role of a deposed king, 'stripping himself of kingly vanities, the pomps and glories of temporal rule; . . . and yet, vanity of vanities, still making himself the focus of a dramatic contemplation of the essential human vanity, persistent though the robe is stripped, the mirror shivered.'[11]

We cannot admire, we cannot even consistently pity, this sentimental egotist who sets himself up as hero on the basis of his suffering rather than of any heroic response to it. All through his career, he tries to conform to an external image—the misunderstood, thwarted king—rather than to develop the innate potential of his character. He cannot develop this potential in the role of king; he cannot bring himself to realize it in any other way. His failure as king—like Henry's success—thus frustrates his basic humanity.

Traditionally, the figure of the king was taken to top the scale of human perfection. Both Richard II and Henry V hold this view. But for Shakespeare himself, this ideal of royal perfection has lost its wholeness, degenerated into a goal of either ceremonial status or politic success. Both Richard and Henry, in their different ways, surrender to externals. The highest human faculties are suppressed or corrupted; there is no genuine development of the self.

Henry's ideal, indeed, bears much that is laudable. He subordinates himself to the social order, as represented—one may almost say symbolized—by the Lord Chief Justice:

> My voice shall sound as you do prompt mine ear;
> And I will stoop and humble my intents
> To your well-practis'd wise directions.
> (H. IV, Pt. II, V. ii. 119-21)

In contrast to Hotspur and Glendower with their competitive view of society, each element struggling against every other, Henry fosters charity and harmony by his rule:

> Not Amurath an Amurath succeeds,
> But Harry Harry.   (H. IV, Pt. II, V. ii. 48-9)

It is a constructive ideal, but not a self-constructive one. In many ways, it requires impoverishment of the self, its end being the growth of the polity, not the individual.

This royal ideal sticks too close to orthodox values, involves too great a sacrifice of valid aims and experiences. It does not solve the problems raised by Falstaff's disordered humanity; rather, it complicates the problem by proving an invalid concept, dismissing a possible solution.

The genuine vindication of man comes through a long struggle in the plays of the next two years. It takes a more destructive path, breaking down values and systems, hatching doubt, gloom, and misanthropy, upholding all the premises of Scepticism. We see this in *Hamlet* and, if anything, more deeply in *Troilus and Cressida*. But in *Hamlet* at least, we also find new, deep, perhaps indefinable values coming to replace the old. By destroying the familiar contours of the moral universe, Shakespeare clears a path for the progress of man's innate virtue.

We cannot be sure whether *Hamlet* or *Troilus and Cressida* is the earlier play. I shall deal with *Hamlet* first; but the precise order is not vital to my argument. At this stage of his career, Shakespeare expresses a conglomerate of ideas that are more clearly resolved in later plays. *Troilus and Cressida*

is most purely full of gloom. *Hamlet* and *Measure for Measure,*
in their separate ways, express themes and ideals that are
taken up in *King Lear.*

3. *Hamlet*

I shall base my analysis of *Hamlet* on two truisms that critics
have sometimes denied or ignored. The first assumes the
centrality of Hamlet in the play. The rival claims of 'the
prince' and 'the poem' can only be resolved by granting that
the former dominates the latter, even to an unusual extent.
My second assumption balances the first: Hamlet's importance
is central but not total. The complexity of the action sur-
rounding Hamlet, the relations in which the subordinate
characters stand among themselves, ensure a contrast between
Hamlet's vision and Hamlet's world. We cannot refuse to
participate in Hamlet's interpretation of life, for it is basic
to the play. Yet we cannot understand it without granting
other possibilities, other interpretations. The world is not
what Hamlet sees it to be.

It is indeed a sordid world by any standards. Its controlling
realities are murder, incest, and usurpation. This is supported
by the quotidian banal 'policy' supplied by Polonius, or the
even more vacuous intrigue of Rosencrantz and Guildenstern.
Yet, as readers have felt, it could be a working system, even a
defensible one as the world goes, were it not for Hamlet's
presence, with the indictment he brings to bear upon it from
a different moral universe. Claudius is not an entirely in-
competent ruler. The courtly world has its own values and
ideals, embodied in a Laertes or a Fortinbras. Horatio can
accommodate himself to this world, though he may not be at
home there. Ophelia's simple, even vulnerable, trust counters
Gertrude's incestuous betrayal of her husband's memory,
which for Hamlet epitomizes the evil pervading his world.

Beyond all this we find a succession of figures and images
suggesting many possible vindications of normal humanity
and courtly life. There is the reverend image of the elder
Hamlet in his lifetime; the Players with their accustomed art
that somehow buoys them above their circumstances; the
flowers that Ophelia carries, and those strewn on her grave,

hinting at an immortality over and above their merely senti-
mental appeal. It is not an impossible world by any means.

Hamlet too seems once to have been a model member of
this world:

> The courtier's, soldier's, scholar's, eye, tongue, sword; . . .
>
> (III. i. 151)

For many commentators, this is the sum total of the ideal he
represents. His career is said to reflect the loss of this ideal,
and perhaps its final recovery.

This is a patently inadequate view. It is obvious that all
through the play, Hamlet moves on a plane apart. The world
of the court has become not only inadequate but quite irrelevant to him. The specific evils of the Danish court have been
transformed into a more absolute sense of evil and nullity.

His first outburst illustrates this:

> 'Tis not alone my inky cloak, good mother, . . .
> But I have that within which passes show—
> These but the trappings and the suits of woe.
>
> (I. ii. 77, 85–6)

The speech began as a reproach to his hypocritical mother
and uncle; but here it turns into something more. Hamlet is
reacting not only against hypocrisy but against sincerity as
the world understands it: a suit of black can *never* represent a
mourner's emotion, there will always be a gap between feeling and expression. Even a normally moral and truthful world
will not satisfy Hamlet. Appearances cannot but be false: the
truth is 'that within' him, and is inexpressible.

Hamlet thus sees himself as essentially alien to the world
and its ways. Through Act I Scene ii, he stands beside the
King and Queen as an embodiment of all that is in contrast
and protest against their rule. When he condemns the Danish
wassail to Horatio, it is not the simple criticism of a single
evil custom but the outcome of a deeper revulsion from his
society. He admits the merits of that society; but his gloom,
concentrated upon the wassail, vitiates the whole picture:

> . . . and, indeed, it takes
> From our achievements, though perform'd at height,
> The pith and marrow of our attribute.   (I. iv. 20–2)

On Hamlet in this state there breaks the Ghost's revelation. It causes far more than a simple moral revulsion. It alienates Hamlet from all humanity, even the highest and happiest:

> Yea, from the table of my memory
> I'll wipe away all trivial fond records,
> All saws of books, all forms, all pressures past . . .
>
> (I. v. 98–100)

The perfection of the courtier's dream would not satisfy him: 'the beauty of the world' and 'the paragon of animals' is to him but 'this quintessence of dust'. As this is a vision of total chaos and negation, it provides the rationale (if such we may call it) behind Hamlet's 'antic disposition'; as it is one of total evil, it inspires the vituperation of the 'Nunnery' Scene; as it must of necessity lead him to reject all life, it raises thoughts of death and suicide. It cannot find expression in any positive terms.

The other characters try to define his condition in customary terms, and naturally end in bewilderment. Polonius and Ophelia think that Hamlet is mad for love; Claudius fears the safety of his usurped throne; for Gertrude, her second marriage seems to rankle whenever Hamlet comes into her presence.

Actually these circumstances merely support in Hamlet a vision of total evil formed, we may say, under an artistic impulse rather than a rational or philosophic one. He builds up his undeniable but finite afflictions into a state of melancholy where the degree of external occasion ceases to matter, a melancholy that will have the abstract perfection of a work of art: self-generating, self-justifying, and therefore impregnable. This melancholy will survive even when 'all occasions inform' against it, and in fact find fresh nourishment in this very circumstance. By the same token, all impulse towards corrective action disappears: not only will it be futile in the face of all-pervasive evil, but it will impair the fullness and independence of this artefact of melancholy. 'All mental form being indefinite and ideal, realities must needs become cold, and hence it is the indefinite that combines with passion.'[12]

As I shall later indicate, this view of Hamlet as the self-absorbed artist in misanthropy is not by itself adequate; but it contains an important partial truth, indicating a paradox that is central to the play. The distinctive vision vouchsafed to Hamlet is one of evil, frustration, and melancholy. But being guided by an impulse towards fullness of perception, it becomes not a limiting or destructive vision but a liberating or creative one, involving a greater exercise of the human faculties than the courtly and heroic norms that it supplants. Hamlet would have been a lesser man if he had not had this paralysing vision of evil and futility. We may recall Faustus, who also exercised his superior faculties to create a profoundly unheroic vision of man. But—and here the distinctive Shakespearean movement comes in—Hamlet's melancholy does not lead to despair and self-damnation. He retains a sort of grace, and an ennobling though perhaps indefinable sense of human values.

The same paradox may be observed in another way: and as this has been less remarked, it is worth detailed illustration. Hamlet is in some ways an excellent Renaissance Sceptic: Rossiter explicitly compares him to Montaigne.[13] For Hamlet, the elements of experience do not provide an ordered pattern but an endless flow of combinations, each with its momentary validity. As we might expect, the most daring examples of this fluidity belong to Hamlet's 'antic disposition', even to the point of *reductio ad absurdum*:

> HAMLET: Do you see yonder cloud that's almost
> in shape of a camel?
> POLONIUS: By th'mass, and 'tis like a camel indeed.
> HAMLET: Methinks it is like a weasel.
> POLONIUS: It is back'd like a weasel.
> HAMLET: Or like a whale?
> POLONIUS: Very like a whale. (III. ii. 366–72)

This, of course, is jest or banter. Hamlet is on a hysterical holiday, following upon his elation at the success of 'The Mouse-trap'. With bitter mischief, he simply wishes to bewilder Polonius, also perhaps to have a bit of his own back on a fickle, perplexing world. To some extent, this is always true of the 'mad' Hamlet: there is an obvious intellectual irresponsibility about all his games with learning. But generally (unlike in the last-quoted passage), this irresponsibility is not the initial impulse behind the exercise. Rather, he conceives a

point in all seriousness, but probes it till it appears untenable
or wearisome: and so, with a final bitter touch, he tosses it
away or mockingly overstates it. It has been reduced to a
funless toy.

> HAMLET. . . . What should a man do but be merry? For look you
> how cheerfully my mother looks, and my father died within's two
> hours.
> OPHELIA. Nay, 'tis twice two months, my lord.
> HAMLET. So long? Nay then, let the devil wear black, for I'll have a
> suit of sables. O heavens! die two months ago, and not forgotten
> yet? Then there's hope a great man's memory may outlive his life
> half a year; but, by'r lady, 'a must build churches, then; or else
> shall 'a suffer not thinking on, with the hobby-horse, whose epitaph
> is 'For O, for O, the hobby-horse is forgot!'   (III. ii. 120-30)

Hamlet has many jokes about the flux of things; but unlike
the exchange about the clouds, they are conceived in grim
earnest:

> . . . your fat king and your lean beggar is but variable service—two
> dishes, but to one table. That's the end. (IV. iii. 23-5)

So too with logic. Hamlet can reason well, indeed flamboy-
antly, as a zestful academic exercise. It is largely in this spirit
(though not without a touch of sarcasm) that he wrangles
about 'a shadow's shadow' with Rosencrantz and Guildenstern, ending with an ironic 'I cannot reason' (II. ii. 253-64).
But how grim is the logic of a later utterance:

> HAMLET. . . . Farewell, dear mother.
> KING. Thy loving father, Hamlet.
> HAMLET. My mother: father and mother is man and wife; man and
> wife is one flesh; and so, my mother. (IV. iii. 49-53)

There are other games with logic that Hamlet can play. A
series of conclusions can be neatly undermined by being
shown to depend on a fantastic proviso:

> . . . for you yourself, sir, shall grow old as I am, if, like a crab, you
> could go backward. (II. ii. 201-3)

Or a logical justification can be provided for the reversal of
normal idiom:

> KING. Now, Hamlet, where's Polonius?
> HAMLET. At supper.

KING. At supper! Where?
HAMLET. Not where he eats, but where 'a is eaten;...
(IV. iii. 17–20)

Or a set of statements can be erected into something very like a riddle:

> HAMLET. The body is with the King, but the King is not with the body. The King is a thing—
> GUILDENSTERN. A thing, my lord!
> HAMLET. Of nothing. Bring me to him. (IV. ii. 26-9)

Hamlet builds up a fantasy world of logic and language. This may provide some sort of relief or escape from the stresses of his situation; but more importantly, it demonstrates his sense of the futility of logic itself. The relief, if any, is self-defeating, deepening his sense of exhaustion and vacuity.

The logical pun, so to speak, on 'at supper', leads us on to simple verbal quibbles, conveying the same sense of the instability of all human terms and concepts:

> Is this the fine of his fines, and the recovery of his recoveries, to have his fine pate full of fine dirt? (V. i. 102–4)

It may be no accident that Hamlet joins with the Gravediggers in a long pun on *lie* (V. i. 118 ff.), for words have become lies to Hamlet—philosophic lies that conceal the ineffable flux of existence, where they are not lies in the simple moral sense. The power of expression is as futile as that of apprehension: there is no relation between language and reality:

> —What do you read, my lord?
> —Words, words, words. (II. ii. 190-1)

Yet there is something radically new about Shakespeare's presentation of Scepticism in *Hamlet*. The lampooning of facts and methods is a conscious parody on the part of Hamlet himself, not merely of the author as generally, say, in Rabelais. Within the world of the play, in the hero in person, we have evidence of both critical and creative power, a vindication of the human intellect even while its methods and products are castigated. There is obviously a great intellectual energy in Hamlet. Thwarted in its efforts at meaningful achievement, it expends itself in mental acrobatics. 'Thwarted' may even be the wrong word: again I suggest that there is in

Hamlet the impulse to create an intellectual fantasy-world as a self-complete artefact, fulfilling its nature by deliberately eschewing the test of reality or the goal of action.

Thus the 'paralysis of the will' may in fact be seen as constructive activity at an imaginative or contemplative level. Hamlet fails to impose an order on the world; but at this other level, he achieves a highly individual structuring of experience. He understands and assesses his world, seeing it as a playground of flux, deception, and illogicality. This he expresses through a corresponding grotesquerie of image and language, so that in common terms his vision appears un-balanced, inconsistent, and destructive—in a word, mad.

This is not the final paradox: it represents one half of a more comprehensive one. It would be not merely inadequate but almost perverse to rest content with the figure of Hamlet as a deliberate individualist, defiantly and even suicidally courting the contemplative isolation of the artist-philosopher. Such indeed is the image he presents at times, and it is impor-tant to understand this image; but as important to realize that the secret of such a stance lies in a diametrically opposite group of principles.

We must explore this new direction to discover the basic impulse behind Hamlet's ethos and conduct. His alienation from the world and his attempt at a self-sufficiency of vision are born of a sort of defensive instinct after the failure of a harmonious universal ideal. Beneath his 'madness', and in fact his conduct all through, there lies an impassioned con-viction of moral absolutes which, agonizingly impossible in the context of the play, should ideally be accepted by man-kind and embodied in action.

The passage that may most appear to show Hamlet's Sceptical distrust of absolutes is in fact extremely ambiguous evidence.

> HAMLET. Denmark's a prison. . . .
> ROSENCRANTZ. We think not so, my lord.
> HAMLET. Why, then, 'tis none to you; for there is nothing either good or bad, but thinking makes it so. To me it is a prison.
>
> (II. ii. 242, 247–50)

Is this a genuinely-held philosophic conviction, or merely the ironic use of one to hit at the two time-servers? And what are the 'bad dreams' which prevent Hamlet from achieving infinity in a nutshell? What but his situation and the atmosphere of the court, with the pressure that these exert upon his moral being? He even feels himself born to set right the disjointed times. I am suspicious of any attempt to present Hamlet as being willingly immersed in a subjective world. Rather, he retreats into his private 'antic' world in a desperate attempt to retain something of universal, but now eclipsed, norms. 'This was sometime a paradox, but now the time gives it proof'.

This sense of absolute values provides another differentia from the customary versions of Scepticism. The nature of these values must be clearly realized. At the clearest and most obvious end of the spectrum, they incorporate such concepts as the sanctity of life, the rights of succession, the force of marital ties, the innocence of romantic love. But these grade into a range of subtle attitudes and responses whose under-lying spirit, when all is said and done, it still best approached through Bradley's words:

an exquisite sensibility, to which we may give the name 'moral', if that word is taken in the wide meaning it ought to bear . . . (W)e must call it a disposition to idealise, to see something better than what is there, or at least to ignore deficiencies . . . To the very end, his soul, however sick and tortured it may be, answers instantaneously when good and evil are presented to it, loving the one and hating the other.[14]

Hamlet's morality, in this sense, is not mere adherence to certain principles but a quality of sensibility, a consistent manner of responding to experience. But Bradley's account must be modified by a recognition that, given the pervasive evil of Hamlet's milieu, his hatred of evil appears much more commonly than his love of good. His moral sensitivity is turned inside out, so to speak, in speeches of satire and frenzied denunciation. An outraged ideal takes such contrary and unbalanced forms that we may question its complete validity. *Is* the world nothing but a prison? Are all women breeders of sinners? Must beauty always transform honesty to a bawd? But there is no doubt that through these hysterical overstatements, Hamlet is still showing his attachment to an ideal that had expected the opposite extreme of virtue.

When we first see Hamlet at the court of Claudius, he

conceals his shock beneath a wry, laconic exterior: 'A little more than kin, and less than kind' (I. ii. 65). His one long outburst expresses grief for his father—but obviously conveys even more his shock that his mother does not evince the same grief. At the end of the scene, when he is left alone, his dis-illusionment finds direct expression in the soliloquy 'O that this too too solid flesh . . .' This is also the first expression of his longing for suicide, so that he can preserve his ideal impregnably in death.

Thus Hamlet's first appearance indicates the polarities within which he seeks to preserve his thwarted moral ideal: the caustic, defensive public stance and the free tirade of private condemnation. After his encounter with the Ghost, the former attitude develops into an 'antic disposition'. The chaos of his moral universe has now been confirmed by the supernatural: the Ghost's tragic narrative yields to the grotesque farce of the 'Cellarage' Scene. Tight-lipped senti-mental gloom is no longer an appropriate defence. Hamlet abandons himself to an ironic accentuation of the chaos by the tormented wit of the 'mad' scenes.

Sometimes he scores a victory by his wit, bewildering the chief agents of a dispensation that bewilders him. These are his moments of brief victory over his milieu, when he exults in the quizzical power he enjoys over his fellow men. He cross-examines Rosencrantz and Guildenstern, baits Polonius and mystifies Osric. The success of 'The Mouse-trap' puts him in a position of power; but he reacts with the same apparent abandon:

> For if the King like not the comedy,
> Why, then, belike he likes it not, perdy.   (III. ii. 287–8)

Yet he passes in a few moments to an entirely serious declara-tion of independence in the 'recorders' speech. Finally, when he is left alone, the full weight of his moral purpose returns upon him:

> . . . Now could I drink hot blood,
> And do such bitter business as the day
> Would quake to look on.   (III. ii.380–2)

The same basic stand underlies Hamlet's various and seem-ingly contrary reactions; he may change or merge his attitudes at a moment's notice. His 'antic' foolery may suddenly subside into open world-weariness and longing for death:

> POLONIUS. . . .—My lord, I will take my leave of you.
> HAMLET. You cannot, sir, take from me anything that I will more willingly part withal—except my life, except my life, except my life. (II. ii. 213–16)

The two veins are most extensively combined in the meditative banter of the Graveyard Scene.

In the 'Nunnery' Scene, 'antic' wit and satiric fantasy combine with direct moral castigation in a malign tirade. It leads on to the equally vehement, but more controlled and pertinent abuse of Gertrude in the Closet Scene, and illustrates how Hamlet turns upon Ophelia his resentment towards his mother. At the same time, the 'Nunnery' Scene follows from the misogyny of the first soliloquy: 'Frailty, thy name is woman!' Again we see how Hamlet fights the world, not with practical resources designed to produce action, but with the inbred, overwrought substance of his cogitations. This disturbs the world about him without altering it; but such disturbance is all he hopes for, despairing of any greater success.

As I see it, Hamlet never breaks free from a paralysing adherence to frustrated moral absolutes. His spirit is never decisively modified by his experience of people and events. Hence his 'madness', his moral passion, his occasional tenderness or self-discipline cannot be arranged in any pattern of development. They form a spectrum of improvised expressions of the same underlying attitude, and he moves from point to point of the spectrum as the occasion demands or his mood takes him. The exact reaction at any point may be unpredictable, as are the tortuosities of the action itself. But all through we have the same dramatic impression of sustained chaos. The episodes of the action, and even more Hamlet's commentary upon them, function as a sort of fugue upon this theme. We are drawn back every time to the same unsolved confrontation between Hamlet and his world.

It is unsolved because we never find out what Hamlet desires by way of solution: he does not seem to know. He never succeeds in defining his ideal; it seems beyond description, let alone embodiment. As I said earlier, it suggests a

different moral universe. On the parallel of 'negative theology',
we may perhaps call this a sort of 'negative morality' that can
find expression only through reversal and rejection of normal
patterns of conduct. It is almost as impatient of orthodox
moral courses as of evil ones. Hamlet does not question his
duty of revenge, but the ideal cannot fire him. Ophelia's
simple goodness maddens him: it has become meaningless,
incapable of countering his mother's carnality but rather
reflecting it in embryo. Yet he loves Ophelia:

> . . . forty thousand brothers
> Could not, with all their quantity of love,
> Make up my sum.   (V. i. 263-5)

Paradoxically, his supremely sensitive moral ideal has robbed
him of all discrimination: his love, while pathetically recog-
nizable as such, cannot escape the taint of his great revulsion
from all experience.

So too in the Graveyard Scene, Hamlet deeply perceives
the common lot of man: 'That skull had a tongue in it, and
could sing once' (V. i. 75). Yet he shuns the memory of being
borne by Yorick. The basic tone of his speech is not humane
but destructive. He turns the thought of death, like Ithuriel's
spear, in satire against one class of society after another: the
politician, the courtier, the lawyer, the lady in her chamber.
This is in the tradition of the medieval Dance of Death; but
the Dance admitted the possibility of repentance, the implicit
promise of Heaven. In Hamlet's vision, defeat and futility are
rendered absolute.

From time to time, he attempts to define his ideal in more
positive terms; but he never truly succeeds. There is nothing
inherently futile about these attempts; in fact they are
frequently realized in some minor character. But they all miss
something of the subtlety and complexity of Hamlet's ideal.
They are no more than hints and sallies, delimiting one
corner of his field or merely indicating it from afar.

Hamlet's praise of Horatio is one obvious attempt at defining this ideal. Another is his fitful admiration for the 'Fortinbras values', which appears to conceal a yearning for the deeper
values of his own ideal. Yet another is the trust in providence, and consequent 'readiness' to meet one's destiny, that
Hamlet evinces intermittently after his return from England.

Of all these attempts at realizing his ideal, the most interesting is the concept of 'honour' that Hamlet evolves out of the grosser and more politic premisses of the 'Fortinbras values'. Just as Hamlet's melancholy exceeds its logical causes, so also this counteracting 'honour' demands a field of expression greater than the sordid world can allow. It can therefore realize itself only *in vacuo*, fighting 'Even for an egg-shell'. This cultivation of honour may appeal as an abstract ideal; like the cultivation of melancholy, it can serve as a moral process providing a basically aesthetic fulfilment. But in terms of action or effect, it is an exercise in futility. 'Honour' is at once the crowning glory of man and the strongest proof of his inconsequentiality.

Meanwhile, the enterprise actually offered to Hamlet remains unfulfilled as being unfit to express his humanity. This is Hamlet's dilemma. He is apparently given the chance to realize his ideal through the act of revenge; but in fact, to be so realized, his ideal must suffer a degeneration that destroys its very nature. It is a basic condition of revenge tragedy that the avenger, thwarted by pervasive evil from leaping to his revenge, must instead pursue it through devious paths, partially adopting the very cynicism and duplicity that he seeks to destroy. *Hamlet* retains some of these devious methods in their externals: in particular, assumed madness and a play-within-a-play. But Shakespeare's hero is unique in being utterly unable to make the moral compromise such deviousness implies. His task of revenge is obstructed by the outraged contemplation of insurmountable evil.

Hamlet thus presents us with a duality: human potential of great subtlety and infinite extent, and a human situation that must of necessity frustrate it. An ideal is proposed but apparently found impossible: to be valid and comprehensive, it must take note of an extent of evil that renders it impotent if not, paradoxically, invalid. We may recall the state of Ficino's Prometheus.

This is why the play ends on a curiously dissatisfying note. The wrongdoers die, and die at Hamlet's hand; but this is an external simulation of the revenge-play ending, bringing nothing of the moral satisfaction such an ending should inculcate. Shakespeare has raised problems deeper than the

mere restoration of order or punishment of crime. He has
evoked an infinitely complex, infinitely suffering moral ideal,
incompatible with the very terms of human existence, let
alone the adverse circumstances of the Danish court. This
ideal is not realized by Hamlet before his death; the institution
of Fortinbras destroys the possibility for ever. The moral
vision of the play remains unfulfilled.

All the same, it survives as a vision or ideal—and as such,
perhaps most valuable by its very impossibility. Its optimism
approaches the infinite, and therefore fails of practical fulfilment. In *Troilus and Cressida*, the ideal itself is exploded.
The play marks Shakespeare's closest approach to total
negation.

4. *Troilus and Cressida*

Few readers will deny that *Troilus and Cressida* is full of
doubt, gloom, and frustration. At its simplest, this appears in
an opposition between the idealistic and the pragmatic, the
emotive and the rational, and mourns the fall of the former
elements in the conflict. Undoubtedly too, there is a deep
sense of the destructive power of time. But the gloom of the
play penetrates deeper than such a simple account can
suggest. The ideal is not merely threatened, but shown to be
corrupt and invalid.

Several times in the play, 'truth' appears as a weakness that
thwarts success and even survival:

> I am as true as truth's simplicity,
> And simpler than the infancy of truth.   (III. ii. 165–6)

The play on 'simplicity' casts a doubt on the virtue of 'simple'
or single, pristine truth. We touch upon the philosophic or
metaphysical doubt that lurks all through the play. Troilus
repeats the self-deprecating pun:

> CRESSIDA. My lord, will you be true?
> TROILUS. Who, I? Alas, it is my vice, my fault!
> Whiles others fish with craft for great opinion,
> I with great truth catch mere simplicity; . . .
> (IV. iv. 100–3)

Troilus's 'vice' is Hector's too. The supreme exemplar of 'honour' embodies the same weakness:

> TROILUS. Brother, you have a vice of mercy in you
>   Which better fits a lion than a man.
> HECTOR. What vice is that, good Troilus? Chide
>   me for it.
> TROILUS. When many times the captive Grecian falls,
>   Even in the fan and wind of your fair sword,
>   You bid them rise and live.   (V. iii. 37–42)

In fact, *Troilus and Cressida* presents us with a specially disturbing version of the basic problem of all tragic heroism. The heroic values, originally no doubt a code of survival, turn into the contrary, making the hero pay for honour with suffering and death. His ideal proves incompatible with the terms of human existence.

The Trojan concept of honour (put forth most clearly in the Trojan Council of II. ii) reflects a decline of idealism far beyond anything in *Hamlet*. Basically, Troilus's ideal is that which Hamlet fitfully admires, of daring death for an egg-shell 'When honour's at the stake':

> Weigh you the worth and honour of a king,
> So great as our dread father's, in a scale
> Of common ounces? Will you with counters sum
> The past-proportion of his infinite . . .   (II. ii. 26–9)

But in *Troilus and Cressida*, this honour is denigrated as it never is in *Hamlet*. For one thing, it is shown to run counter to morality in the simple and obvious way. Nowhere in *Hamlet* do we find that the hero considers his father's revenge to be wrong or sinful in a straightforward sense: that is a fancy of the critics. But in *Troilus and Cressida*, Hector clearly points out that Troilus's honour contradicts the basic principle of marriage and in fact all morality:

> The reasons you allege do more conduce
> To the hot passion of distemp'red blood
> Than to make up a free determination
> 'Twixt right and wrong; . . .   (II. ii. 168–71)

The moral justification for 'honour' being removed, the rational absurdity becomes intolerably plain:

> . . . 'Tis mad idolatry
> To make the service greater than the god;
> And the will dotes that is attributive
> To what infectiously itself affects,
> Without some image of th'affected merit.   (II. ii. 56–60)

The last three lines are particularly interesting in the light of my reading of *Hamlet*. There we see a concept of honour that was independently conceived and maintained, without reference to external circumstances, like a work of art with its self-contained perfection. In *Troilus*, this is shown as an irrational and dangerous ideal. That is why Hector's final volte-face in the Council Scene is not made valid by heroic emotion. It is not that Shakespeare's poetic power suddenly deserts him: the succeeding speech by Troilus ('Why, there you touch'd . . .') is full of enthusiasm. But Hector's words are deliberately kept free of the romanticism that lends a momentary appeal to the ideal: its irrationality comes out clearly through his plain, almost listless acceptance of the war.

The bitter Diomedes provides the best comment, in a later scene:

> He merits well to have her that doth seek her,
> Not making any scruple of her soilure,
> With such a hell of pain and world of charge;
> And you as well to keep her that defend her,
> Not palating the taste of her dishonour,
> With such a costly loss of wealth and friends.
>
> (IV. i. 57–62)

Again, it is Diomedes who declares that in the Greek camp, Cressida shall be prized 'to her own worth' (IV. iv. 134). Hector too had at first argued the need for 'affected merit' to justify the pursuit of honour.

Interestingly though, the crucial parody of Trojan honour comes from the Greek camp. Achilles' sulks indicate the same concern with individual honour, even in opposition to common values and the general good, that Troilus had commended and Hector acquiesced in:

> . . . in self-assumption greater
> Than in the note of judgement; . . .   (II. iii. 120–1)

The Trojans will defend a rape to the ruin of the public weal;

Achilles will maintain his selfish dudgeon even if it costs the Greeks their victory. In both cases, private honour is asserted in defiance of common norms. It is shown to be the outcome of pride.

The Grecians' comments on Achilles may apply *mutatis mutandis* to the self-instituted Trojan honour as well:

> AGAMEMNON. . . . . He that is proud eats up himself. Pride is his
> own glass, his own trumpet, his own chronicle; . . . (II. iii. 150–1)

Ulysses is clearer still:

> Shall the proud lord
> That bastes his arrogance with his own seam
> And never suffers matter of the world
> Enter his thoughts, save such as doth revolve
> And ruminate himself—shall he be worshipp'd
> Of that we hold an idol more than he?   (II. iii. 179–84)

Surely this is no accidental echo of Hector's 'mad idolatry'. It is the most telling exposure of Trojan honour that, for all the generosity, refinement and genuine sacrifice of its exponents, its essential nature can be analysed into such close conformity with the conduct of the cur Achilles.

There is another imperfection about Trojan honour. Though admirable in many (ultimately untenable) ways, it is something fully-formed, static, antique—even outdated. In *Hamlet*, the 'Fortinbras values' imply a certain growth or dynamism: they suggest the inexpressibly superior ideal that Hamlet is struggling to embody. But the spirit of Troy has exhausted its potential. It may still command a nostalgic golden-age admiration if the participants can pass outside time:

> What's past and what's to come is strew'd with husks
> And formless ruin of oblivion;
> But in this extant moment, faith and troth,
> Strain'd purely from all hollow bias-drawing,
> Bids thee with most divine integrity,
> From heart of very heart, great Hector, welcome.
> (IV. v. 166–71)

But within the time-bound action of the play, the old ideal is doomed. Time can only destroy: it cannot evolve or fulfil.

The lines I have just quoted are actually spoken by Agamemnon. But the spirit of antique honour pervades Greek

and Trojan alike in this scene, and there is something of this
honour about Agamemnon and Nestor in any case. The distinctive 'Grecian honour' finds its chief exponent in Ulysses.

If Trojan honour is proud, self-generated, and self-contained, Grecian honour as preached by Ulysses is social or
communal:

> . . . no man is the lord of anything,
> Though in and of him there be much consisting,
> Till he communicate his parts to others; . . .   (III. iii. 115–17)

But this is not permitted to grow into an ideal of charity and
fellow-feeling of the sort that appears fitfully in the History
Plays or *Hamlet*. Ulysses' next words bring us back to the
standard level of the play:

> Nor doth he of himself know them for aught
> Till he behold them formed in th' applause
> Where th'are extended; . . .   (III. iii. 118–20)

Just as Trojan honour was lowered to the level of pride, so
Ulysses' honour is equated with 'esteem':

> Nature, what things there are
> Most abject in regard and dear in use!
> What things again most dear in the esteem
> And poor in worth!   (III. iii. 127–30)

It is this that touches Achilles to the core:

> I see my reputation is at stake;
> My fame is shrewdly gor'd.   (III. iii. 227–8)

And no doubt it is the same concern for reputation that
makes him claim personally whatever merit accrued from the
gang slaughter of Hector by the Myrmidons:[15]

> On, Myrmidons, and cry you all amain
> 'Achilles hath the mighty Hector slain'.   (V. viii. 13–14)

The common reason that the Trojans had rejected proves, as
cultivated by the Greeks, to be a purely external esteem,
equally unfit to pass Hector's criterion of

> estimate and dignity
> As well wherein 'tis precious of itself
> As in the prizer.   (II. ii. 54–6)

We may again cross sides[16] to record a telling comment by

the Trojan Pandarus: 'Grace! not so, friend; honour and lordship are my titles' (III. i. 15–16).

Two opposite ideals of honour are thus proposed and dismissed. This double dismissal has interesting affinities. It would be absurd to suggest that *Troilus and Cressida* is a conscious critique of Renaissance Scepticism. But obviously, the two honours bear some resemblance to the two standard ideals of Sceptic conduct: an individual code of values, and an implicit conformity to social norms. Shakespeare has taken the same two paths as the Sceptics to solve the problem of human conduct in a confusion of values and circumstances. Both ideals are denied even the tentative validity that they bear in the work of a balanced Sceptic like Montaigne.

We may probe deeper still. The characters appeal to external standards of judgement because of the impossibility of a genuine moral assessment. This moral frustration, more than anything else, causes the unrest and speculation at the core of the play. As has often been noted, the characters speak in an unusually analytic, contemplative tone: they are constantly seeking the motives of their own conduct and looking for values to guide them. They are struck by the contrast between the cruel frivolity of 'wars and lechery' and the power and beauty of the ideals, such as honour and love, born out of that unreason. They can neither accept nor eliminate this contrast, but analyse and theorize in attempts to do so. (Perhaps, on the whole, the Trojans aim at acceptance, and the Greeks at elimination.) To risk a slightly flamboyant paradox, they are struck by the power of human weakness.

All human virtue being untenable and uncertain, characters lose their moral identity. A. P. Rossiter makes an acute comment on Cressida:

. . . for every participant in the scene there is a phenomenon called 'Cressida': Thersites' is no more Ulysses' (though both think her a mere flirt) than Diomed's is Troilus'; nor is Cressida's Cressida like any of these. In each, the individual consciousness spontaneously generates its own norms, and enjoys complete freedom in 'making its own existence'. But this is the same as showing that there are *no* norms, in the sense in which traditional philosophy assumes them. The absolutes are myths.[17]

This is the proper Sceptical predicament, classically expressed by Montaigne: characters constantly change and remake their identities. Human nature is an endless flux, so that it is impossible to judge people by absolute moral standards or in fact to formulate such standards at all.

The uncertainty of human identities ultimately reaches a point where (at least in metaphor) we approach the Sceptic distrust of the senses:

> Shall I not lie in publishing a truth?
> Sith yet there is a credence in my heart,
> An esperance so obstinately strong,
> That doth invert th' attest of eyes and ears;
> As if those organs had deceptious functions
> Created only to calumniate.   (V. ii. 117–22)

'This is, and is not, Cressid' (V. ii. 144). I repeat that I do not wish to present the play as an expression of formal Scepticism; but Shakespeare is touching upon many of the same concerns, with a distinctive emphasis. The Sceptical premisses are given a specially *moral* orientation. The bewilderment is not caused by the weakness of the human senses or the inscrutability of the external world: it is due to the moral corruption of man.

As we saw, even in standard Scepticism, the epistemological problems were held to be caused by sin—ultimately by the fallen state of man. It is as though Shakespeare were dramatizing this central moral corruption. The intellectual failure provides an accompaniment, through the imagery and in subsidiary thematic motifs. Moral falsity leads to a sense of metaphysical falsity: the former is the basic problem, the latter its philosophic reverberation. Hamlet's 'Words, words, words' expresses an intellectual frustration; Troilus' 'Words, words, mere words' (V. iii. 108) shows moral disillusionment at Cressida's faithlessness.

The ultimate disillusionment emerges in the speeches of Thersites. One can scarcely call Thersites a disillusioned moralist: his brutal raillery is far removed from all moral conceptions whatsoever. This is the most disturbing feature of Thersites' rant. On the one hand, it hits home, unquestionably exposing the sordidness, hypocrisy, and futility of the war and of the Greek camp in particular. On the other hand, it exposes it not to induce balance or correction, but to cast us out upon a still more frightening, utterly disordered and cynical world. Thersites does not merely sum up the evil in the rest of the play; he adds another dimension to it.

His raillery is too deeply rooted in reality to be dismissed as a misanthrope's fantasy:

> Here is such patchery, such juggling, and such knavery. All the argument is a whore and a cuckold—a good quarrel to draw emulous factions and bleed to death upon. (II. iii. 67-70)

This is no more than what everybody from Hector downwards is saying: no more than we all feel. In a way, Thersites brings out the basic spirit of the play. His images of animals, sickness, sores, and putrefaction bear an obvious symbolic relation to the general conduct of affairs. His direct association of war with lechery compresses the military consequences of the rape of Helen into a symbol for the sordid tangle of motives governing the action. Thersites responds to Cressida's betrayal of Troilus just as he does to Achilles' sulks and the consequent intrigue: it is all wars and lechery (II. iii. 81-2, V. iv. 34). When Menelaus and Paris fight, or Troilus and Diomedes, this throws into focus the general cause of the war: 'The cuckold and the cuckold-maker are at it' (V. vii. 9); '. . . lechery eats itself' (V. iv. 34). This is a literal realization of the sexual motive with which, more obliquely, Thersites associates the martial instinct at all times. It reflects Shakespeare's own design in using a story of pandered and betrayed love to open up a perspective upon war.

Yet it would be preposterous to take Thersites as the dramatist's mouthpiece, directly expressing the theme of the play. He is himself the most despicable character of all.[18] Beyond the evils that he castigates, he evinces another peculiar to himself. His railing rhetoric, the luxuriance of his gross satiric fantasy, argue for an independent impulse to pervert and befoul, a degraded but active imagination. His vision of total evil overcomes his own nature. We may even feel it emanates from his nature: 'a bastard begot, bastard instructed, bastard in mind, bastard in valour, in everything illegitimate' (V. vii. 16-18).

In the other characters of the play, we mark the exposure of false and hollow values. In Thersites there is a total absence of all moral referents, a seemingly endless capacity to absorb the sordid and the evil. This makes him a telling critic of the evil world of the play; but it opens up the prospect of a still greater degeneration. The vision of folly and evil that he fosters is true in any case, but he renders it even truer than it would otherwise have been. The whole structure of reassuring beliefs and ideals—demonstrably overthrown in the rest of the play—is desecrated by Thersites with a violence that provides a new shock, a new despair.

We are thus placed in a conflict. It seems inevitable that we should accept Thersites' view of man; yet we are repelled by his character, we abhor any concurrence with the position he holds. Such concurrence would be the ultimate humiliation of man in the play. Shakespeare reveals mercilessly quite how sordid it would be; but he leads us to the point where we wonder whether we can escape the identification.

This 'classical' play bears no explicit reference to the Fall or to any other Christian doctrine, but it presents mankind in what can only be called the fallen state. Further, it frustrates all the ideals by which man seeks to overcome this state; going beyond, or beneath, *Hamlet*, it practically denies the presence of virtuous power in man. *Measure for Measure* presents us with new problems, but also new hope.

5. *Measure for Measure*

Although *Measure for Measure* is profoundly disturbing in many ways, Shakespeare eschews the easy iconoclasm with which modern critics and producers tend to credit him. Nothing could be more misguided than to consider the play as a simple anti-establishment tract. Nowhere does Shakespeare dismiss the concept of justice or the need for order and authority. On the contrary, the root evil of the play, which gives rise to the entire sequence of moral problems, is 'too much liberty':

> ... our decrees,
> Dead to infliction, to themselves are dead;
> And liberty plucks justice by the nose;
> The baby beats the nurse, and quite athwart
> Goes all decorum.   (I. iii. 27–31)

It is the same problem as in *Troilus and Cressida*: degree has been lost. Accordingly, there is imperative need for order

and justice. Angelo's initial standpoint has a stern consistency
about it:

> You may not so extenuate his offence
> For I have had such faults; but rather tell me,
> When I, that censure him, do so offend,
> Let mine own judgement pattern out my death,
> And nothing come in partial. (II. i. 27–31)

He retains this consistency even in his fall:

> . . . I crave death more willingly than mercy;
> 'Tis my deserving, and I do entreat it. (V. i. 474–5)

Most important, the Duke himself concurs, in those cryptic
couplets which, however primitive and undramatic, undoubtedly form a nodal point in the play:

> More nor less to others paying
> Than by self-offences weighing. (III. ii. 247–8)

There are moments when mercy itself must be stern:

> ISABELLA. Yet show some pity.
> ANGELO. I show it most of all when I show justice;
>   For then I pity those I do not know,
>   Which a dismiss'd offence would after gall . . .
>   (II. ii. 99–102)

Even after Angelo falls, the same point is made by the Duke
himself:

> The very mercy of the law cries out
> Most audible, even from his proper tongue,
> 'An Angelo for Claudio, death for death!' (V. i. 405–7)

This is not the final spirit of the play, but it is an important
phase in its development. Shakespeare's stand in this play
shows a striking resemblance to the orthodox Sceptic view of
the social order, though I should hardly like to propose any
direct influence. The Sceptic doubts the principles on which
society rests, and the possibility of ever arriving at any valid
principles whatsoever. But in practice, he accepts this order
as an indispensable condition of existence. Shakespeare, too,
here proposes fairly orthodox norms of social conduct and
community rule, whatever his ultimate philosophic conclusion
may be.

What invalidates this authority is not any flaw in the ideal itself, but the impossibility of finding a man 'as holy as severe'. It is not that the woman has not sinned through adultery, but that there is no innocent man to cast the first stone.

> Go to your bosom,
> Knock there, and ask your heart what it doth know
> That's like my brother's fault.   (II. ii. 136–8)

Escalus had said the same thing earlier:

> Let but your honour know,
> Whom I believe to be most strait in virtue,
> That, in the working of your own affections,
> Had time coher'd with place, or place with wishing . . .
>   (II. i. 8–11)

The second line quoted thus takes on a fine irony. It is one of the several early passages where personal virtue is treated with a doubt that later develops into total distrust.

The exercise of authority becomes an instance of pride, as Isabella declares in her speech on 'Man, proud man . . .' We are thus faced with a paradox. Social order is necessary to suppress the vicious instincts of fallen man. To ensure this order, man may command or subjugate his fellow-beings. He may even assume the exercise of divine prerogatives, but this cannot remove his basic corruption. On the contrary, it becomes an instance of pride that aggravates the corruption. In the figure of the Duke, we seem indeed to have an unsullied and divinely sanctioned image of authority; but this holds true only while we regard him as an allegorical or symbolic character, which we can scarcely do with any consistency. He is too clearly less than superhuman, aware of his own patent shortcomings (''twas my fault to give the people scope') and entirely ready to adopt devious shifts and policies.

Thus at one level, the play creates a deep sense of frustration. The ideal of virtuous authority becomes an external, projected image, barely tenable on the plane of social organization, while the intractable reality of human nature rankles beneath it. The Duke's dismissal of life and Claudio's terror of death (III. i. 5 ff. and 119 ff.) apparently conform to standard patterns of Christian meditation; but in fact, they create between them a sense of total futility, a metaphysical void.

This bewilderment and moral negation threaten to destroy the very terms of human virtue. Good and evil usurp each other's functions. Admiration for Isabella's virtue leads Angelo to his fall:

> Most dangerous
> Is that temptation that doth goad us on
> To sin in loving virtue.   (II. ii. 181-3)

There is a deeper sense too in which 'some by virtue fall'— the sense in which Escalus actually intended these words (II. i. 38). Even where moral rigour is successfully practised, it implies a denial of humanity, leads to grave injustice, and appears no less than monstrous. Lucio holds the novice Isabella as 'a think ensky'd and sainted'; but he describes the same celibacy in Angelo, a few lines later, in very different terms:

> . . . a man whose blood
> Is very snow-broth, one who never feels
> The wanton stings and motions of the sense,
> But doth rebate and blunt his natural edge . . .
>   (I. iv. 57–60)

Human nature is incompatible with the practice of virtue, and the contrast is *made to tell against virtue*.

The temptation of Isabella reveals this most elaborately. Her problem is far greater than Angelo's. Angelo falls unwittingly; and his temptation is obviously to evil. But Isabella has to make a conscious choice, and something like a Hegelian choice between two goods. We should not lessen the difficulty of the choice by regarding her ideal of chastity simply as a craven and selfish scruple. This is to pre-date the permissive age in a manner illegitimate even for the producer and indefensible in the scholar. Yet we can hardly regard Isabella as an entirely saintly figure. Her state is undoubtedly less than ideal, a morbid degree of 'physical self-regard'[19] asserted with the hysterically inflexible stand of a person facing an exasperating problem with an inadequate code of values. Her situation relative to Angelo is now reversed, and he can point out that *her* unbending virtue is an instance of pride:

> Be that you are,
> That is, a woman; if you be more, you're none; . . .
>
> (II. iv. 134-5)

Isabella's own words do not belie the charge:

> More than our brother is our chastity.   (II. iv. 185)

How easily, too, does her love of Claudio turn to hate, once
he ceases to be a tractable element in her private and com-
fortable moral dispensation:

> Wilt thou be made a man out of my vice?
> Is't not a kind of incest to take life
> From thine own sister's shame? . . .
>   . . . Take my defiance;
> Die; perish. Might but my bending down
> Reprieve thee from thy fate, it should proceed.
> I'll pray a thousand prayers for thy death,
> No word to save thee.   (III. i. 139-41, 144-8)

Angelo falls to temptation; Isabella offends by resisting it.
Yet the fault appears to lie less with Isabella as a person than
with the necessary moral implications of her situation. The
disturbing rigidity of her virtue, her sisterly love turned to
such violent hate, her sudden and inept plea for Angelo's
forgiveness—all this constitutes an unsatisfactory response,
but no more unsatisfactory than any other, to a frighteningly
complex moral problem. Shakespeare is not merely saying
that virtue is twin with priggishness. He is concerned with the
profound interrelation of good and evil, their mixture in
all human motives, and the utter inadequacy of all moral
categories. The point is not that Angelo and Isabella are
hypocrites; it is that their vices are the inescapable obverse or
concomitant of their virtues.

'Prayers cross' over and over again in the play. 'Heaven
grant us its peace, but not the King of Hungary's!' says
Lucio's companion (I. ii. 4); and Isabella knows the same
mixed motives:

> There is a vice that most I do abhor,
> And most desire should meet the blow of justice;
> For which I would not plead, but that I must:
> For which I must not plead, but that I am
> At war 'twixt will and will not.   (II. ii. 29-33)

Or, as she says elsewhere,

> It oft falls out,
> To have what we would have, we speak not what we mean: . . .
>
> (II. iv. 117-18)

The impossibility of resolving such dilemmas comes out in Angelo's strange consolation to Isabella:

> Be satisfied;
> Your brother dies to-morrow; be content.   (II. ii. 104-5)

Such a simplification of issues, such a suppression of one side of the dilemma, is too much for human nature, as Angelo himself comes to realize: 'Blood, thou art blood.'

There is more than malapropism in Elbow's confusion of 'benefactor' and 'malefactor'. Virtue and vice mingle all through *Measure for Measure*. The play is full of expressions like 'charity in sin', 'foul redemption', 'to sin in loving virtue'.

> What sin you do to save a brother's life,
> Nature dispenses with the deed so far
> That it becomes a virtue.   (III. i. 135-7)

This is associated with another aspect of the theme of authority. If all men are equal in sin, 'Which is the wiser here, Justice or Iniquity?' Good and evil, virtue and vice, become a purely social or verbal distinction.

> 'Twas never merry world since, of two usuries, the merriest was put
> down, and the worser allow'd by order of law a furr'd gown to keep
> him warm; . . . (III. ii. 6-9; cf. II. ii. 130-1, II. iv. 12-17)

Angelo and Isabella prove kin to Claudio and Juliet, and indeed to Pompey and Mistress Overdone.

In fact, in one respect the latter pairs are superior. For the seeming-virtuous, the moral tangles of real life can be cut only through sterility and death—Claudio's or their own. Angelo in his ignominy can only plead for death, and Isabella longs for such a simple answer to the moral challenge of her situation:

> O, were it but my life!
> I'd throw it down for your deliverance
> As frankly as a pin.   (III. i. 105-7)

The baser characters, however, stand for life and growth:
'thou art to continue now, thou varlet; thou art to continue.'
Through their transgressions we have fitful glimpses of zest,
humour, and (as I shall soon indicate) true charity and
fellow-feeling.

This deepens our moral bewilderment and destroys all
faith in absolutes. For Angelo, the law is an unchanging,
impersonal force:

> It is the law, not I condemn your brother. . . .
> The law hath not been dead, though it hath slept.
>
> (II. ii. 80, 90)

Isabella, however, sees it only as the strong man's means of
obtaining his desires:

> Bidding the law make curtsy to their will;
> Hooking both right and wrong to th' appetite,
> To follow as it draws!   (II. iv. 175–7)

And for Pompey the law is an unhallowed and purely for-
tuitous code, changeable at will and implying no moral judgement at all:

> ESCALUS. . . . What do you think of the trade, Pompey? Is it
>   a lawful trade?
> POMPEY . If the law would allow it, sir.   (II. i. 213–15)

It will easily be seen that *Measure for Measure* carries
premisses closely analogous to those of orthodox Scepticism.
We see the inadequate and contingent nature of all codes of
value, the inscrutable complexity of human conduct, the very
real superiority of the allegedly base or lowly in certain
regards. All this points to the frightening gap between actual
human nature and the principles set up to explain and control
it. Hence the sudden wildness with which evil may break out
in human affairs, and the futile and self-defeating efforts of
moral curbs. For stern, considered exposure of moral motiva-
tion, the unflinching analysis of the essential evil in man,
Measure for Measure goes further than any other play by
Shakespeare.

But at the same time, the play marks a new and most
important optimism in Shakespeare's concept of man. The
Sceptical bewilderment is not resolved, but it is transcended
by another movement in the play.

Regarded strictly in terms of moral requital, the conclusion cannot but appear unsatisfactory. But surely the title is meant ironically—a contrast to the 'straight' use a simple comedy of intrigue, with a tit-for-tat plot, would require. In this play, 'measure for measure' seems an inadequate code of judgement. The Duke declares this code while condemning Angelo to death (V. i. 408 ff.); but the sentence is not carried out. Instead, Angelo, and everybody else (not excluding Lucio), are judged by another standard altogether.

Juliet, though she appears but seldom, takes part in a dialogue as significant as it is touching:

> DUKE. Love you the man that wrong'd you?
> JULIET. Yes, as I love the woman that wrong'd him.
> DUKE. So then, it seems, your most offenceful act
>   Was mutually committed.
> JULIET.   Mutually.   (II. iii. 24-7)

There is between Claudio and Juliet a love born of a humble sense of sinfulness. This humility, this fellow-feeling in sin, induces a spirit of forgiveness and charity, a happy complement to the exposure of authority:

> You would have slipp'd like him; but he, like you,
> Would not have been so stern.   (II. ii. 65-6)

By contrast, moral rectitude appears to imply a sterile self-centredness:

> . . . if our virtues
> Did not go forth of us, 'twere all alike
> As if we had them not.   (I. i. 34-6)

Angelo's rigour obviously implies a shocking lack of charity; in fact, this seems to be the necessary concomitant of a moral order based on 'measure for measure'. But the merciful dispensation at the end of the play allows every character to be happy once he relinquishes his pride and regards his fellow-men with a chastened love:

> Well, Angelo, your evil quits you well.
> Look that you love your wife; her worth worth yours.
>   (V. i. 494-5)

Such humility and charity answer to God's loving mercy. Shakespeare's themes must be very subtly disentangled here.

Critics have convincingly argued for a symbolic function in
the Duke, whereby he becomes a sort of Christ-figure, and his
rightful secular authority the image of the grace of God. But
I have already suggested that one cannot read the Duke's
character consistently in this way: he displays too many
palpably human traits. It seems to me that Shakespeare, with
the compression habitual in his mature work, is simultaneously
presenting the Christian ideal of authority and the inadequate
vessel through which it finds expression.[20] The Duke is
trying to express an ideal that strains the resources of human
nature. His shifts and stratagems, his self-criticism in at least
the earlier part of the play, and the devious dramatic devices
by which he gradually unfolds his mercy in the last scene, all
seem to indicate his awareness of this inadequacy and his
efforts to overcome it. This makes the Duke an easier character
to understand and accept than if we remove him to a purely
symbolic plane, marked off from the other persons in the play.

Having made this proviso about the Duke *as a character*,
we may none the less enlarge upon the theme of love and
mercy as reflected primarily in his actions. Not entirely,
though: the earliest clear mention of the theme of mercy is
probably in the passing but deeply felt comment by Escalus:

> Well, heaven forgive him! and forgive us all!   (II. i. 37)

Angelo needs double forgiveness: for his own sins (as yet
unknown to himself), and for his unforgiving nature. The
plea for mercy in Heaven's name rings through Isabella's
speeches to Angelo (see II. ii. 49 ff., 110 ff.). The clearest
allusion comes in these lines:

> How would you be
> If He, which is the top of judgment, should
> But judge you as you are? O, think on that;
> And mercy then will breathe within your lips,
> Like man new made.   (II. ii. 75–9)

'Man new made' is of course Christ, the second Adam, or perhaps man as redeemed through Christ. The recurring use of
'grace' all through the play is well known.

It would be going absurdly far to say with Battenhouse[21]
that *Measure for Measure* is an allegory of the Atonement;
but the theme of charity, mercy and self-sacrifice is obviously

central to the play. Shakespeare presents a merciful deity. The sterner doctrine of arbitrary predestination is clearly hinted at once at least, but dismissed with obvious bitterness:

> Thus can the demigod Authority
> Make us pay down for our offence by weight
> The words of heaven: on whom it will, it will;
> On whom it will not, so; yet still 'tis just.   (I. ii. 114–17)

The speaker's own fate belies the truth of this unmerciful doctrine.

The ethical confusion of the play is never sorted out in rational terms; but it is covered over by the power of mercy, so that all questions of duty, justice, sin, and punishment finally become irrelevant. The first half of the play chiefly explores the ethical problem; the second half presents the dispensation of mercy. I think this explains the undoubted difference of texture: subtle and disturbing analysis in the first half, and a simpler ordering of the action in the second, with a corresponding change in the presentation of the Duke.

Measure for Measure presents a distinctive version of the standard Renaissance dilemma. When man functions as an independent and responsible moral agent, his efforts end in disorder and bewilderment. A moral order—or at least a stable moral standpoint—is possible only when, weak and chastened, man supplicates for mercy through divine grace.

The advance from *Troilus and Cressida* lies in that order or stability is at least considered possible. A moral resolution is not totally beyond reach; and when Shakespeare attains the final synthesis of the last plays, it reflects somewhat the same terms of grace and providence, though changed almost beyond recognition.

But Shakespeare reaches this final order only after combating a still more anguished vision of evil, suffering, and bewilderment. The futile humanity of the History Plays has given way to the far deeper but still unsatisfying solution of *Measure for Measure*; Shakespeare has at least as far to go again. For while *Measure for Measure* grants the possibility of a moral ordering of life, it rejects all thoughts of exceptional virtue in man. We all stand in need of heaven's forgiveness.

In *Othello*, *King Lear*, and *Macbeth*, Shakespeare achieves a unique and paradoxical feat. Through the spectacle of folly, sin, and suffering, he builds up an image of heroic man, with titanic powers of both perception and action. It is the most impressive step in Shakespeare's rehabilitation of man.

6. *King Lear*

I shall pass over *Othello* with what may appear a strange neglect. This is because I find few significant features in Othello's heroism which do not appear in some other play in more memorable form. Suffice it to say that after the unmixed humility of *Measure for Measure*, *Othello* initiates the supremely Shakespearean tragic pattern where the hero's weakness is coextensive and indeed identical with his greatness. The ease with which Othello is inveigled into jealousy, and the extent of that jealousy, argue for a depth of feeling, a profound and complex apprehension of love that embraces the entire moral and physical order:

> Perdition catch my soul
> But I do love thee; and when I love thee not
> Chaos is come again.   (III. iii. 91–3)

A lesser man would not so easily have fallen victim to Iago, because a lesser man could not have conceived of the self-contained, unearthly perfection of Othello's world of love, destroyed by the least hint of impurity. Not that there is anything philosophic about this love. It is erotic and full-blooded, with a wordless intensity that makes it difficult to write about. We discover the force of Othello's love largely through the expression he gives to his jealousy and hate. Here perhaps *Othello* is unique: it presents an image of heroic power that springs startlingly close to the sources of animal energy, the *feritas* in man. No author of comparable depth or responsibility would have based his vision of man on such unpromising material.

A sordid crime takes on heroic dimensions from the power of love that lies, frustrated, at its root. Othello's sin is born out of a strange innocence, a pure concentration of passion untouched by the world and therefore blind against it. Again, with what intensity does Othello repent—an intensity possible only where the innate moral sense is far more entrenched and vigorous than the vice that torments it. We had first observed in *Doctor Faustus* this common predicament of the Renaissance tragic hero. His initial spurious heroism leads to sin and frustration; but the perception of this evil within himself inspires a moral vision, with the will to enforce it even to the point of self-destruction, and in this lies his true heroism.

In the course of two speeches (V. ii. 262 ff., 341 ff.) Othello discovers his sinful state, condemns himself to hell-fire, and inflicts upon himself a violent death whose ignominy cannot conceal a stoic dignity. These two speeches touch the height of his moral being, and display his renewed control over events a moment before he relinquishes it. He has fully realized his innate moral resources in his response to the situation—yet the situation was created by his own heroic deficiencies.

Two speeches is too brief a compass to bring out the full scope of this moral design. In *King Lear*, Shakespeare gives himself room enough to develop the same exaltation through self-castigation, the same growth of moral being from suffering induced by one's own fall.

In *Othello*, a domestic tragedy was heightened to grand moral dimensions. This is only a foreshadowing of the apocalyptic scale of events, values, and imagery in *King Lear*. The play touches depths and heights scarcely ever contemplated before without the supporting framework of explicit Christian doctrine.

The 'fairy-tale' opening actually assists in this. The mood of the opening scene varies between the narrow, mundane spirit of the court and the predictable formula of the fairy-tale ritual. Presently we realize the moral change in the apparently unexceptional situation. The contrast brings out in the most telling possible way the unfathomed implications of human action, the level of moral intensity at which the play works.

It is the same all through.

> The gods are just, and of our pleasant vices
> Make instruments to plague us: . . .   (V. iii. 170-1)

These lines are often used to help define the moral order of the play. Another significance is generally overlooked. The *pleasant* vice is punished by a pestilential evil (surely 'plague' is used here in no light sense). Man cannot gauge the effects of his deeds: his power to work evil is matched by his imbecility. (The play progresses to the opposite situation where, robbed of power, man attains to moral insight at last.) Hence the easy transgression of the unvicious Gloucester creates in Edmund a monstrous concentration of evil. In the symbolic design of the play, this is opposed by a power of heavenly goodness: the figure of Cordelia. The opposed moral impulses in man are raised to an ideal or symbolic purity and concentration: the devil and the angel potentially within us are made actual, and our full capacity for good or evil thus brought out.

In characters that retain the human admixture of good and evil—Lear, Gloucester, and Edgar, at three levels of dramatic function—we find an archetypal concentration of passion and suffering, as in the heroes of ancient myths. They suffer with an intensity unknown in the experience of an individual, and analyse their state and remould their moral being with a rare degree of heightened, symbolic validity. It is as though an individual is being invested with the experience and achievement of the entire human race. No doubt this is true of all tragedy; but in *King Lear*, the accidents of individual character and situation are unusually overwhelmed by the sense of collective experience. The capacities of the individual are heroically enlarged.

The nature of this enlargement must be properly appreciated. It is not a simple idealization of man by the emphasis of some superior faculty or attribute, a goodness outweighing the evil or inferior elements in human nature and bringing man close to the angels. Such selective development was, of course, the common assumption of some varieties of Renaissance idealism—as in the classic metaphor of the seeds in Pico's *Oration on the Dignity of Man*. In *Lear*, however, evil and suffering are as gigantic as the spiritual or benevolent forces. There is a total expansion of scale. Heroic man is compounded of both god and beast.

In this all-inclusive humanity, the entire range of man's experience serves to aggrandize him; sin, pain, and loss are seen to stimulate and expand the faculties. Standard moral concepts grow meaningless here. Ideals such as gratitude, obedience, sexual purity, justice, and mercy are constantly invoked; but they are recast into concepts unrelated or even opposed to conventional values. The art of Michelangelo provides the only valid parallel for the gigantic sweep and unfamiliar contours of Shakespeare's moral setting, and against it the elevation of the total unordered reality of the human state.

Strangely, this unfamiliar world may be best introduced by some points not unique to the play, points that it shares with *Measure for Measure* in particular. In mundane terms, the great revelation that comes to Lear upon the heath, as to Angelo in his chamber, is the sense of our common sin and frailty. Having 'ever but slenderly known himself', Lear had set out with a proud assumption of his power to judge people and dispense reward and punishment. In his madness, he still invokes his invulnerable power in pitiful snatches:

> No, they cannot touch me for coining; I am the King himself.
> (IV. vi. 83–4)

But

> To say 'ay' and 'no' to everything that I said! 'Ay' and 'no' too was no good divinity. When the rain came to wet me once, and the wind to make me chatter; when the thunder would not peace at my bidding; there I found 'em, there I smelt 'em out. (IV. vi. 98–103)

Angelo's discovery breaks upon Lear too:

> Thou rascal beadle, hold thy bloody hand.
> Why dost thou lash that whore? Strip thy own back;
> Thou hotly lusts to use her in that kind
> For which thou whip'st her.   (IV. vi. 160–3)

Yet there is a radical difference in the treatment of this theme in *King Lear*. Lear's experience is indeed one of self-discovery; yet obviously, he does not suffer from Angelo's acute sense of a personal fall. His perception of common human frailty is therefore more philosophic; it bears less of shame and self-hate and is more purely an exercise in charity and human understanding. In other words, Lear's assertion of mankind's endemic sinfulness is carried out in a spirit that partly denies its own premises. It is not merely a fellow-feeling in sin; it inspires a love that can raise and strengthen man's moral being.

The classic instances of this love are, of course, Lear's call
to the Fool to enter the hovel (III. ii. 68) and later, his
general apostrophe to the 'Poor naked wretches, wheresoe'er
you are' (III. iv. 28 ff.). The perception of human misery is
accompanied by the urge for action, a plea for moral change:

> Take physic, pomp;
> Expose thyself to feel what wretches feel,
> That thou mayst shake the superflux to them,
> And show the heavens more just.   (III. iv. 33–6)

This passage well illustrates the difference in spirit between
Measure for Measure and *King Lear*. In the former play we
had a static ideal of forgiving coexistence. Angelo undergoes
revelation and self-discovery, but there is no enlargement of
his sensibility: he merely condemns himself by the same
standards he had earlier used to condemn others. He may
desist from moral tyranny, but neither he nor any other
character gives evidence of spiritual growth.

In *King Lear*, on the contrary, there is a genuine revaluation
of norms: the sense of pervasive evil passes into the declaration
that '*None* does offend' (IV. vi. 168). This may even be
thought to harmonize with the ideal innocence of the natural
order:

> The wren goes to 't, and the small gilded fly
> Does lecher in my sight.   (IV. vi. 112–13)

So too with Lear's sense of his own moral state. It finds its
climax in an agonizing sense of sin:

> . . . I am bound
> Upon a wheel of fire, that mine own tears
> Do scald like molten lead.   (IV. vii. 46–8)

But Lear emerges from this agony into a new ideal of harmony, a little world created out of a new and blessed human
relationship where the traditional roles of father and daughter
do not count:

> When thou dost ask me blessing, I'll kneel down
> And ask of thee forgiveness; . . .   (V. iii. 10–11)

Behind the sin and suffering, *King Lear* presents us with the
constant possibility of peace and innocence, the ideal of a
transcendent order.

It contrasts in this respect with the theme of *Hamlet*. Hamlet's sensitive moral being could not absorb the evil it perceived: his moral energies drove him to alienation and the vision of death. In *Lear* too, there is a very real alienation imposed upon the hero by the sheer magnitude of his tragic experience—a matter to which I shall later revert. But essentially, his experience is constructive, purgatorial. It brings him closer to humanity; it makes him discover the possibility of new ideals, whereas Hamlet saw only the disintegration of old ones. He was doomed by a heroic inflexibility in principles present in him from the outset; Lear changes and grows, gradually evolves his moral conceptions, admitting the full reality of human experience and even enlarging its boundaries.

'Here's grace and a cod-piece,' says Lear's Fool. This duality can at times induce a hysterical sense of the irredeemable foulness of man, the constant impediment of the flesh:

> Down from the waist they are centaurs,
> Though women all above;
> But to the girdle do the gods inherit,
> Beneath is all the fiends'; . . .   (IV. vi. 124-7)

Physical repugnance may unite with moral contempt:

> . . . unaccommodated man is no more but such a poor, bare, forked animal as thou art. (III. iv. 105-7)

But once again, the power of 'grace' can counter and absorb this foulness. The repugnance is united with profound pity for Edgar's condition:

> Why, thou wert better in thy grave than to answer with thy uncover'd body this extremity of the skies. (III. iv. 100-2)

From this, Lear is led on to a wild act of identification with the basic lot of man:

> . . . Off, off, you lendings! Come, unbutton here. (III. iv. 108)

The perception of man's foulness and helplessness actually intensifies the action of 'grace' and charity. We have seen in Sceptics like Montaigne and Rabelais the willing though unheroic acceptance of the 'amphibious' nature of man. In Shakespeare this duality is startlingly exploited to create a unique impression of power and growth. It is by accepting the lower faculties that we truly exercise the higher ones and create a superior order of existence.

This leads on to another important aspect of Lear's suffering, where a contrast with *Measure for Measure* may again prove useful. To Angelo, each stage of his self-discovery comes as a reluctant and horrifying revelation. Lear, on the contrary, deliberately draws upon himself an increasingly intense weight of suffering.

> Then let fall
> Your horrible pleasure. Here I stand, your slave,
> A poor, infirm, weak and despis'd old man; . . .
>
> (III. ii. 18–20)

He appears to call down upon his own head the suffering due for all man's evil. It is a sort of communal purgation or expiation. Though 'more sinn'd against than sinning', Lear identifies himself with sinful humanity. He stands upon the heath as a king and representative of man, suffering as a royal duty, almost a prerogative. 'Pour on; I will endure' (III. iv. 18).

It is dangerous to propose Christian analogues for such a complex play—there is too much temptation to simplify it in terms of clearly defined doctrine—but we have here an obvious approximation to the suffering of Christ himself. In fact, Lear seems to unite the characters of the first and the second Adam, and draw upon himself the suffering of both. It is his fall from reason and duty that sets in motion the chain of disasters, involving his own alienation and banishment; there comes to rest upon his head a collective, primordial guilt; and its atonement and forgiveness are ensured by his own agony and death.

This combination of two opposed but complementary roles brings out the paradoxical compound of Lear's heroism, the spiritual strength that transforms the nature of vice and frailty by an indomitably suffering acceptance. By this paradox, the profoundest capacity to discover and accept truth, to endure and evolve, to draw upon inexhaustible spiritual resources, is expressed in words like these:

> I am a very foolish fond old man, . . .
> And, to deal plainly,
> I fear I am not in my perfect mind.   (IV. vii. 60–3)

However, in spite of this humility, in spite of the love and harmony that it inspires, there is in Lear a supreme heroic isolation. By the very extent of his participation in the human lot, he acquires the status of saint or superman, beyond the reach of normal human values and relationships. He is marked out by the unique intensity of his experience. Hence although he evolves a life-giving vision, his moral faculties go on to achieve a degree of perception that human life cannot accommodate.

> The oldest hath borne most; we that are young
> Shall never see so much nor live so long.   (V. iii. 325-6)

Thus Lear's career ends in loss, alienation, and death.

During the revelation on the heath, and after the meeting with Cordelia, Lear discovers a new moral order that implies the destruction of the orthodox one. But the death of Cordelia shatters the possibility of this new order as well. It appears that Lear's moral perception cannot be embodied in any conceivable order of events. He can only bear the burden of his wisdom into the next world.

The strength with which he bears it is perhaps debatable. His final madness and death—whether of heartbreak or of a deluded joy—apparently indicate a collapse of power. But I wonder if one should not emphasize, more than this apparent collapse, the stark, hopeless strength with which he earlier accepts the deepest measure of his loss.

> Howl, howl, howl, howl! O, you are men of stones!
> Had I your tongues and eyes, I'd use them so
> That heaven's vault should crack. She's gone for ever.
> I know when one is dead and when one lives;
> She's dead as earth.   (V. iii. 257-61)

The capacity to face the full truth of life and death reaches its greatest extent in these lines. Nor does Lear suffer complete disintegration after it. His last speech still reflects the starkest question in human experience:

> Why should a dog, a horse, a rat have life,
> And thou no breath at all?   (V. iii. 306-7)

By the time Lear dies, he has stretched every moral fibre to the uttermost. His very death, with its 'Look there, look

there!', seems to come as a final straining of the faculties, a
still more breathtaking assault upon 'the mystery of things'—
a climax, not an escape. Lear dies searching, striving, enduring.

And by this time, it is obvious that he searches and endures
alone, unsupported by any external moral order. Outside
human apprehension, all is chaos. This sense of chaos had
already developed in the storm scenes. At times, Lear might
consider the storm to be the herald of cosmic justice:

> Let the great gods,
> That keep this dreadful pudder o'er our heads,
> Find out their enemies now. Tremble, thou wretch,
> That hast within thee undivulged crimes
> Unwhipp'd of justice.   (III. ii. 49-53)

But more often, it is the agent of heaven's undiscriminating
tyranny:

> But yet I call you servile ministers
> That will with two pernicious daughters join
> Your high-engender'd battles 'gainst a head
> So old and white as this.   (III. ii. 21-4)

The natural order disintegrates along with the normal moral
and social order. This total collapse is an obvious reflection
of the fallen state of man, with the concomitant 'fall' of the
entire natural order.

The death of Cordelia gives the final negative answer to the
debate on heaven's justice that runs throughout the play.
Moral forces seem to have no validity outside mankind. On
this point indeed, Edmund's belief is supported by the play
as a whole.

> Fut, I should have been that I am, had the maidenliest star in the fir-
> mament twinkled on my bastardizing. (I. ii. 125-7)

Edmund sins not by denying an external order, but by himself participating in the external disorder and thereby sur-
rendering his claims to a superior humanity.

This may serve to introduce the most remarkable innovation in Shakespeare since *Measure for Measure*. Mercy and
forgiveness are an important concern in *King Lear*, but divine
mercy has ceased to be an operative force. The moral centre
has passed within man. The perception of his fallen state, and
the chaos that surrounds him, involves the release of moral

energies whose unbearable intensity may finally destroy him, but none the less permits him to transcend his original state. Man becomes master of his own soul, winning this right by the exceptional power of his experience. This creates in him a heroic resilience to personal suffering, external disorder, and alienation from general humanity, in whom this power remains unrealized.

This isolated grandeur, this superman-stature of a representative yet exceptional individual, marks a new phase in Shakespeare's conception of man. Granville-Barker, in a memorable phrase, calls it the 'exalting of the solitary dignity of the soul'.[22] We find it in *Macbeth*, in *Coriolanus*, in *Antony and Cleopatra*. This conception of man falls short of Shakespeare's final position in two important ways. It implies the neglect or the explicit denial of any wider, absolute order; and in *Macbeth* at least, it involves a sense of sin inseparable from the aspiration. In fact, this conception is an exceptionally intense version of the standard vein of Renaissance idealism which elevates the human faculties at the expense of the total order. These imperfections are gradually cast out, and in the last plays we find a human ideal that is pure and harmonious but less inclusive, less titanic. It is in the tragedies that Shakespeare attains his greatest sense of the power and dignity of man.

7. Macbeth

Much recent criticism regards *Macbeth* as a sophisticated morality play. Macbeth is pictured as a figure of evil and disorder, expelled by the forces of order and regeneration. It is, however, a moot point how far this simple triumph of good over evil—Aristotle's non-tragedy of 'an extremely bad man . . . falling from happiness into misery'—could produce the complex impact actually created by the play. Moreover, the dramatic focus remains on Macbeth all through. This reversal of the usual moral perspective cannot but affect the values of the play.

Not that a moral pattern—even a 'morality pattern'—does not exist in *Macbeth*. Its presence is too patent to need pointing out. Yet we may feel that many of the reconciling elements

in the play derive from Macbeth's active career and not
merely his defeat. He induces an enlargement of vision: the
reader may even be tempted at times to identify himself with
the hero.

Critics who admit this generally rest content with a compromise. Either (like Bradley) they stress Macbeth's initial
virtues, which largely disappear in the course of the play. Or
else they point to Shakespeare's supposed emphasis upon
neutral or mitigating circumstances, his suppression of the
most repugnant features of the crimes, or his alleged postula-
tion of a fatal spell cast by the Witches. In fact, the reconciliation appears to be a far subtler process, requiring a full
recognition of Macbeth's criminality, as Macbeth himself
recognizes it.

The principal difficulty in tracing this process is the
absence of suitable terms to use. The only words that offer
themselves are fraught with moral implications. Not that such
implications are irrelevant in the total context of the play: in
fact, they are vitally important. But in the particular aspect I
now intend to examine, the principles involved are so anti-
moral, so contrary to the accustomed values for which alone
we have an adequate language, that one is left with no
alternative but to issue an initial warning to the reader and
proceed in terms that, however carefully protected from
moral connotations, still hold out a grave risk of misinter-
pretation. The very word 'moral' must be taken simply as
referring to the sector of experience usually treated by
orthodox moral values: it does not imply any adherence to
such values.

The basic moral situation of Macbeth is much the same as
that of Faustus. He commits a cardinal sin to achieve an end
by which he will, supposedly, more completely realize and
fulfil himself. In fact, he releases forces of evil and disorder
that engulf his community, while he himself is driven to
suffering, failure, and death.

Here ends the resemblance to Faustus. Once Faustus
understands the moral implications of his act, he is at once
reduced to frustration and paralysis. The understanding
itself marks his highest moral achievement: its force and
penetration constitute his glory and at the same time his

ruin. Man surrenders to a self-created image of his weakness and foulness.

There is the same image in *Macbeth*—the recurring figure of the 'man of blood' that suggests both crime and retribution. Macbeth's sense of the foulness of his crime, both before and after the commission, is far intenser than Faustus'. It is fomented by the bloody details of the murder: Faustus' sin was of an abstract, intellectual nature. When Macbeth cannot say 'Amen', his 'hardening of the heart' exceeds any agony that Faustus suffers; and his subsequent despair comes out in speech after speech:

> I am in blood
> Stepp'd in so far that, should I wade no more,
> Returning were as tedious as go o'er.   (III. iv. 136–8)

But the play differs from *Faustus* in Macbeth's dichotomous response to this situation. Before the commission of the murder, he is divided between moral horror at a *voluntary* crime and the strong though unexpressed sense of an 'appalling duty'[23] imposed by his situation. Once committed, then, the murder leads to another ambiguity of response. On the one hand, it freezes him in an unalterable moral state, a sinful relation to his fellows that he may intensify through further crime but cannot unmake or rectify. This is undoubtedly a situation of his own creation. He cannot and does not disown it, but rather accepts it as the basic condition of his future existence. But on the other hand, it is created by the suppression of some of his strongest impulses, and once created, takes on an unchangeable, inevitable nature. He therefore seems to treat it as something 'given', imposed: organic and yet alien. 'The deed, which was his own, has now acquired a life of its own and it threatens the tenderest quick of his being.'[24] It is a weight he must carry through life, though his supremely sensitive moral imagination recoils from it at every step.

> My strange and self-abuse
> Is the initiate fear that wants hard use.   (III. iv. 142–3)

The deed born of his 'self-abuse' rises continually to put his true self to trial and agitation.

The murder of Duncan thus proves to have a double

function. From one point of view, it is the protagonist's own conclusive reaction to the initial circumstances in which he was placed: the Witches' prophecy, Lady Macbeth's incitement, his own ambitious dreams. Once the murder is committed, his fate follows swiftly and inevitably from it. From another point of view, however, the murder is itself a starting-point, an imposed or external factor, providing the protagonist with an agonizing stimulus to which his subsequent career will be the response. From this angle, Macbeth's crime does not seal his doom or lay down the limits of his being; rather, it requires a new response, carries scope for the growth of being. How does Macbeth answer the challenge of his self-created situation?

The sense of damnation is vivid in *Macbeth* from the very moment of his crime: 'Macbeth shall sleep no more'. (Contrast Faustus' 'An this be hell, I'll willingly be damned.') Macbeth's moral sense, unlike that of Faustus, is not an external feature, instilled by education and rendered indelible only by generations of ingrained acceptance: it is a basic condition of Macbeth's being. When he reacts to his deeds with moral horror, he is not being held spellbound by an abstract, imposed code of judgement. He is being true to his own nature.

As in *King Lear*, so here too in a different way, the moral centre has passed within man. He generates his own values and impulses. He may still express them in terms of an external order or scale of values: language does not permit moral issues to be discussed in purely individual or subjective terms—which may in fact be said to imply a negation of morality. The common human intellect shrinks from the exercise, and tries to suppress it by denying it the use of language. But as I remarked before, matters which normally induce moral judgement or speculation are here treated in this anti-moral mode.

Macbeth himself hardly admits, perhaps hardly realizes, the purely individual values to which his innermost being is pledged. This emerges most clearly from the soliloquy 'If it were done . . .' He attempts to justify his horror of the murder in terms of rational morality: 'He's here in double trust . . .' But in the visionary poetry that follows, he reveals

his real psychic impediment: the deed will release the apocalyptic fancies of his own imagination—fancies which, while
certainly including moral issues, engulf them as a stream is
engulfed in a whirlpool.

What Macbeth values above all is the full truth and power
of his individual being. He abhors his crime less as the murder
of Duncan than as the destruction of his own moral entity:

> I dare do all that may become a man;
> Who dares do more is none. (I. vii. 46-7)

'A man' is here pictured in the image of orthodox 'honour':

> . . . I have bought
> Golden opinions from all sorts of people,
> Which would be worn now in their newest gloss,
> Not cast aside so soon. (I. vii. 32-5)

But another, equally authentic impulse drives him towards
the deed. His supreme loyalty to the self generates an ambition
that leads him beyond the orthodox ideals of honour and
morality:

> The Prince of Cumberland! That is a step,
> On which I must fall down, or else o'er-leap,
> For in my way it lies. Stars, hide your fires;
> Let not light see my black and deep desires. (I. iv. 48-51)

His most obscure and aberrant desires are made to prevail
over universal order. Already we see the impulse that will
later appear with frightening violence:

> But let the frame of things disjoint, both the worlds suffer,
> Ere we will eat our meal in fear . . . (III. ii. 16-17)

It is the terrifying egocentrism born of *virtù*, a craving for the
full satisfaction of one's faculties at no matter what external
cost:

> For mine own good
> All causes shall give way. (III. iv. 135-6)

We might feel we are again returning to the primitive ambition
of *Tamburlaine*—were it not that in *Macbeth*, this ambition is
accompanied by a horrifying sense of sin.

From the outset, the fullness of Macbeth's humanity agi-
tates him between an impossible range of contraries: honour

and ambition, moral horror and irresistible temptation. Lady Macbeth knows of this conflict, but sees it, with her typical simplification of issues, as a failure of spirit, rather than an excess of energy seeking contrary but simultaneous expressions:

> What thou wouldst highly,
> That wouldst thou holily; wouldst not play false,
> And yet wouldst wrongly win.   (I. v. 17–19)

This is the dilemma in which Macbeth has to take his first moral decision.

I do not think it too paradoxical to say that this decision is taken *after* the murder of Duncan. From the moral-theological viewpoint no doubt, Macbeth undertakes the murder of his free will, with full responsibility. But from a subtler psychological viewpoint, he is driven to the deed by a variety of factors (among them his own subconscious urges) that he can scarcely comprehend, and against which he fails to assume a definite stand. Even the declaration

> I am settled, and bend up
> Each corporal agent to this terrible feat.   (I. vii. 79–80)

seems a momentary, short-circuited decision, seizing upon one supremely attractive possibility as a way out of his dilemma, rather than a genuine solution based upon a comprehensive understanding. Such an understanding, and a moral stand based upon it, are born out of the deed itself.

This reaction makes a contrast to Faustus' despair. Theologically, Macbeth also despairs; but this despair does not lead to the paralysis of power or suicide of the spirit that we find in Faustus. Faustus can only offer himself as expiatory sacrifice to the external power he feels he has offended. But for Macbeth, as I have said, the moral centre lies within himself. His crime disturbs him so profoundly because it has destroyed the peace and integrity of his own being. His allusions to the deed constantly bring this out:

> To know my deed, 'twere best not know myself.   (II. ii. 73)

> The wine of life is drawn, and the mere lees
> Is left this vault to brag of.   (II. iii. 93–4)

> . . . on the torture of the mind to lie
> In restless ecstasy.   (III. ii. 21–2)

The specifically moral suffering, the sense of guilt or wrong-doing, appears to play a subsidiary part to this, important only in so far as it contributes to this inner disturbance. Macbeth has only to placate his own being, to restore his unity of self. He need not preserve the sanctity of an external moral order: in fact, he seeks to overthrow it so as to cancel one side of the dilemma and achieve a bleak peace of spirit, a purely amoral harmony of being.

In his case, accordingly, the consciousness of his crime inspires growth and activity. He is assisted by the fact that his crime makes him king and thus grants him apparently un-limited power over external circumstances. It therefore seems possible for him to undertake crime after crime until their cumulative force can expel or suppress all contrary impulses, creating a trans-moral stage where he can contemplate his power with a purely factual sense of achievement, where indeed

> this blow
> Might be the be-all and the end-all here . . .

Needless to say, the impediment cannot be removed. Instead of amorality, he can achieve only a conscious defiance of morality. Before the murder, he had formed with evil only an awestruck, hesitant, protesting association. Now he undergoes a conscious, willing dedication to the powers of evil, an identification with them. 'Things bad begun make strong themselves by ill' (III. ii. 55).

The nature of this identification does not seem to be generally understood. It is commonly taken as the absolute or culminating point of Macbeth's career. He is pictured henceforth as a figure of pure evil, opposed to the forces of goodness, so that the entire play can be interpreted morality-fashion. As I see it, however, the dedication to evil is merely a stage in Macbeth's growth. The actual dedication is less significant than the fact that, as the denial or rejection of good, it indicates Macbeth's attempt to curb the disturbing, self-castigating elements of his own nature. It is the first great step by which he alienates himself from mankind and its values:

> Cancel and tear to pieces that great bond
> Which keeps me pale.   (III. ii. 49–50)

He needs to destroy the traditional order if he is to assert
his own being, which has revolted against that order. I have
already shown how a violent urge for self-assertion and self-
fulfilment underlies the images of chaos in which he indulges
at this stage:

> But let the frame of things disjoint, both the worlds suffer . . .
>
> (III. ii. 16)

Similar invocations to chaos occur later in the play:

> Though bladed corn be lodged and trees blown down;
> Though castles topple on their warders' heads;
> Though palaces and pyramids do slope
> Their heads to their foundations; though the treasure
> Of nature's germens tumble all together,
> Even till destruction sicken—answer me
> To what I ask you.   (IV. i. 55–61)

By this stage, however, there is another development that
most readers and critics seem to miss. Macbeth is now speaking *entirely on his own behalf*, without any sense of identification with a greater power of evil. He now curses and
defies the evil forces themselves. They become something
alien, almost inimical:

> I will be satisfied. Deny me this,
> And an eternal curse fall on you!   (IV. i. 104–5)

And when the apparitions come:

> Filthy hags!
> Why do you show me this?   (IV. i. 115–16)

Earlier, the hags' prophecies had synchronized with his own
aspirations. Now they thwart his vision: fate seems to con-
spire against him, and the evil powers oppose him in their
traditional role as instruments of moral retribution. He passes
into a total reliance on his own strength.

In *King Lear*, we had seen how endless resources of human
fortitude appear out of helpless suffering. In *Macbeth*, a
similar power appears when an ineradicable sense of guilt
combines with the threat of worldly failure. Condemned by
every code of values that has a name, outlawed by providence,
alienated from the very powers of evil, Macbeth displays an

indefinable and inexplicable resilience. He can still sustain our faith in the power of man.

This is perhaps Shakespeare's most breath-taking feat, surpassing even *King Lear*. In Lear there had been weakness but not sin. We did not have to overcome a profound moral repugnance, but rather felt a pity that, though incompatible with our ultimate admiration, could help to enlist our sympathy. In *Macbeth*, the hero is deprived of any possible support from any external quarter. There is no cause why such power should appear in him, for he is already in a state of despair. Nor does it have any function to justify its appearance, for it cannot redeem him from that despair. It simply *is*.

This power and growth does not consist only in the celebrated 'Promethean grandeur', the mood of desperate defiance:

> Lay on, Macduff;
> And damn'd be him that first cries 'Hold, enough!'
> (V. viii. 33–4)

Macbeth does indeed take such a stand from time to time; but it is combined with so many other elements that his final state must be assessed in very different terms. We have also to consider the Macbeth who is 'sick at heart', who frightens the Doctor and bullies his servant as an outlet for his own terror.

Two contrary factors must be remembered. First, in spite of partial evidence to the contrary, it cannot be denied that Macbeth does evince a gradual hardening or anaesthetizing of his moral responses. He now plans his crimes in minute and far-sighted detail, all pity and moral scruple blanked off with a deliberation that Duncan's assassin could scarcely have conceived:

> The time has been my senses would have cool'd
> To hear a night-shriek . . .
> . . . I have supp'd full with horrors;
> Direness, familiar to my slaughterous thoughts, ·
> Cannot once start me.   (V. v. 10–11, 13–15)

But at the same time, his basic moral sensitivity remains as acute as ever: in fact, it appears in its most impressive form *after* the frenzy of the murder is over, when nothing is left but the yearning contemplation of a now impossible alternative.

This chastened clarity of moral perception appears for the first time in the speech 'Had I but died . . .' (II. iii. 89 ff.). It appears in 'Duncan is in his grave . . .' (III. ii. 22 ff.); in 'I have liv'd long enough . . .' (V. iii. 22 ff.); in his address to the Doctor (V. iii. 40 ff.); and, no less than in 'To-morrow, and to-morrow' (V. v. 19 ff.), in the brief comment on his wife's death that prefaces it:

> She should have died hereafter;
> There would have been a time for such a word.
>
> (V. v. 17–18)

Most telling of all are his words to Macduff before the final duel:

> But get thee back; my soul is too much charg'd
> With blood of thine already.   (V. viii. 5-6)

Whether a touch of 'real conscience' or not, this certainly shows his persistent attraction towards the spurned alternative of orthodox morality. To the end, this aspect of his sensibility remains acutely alive.

Putting these contrary elements together, the hardening of Macbeth's nature appears less as an inevitable and unconscious degeneration than as a deliberate control of certain aspects of his being, like an evil parallel to moral discipline. One may even call it a sort of unsanctified asceticism, a refusal to permit oneself the least distraction of a moral or emotional indulgence. Instead, there is a forced concentration upon the stark void horror of his situation, an attempt to turn *that* into a positive basis for conduct: defeatist, unavailing, but vindicating even in a state of damnation what we can only call the resilience and moral honesty of human nature. He preserves something of the dignity of his noblest impulses while owning the entire body of his actions. To disown or repent even his basest act would tarnish the loyalty to the full truth of his being that, however reprehensible in his state of sin, is the essence of his nobility. The highest part of his nature demands, even if suicidally, that the basest part should be unflinchingly accepted and recognized.

From time to time the effort breaks down, and we have speeches like those I alluded to above. At other times the strain comes out indirectly, in scenes of nervous agitation and petty tyranny. The whole exercise goes against Macbeth's grain, it involves a denial of his nature and a sacrifice of his most cherished values; but he makes the sacrifice, as others do for more obviously virtuous causes, in grim loyalty to the consequences of his deed, attempting to restore his integrity by unflinching acceptance of his shame. He tortures and suppresses his higher nature so that he might reconcile it with the lower and achieve a unity of being.

If he grasps the reality of the deed he is alienated from himself and can no longer recognise the bloody hand as his own. . . . Very well, he will know his deed. He will make his peace with it, build his life around it, accept it as a fact. What he will not do is *own* the deed—acknowledge it as the work of the general, Macbeth, loyal vassal of the gracious Duncan. To that self he bids an anguished farewell . . .[25]

Now indeed, though he stands defiant before fate and his adversaries, he is truly humble, prizing his career for no more than it is worth. But he wears this humility with an unassailable dignity of spirit.

That is why his final stand, misguided and desperate though it is, affects us as something more than mere villainy. It is a conscious effort of strength, commanding our tacit and almost unperceived admiration, even after all moral reason for admiration has disappeared. He now asserts almost solely his baser qualities, having largely suppressed the finer ones; but the very assertion becomes a proof of strength, a terrifying but indomitable vitality born out of a sort of creative despair. He is, so to speak, not only literally but morally in a state of siege. His resources are exhausted, but he faces perdition with unflagging spirit.

It will easily be seen that this account of Macbeth's human energy does not at all preclude the moral interpretation of the play, with Macbeth leading the defeated powers of evil. Rather, the two interpretations are complementary: the heroism takes on meaning only when placed against its necessary concomitants of guilt and despair. And in another perspective—one we have not adopted here—this sin and despair, and the moral order that judges and opposes them, take on something like absolute validity. Unlike Faustus, Macbeth does not only condemn himself. He is far more violently condemned by society and the entire cosmic order.

The play incorporates two simultaneous movements, the 'moral' and the 'heroic'. Neither can be ignored. Like Marlowe's *Tamburlaine*, *Macbeth* revolves upon the two poles of the Renaissance philosophy of man: the sense of a moral order, and the power of man that cannot be confined within it.

To be sure, the two elements are still mutually exclusive or antagonistic, as they were in *Tamburlaine*. It is only in Shakespeare's last plays that man achieves growth of being in harmony with the cosmic order. Before that, however, Shakespeare purges humanity of the taint of sin by a heartening subterfuge, if ultimately an imbalanced and inconclusive one: he practically dissolves the frame of moral values. This is what happens in *Antony and Cleopatra*.

8. *Coriolanus: Antony and Cleopatra*

With *Macbeth* and *Antony and Cleopatra* goes *Coriolanus*, but that is a story of heroism *manqué*. Coriolanus, like Macbeth, seems to seek self-expression against all normative restraints; but his individualism is of quite a different nature. In fact, it cannot be described as self-expression in any true sense. Macbeth's ambition rises from the innermost impulses of his being, and insists on asserting itself against the equally innate and vital moral elements of his nature. Coriolanus' ambition, on the contrary, is not an assertion of his deepest nature but an attempt to conform to an external image of the patrician warrior–hero. Although he appears to assert his distinctive spirit against social and ethical norms, this spirit is in fact an extreme version of the heroic ideal of Roman society—an instilled, not an innate virtue.

Thus Coriolanus' initial heroism proves shallow and untested, valid only as long as it can be sustained by physical acts of valour. Unlike Macbeth's heroism, it cannot survive opposition, for it consists essentially in *being accepted as* a hero. Coriolanus can only withdraw, and attempt to fight back by the same inadequate weapon of physical valour. There is no growth or adaptation. Nor, unlike Macbeth, does Coriolanus recognize how far his ambition ignores the contrary impulses in his own nature: paradoxically, his single-mindedness proves the feebleness of his ideal, indicating its narrow and inadequate base. Macbeth's ambition is tested and reinforced by the very conflict within his nature.

Hence Coriolanus' self-created image crumbles away at the first genuine moral conflict that he faces, in the women's visit to his camp outside Rome. Instead of stimulating him like Macbeth to a growth of being, it finishes him off. He can no longer play the unflinching hero; at the same time, he cannot forge a fresh identity out of the newly revealed tender elements in his character. It is difficult to agree with Bradley's reading of the play, that by his act of mercy Coriolanus fulfils his nature, so that his subsequent fate becomes a matter of indifference.[26] No such sense of fulfilment emerges from Coriolanus' speeches either at the end of the mercy-scene or upon his single appearance after that. If any impression is left by these, it is a sense of purposelessness, an unprecedented lack of zeal and domination. There is even an element of apology, a perceptible attempt to excuse or justify his conduct:

> Hail, lords! I am return'd your soldier;
> No more infected with my country's love
> Than when I parted hence, but still subsisting
> Under your great command.   (V. vi. 71–4)

His occupation is gone, and has not left behind any memory of a valid standpoint at any stage of his career.

Genuine development after *Macbeth* is apparent in *Antony and Cleopatra*. The conduct of Antony and Cleopatra can of course be described by simply heightening the terms of normal sexuality; but this seems to miss the distinctive values of the play, undefinable in standard ethical terms.

This singularity is epitomized by a feature that must strike even the casual reader, in a speech like this:

> . . . since my lord
> Is Antony again, I will be Cleopatra.   (III. xiii. 186–7)

They have been defeated, and they have quarrelled violently over the defeat and Cleopatra's alleged infidelity. But this is more than a petty squabble between two failures. There may indeed be a hint at this unheroic possibility, but in the primary movement of the dialogue, the fury of the speakers points to a grandeur and growth of being. The passionate reconciliation that now follows may be logically felt as a contradiction, a sudden change in the enslaved Antony at a single speech from Cleopatra ('Ah, dear, if I be so . . .': III. xiii. 158 ff.). But as an exercise of emotional energy, the whole contradictory sequence appears as a sustained, consistent development. Cleopatra makes overtures to Caesar; she also declares a passionate attachment to Antony. Both these are expressions of the same vital process by which she is continually trying to preserve and surpass *herself*. The same, in Antony, are the successive loathing and devotion—at either stage, he is being truest to the demands of his own nature, consistently seeking a sincere expression of his spirit through mercurial change of means.

She (Cleopatra) is like Antony in . . . that she has never learned to compromise with life, nor had to reconcile here own nature's extremes. To call her false to this or to that is to set up a standard that could have no value for her. She is true enough to the self of the moment; and, in the end, tragically true to a self left sublimated by great loss.[27]

This points to the most interesting feature of my quotation from Cleopatra's speech. Like lesser mortals, Shakespeare too seems unable to find terms for the distinctive plane of values on which the play moves. He can suggest the spirit of his hero and heroine only by using their own names.

> Sir, sometimes when he is not Antony,
> He comes too short of that great property
> Which still should go with Antony.   (I. i. 57-9)
>   . . . t' imagine
> An Antony were nature's piece 'gainst fancy,
> Condemning shadows quite.   (V. ii. 98-100)

We may also compare the First Folio reading of V. ii. 87:

> . . . an Antony it was,
> That grew the more by reaping: . . .

Such supremely individual characters cannot be defined in terms of general validity.

The conception is best described by returning for a moment to *Macbeth*—where too we were greatly hampered by the absence of descriptive terms. In an early scene, Ross describes Macbeth's prowess in battle:

> Till that Bellona's bridegroom, lapp'd in proof,
> Confronted him with self-comparisons . . .   (I. ii. 55-6)

Without dismissing the usual interpretation of the line, one may suggest a further meaning: Macbeth's prowess is so great that he can only be compared with himself—his values are only to be named, not related through description and analogy. In *Antony and Cleopatra*, such 'self-comparisons' reach their climax.

I say 'climax' because within the framework of the play, Shakespeare allows the individual engagement with experience a dominance that certainly does not exist in *Macbeth*. There, the hero's unique values and responses were born out of conflict with normative moral principles. But Antony and Cleopatra are totally absorbed in their individual response. The normative values are evoked, not so much to be flouted as to be dismissed as an utter irrelevance.

> . . . for vilest things
> Become themselves in her, that the holy priests
> Bless her when she is riggish.   (II. ii. 242–4)

Dishonour is knowingly accepted in the play. Coquetry, faithlessness, anger, and cowardice cannot be judged in normal terms, but add up by a strange mathematics to a pristine, amoral, almost barbaric emotion. It is not that Antony is incapable of valour, or Cleopatra of faith in love; but the same force of emotion that makes this possible leads them further, from time to time, to ignore and dismiss the standard canons of conduct. Their deviations testify not to weakness or failure but to a positive drive towards self-expression.

There is no sense of an absolute or cosmic order that can authenticate the orthodox moral values. *Antony and Cleopatra* offers a contrast to *Macbeth* in this respect. The nearest approach to a supernatural force is 'Fortune', and this is an inferior, sublunary power ruling only over men who confine themselves to the mundane:

> 'Tis paltry to be Caesar:
> Not being Fortune, he's but Fortune's knave,
> A minister of her will; . . .   (V. ii. 2–4)

For Antony and Cleopatra, the cosmic powers appear to be at their command:

> His face was as the heav'ns, and therein stuck
> A sun and moon, which kept their course and lighted
> The little O, the earth.   (V. ii. 79–81)

At Antony's death, the very universe seems to dissolve:

> The crown o' th' earth doth melt. My lord!
> O, wither'd is the garland of the war,
> The soldier's pole is fall'n! . . .   (IV. xv. 63–5)

Surely the first line refers not merely to the imperial crown but to the melting of the pole; and the withering garland signals a general infertility, the negation of

> For his bounty,
> There was no winter in't; . . .   (V. ii. 86–7)

How swiftly, almost casually, such forces are evoked: 'Let Rome in Tiber melt . . .'; 'Melt Egypt into Nile!'; 'Moon and stars! whip him.' These are inferior and subordinate powers: Antony and Cleopatra are the only gods, their love the supreme value. The ultimate order of the world is generated from purely human and purely individual energies. Of any greater or truly absolute order, there is no suggestion at all.

It may be seen from this that in *Antony and Cleopatra* we have the concepts of standard Scepticism, raised to epic power and thereby transformed beyond recognition. There is the same overthrowing of standard moral categories, the 'nominalistic' sense of the uniqueness of an experience, the celebration of individual values and individual ordering of experience. What has been lost, or overcome, is the accompanying sense of humble restraint, the tentativeness of the system thus evolved. Man's relation to the world is reversed. He is no longer fashioning a purely personal order in an infinite and bewildering universe; the universe shrinks to a 'little O' that cannot satisfy his demiurgic power.

> Nature wants stuff
> To vie strange forms with fancy; yet t' imagine
> An Antony were nature's piece 'gainst fancy,
> Condemning shadows quite.   (V. ii. 97–100)

The urge for complete expression of this supreme energy comes out in the main dramatic conflict of the play, between 'Egyptian' and 'Roman' values. This is clearly at a far less intense level than the pervasive moral collision in *Macbeth*. In fact, the conflict in *Antony and Cleopatra* can practically be dismissed from the outset because the 'Roman' order is

presented as inadequate. Not that its values bear any intrinsic
defect; on the contrary, they are noble and admirable. What
is in question is their formation into a complete ideal of
conduct, with the subjugation of the self and impoverishment
of the faculties that this implies. In other words, they are
inadmissible only if erected into a total order. The essence
of these values is incorporated, indeed perfected, in Antony
and Cleopatra's own ideal:

> . . . a Roman by a Roman
> Valiantly vanquish'd. (IV. xv. 57–8)
> . . . what's brave, what's noble,
> Let's do it after the high Roman fashion,
> And make death proud to take us. (IV. xv. 86–8)

The conflict between Roman and Egyptian resolves itself
into that between a more and a less comprehensive code.
They are incompatible, not so much by the difference between
their values as by the opposite modes of experience they
imply. Discipline of the self is opposed to the urge for
complete self-expression, a rigid frame of values to a total
refusal to embody or even acknowledge any formulated or
expressible values whatsoever. This is again a heroic heightening of Sceptic 'libertinism', carried beyond the limited,
tentative, purely personal field within which the libertine
principle operated in standard Scepticism. Antony and
Cleopatra wipe away all competing values and responses,
destroy all orthodoxies with a self-assertion that makes one
evoke Nietzsche's concept of the Dionysian.

By an ironical but entirely necessary paradox, this creative
power cannot create anything within the order of the world:
it can find no scope or material. It asserts itself by destroying
all extant values, and then withdrawing completely from the
shattered and discredited order. Inaction becomes a positive
assertion of the spirit—refusing, as it were, to debase one's
power in base engagement with the world. We may recall
Macbeth's strange dark 'asceticism' in his state of damnation.
More closely still, we are reminded of Hamlet's paralysing
misanthropy, his refusal to compromise with reality or with
the stultifying duty of traditional revenge.

The Roman ideal prizes action and the pursuit of fame; it
wishes to make an impact on the external world and enter

into profitable relation with it. Antony and Cleopatra, on the other hand, withdraw from the pursuit, to preserve the pure unique impulse of their being from the essential futility of action.

> Now all labour
> Mars what it does; yea, very force entangles
> Itself with strength.   (IV. xiv. 47–9)

The inaction to which Antony therefore consigns himself suggests something of the coiled, up-gathered energies of a fallen Titan. His powers have failed in external engagement, but they cannot therefore be dismissed: they are brought to act upon his own life with still greater intensity.

Similarly, Cleopatra winds through her series of moods, shifts, and stratagems in an unceasing effort to remain mistress of the changing situation, to subjugate circumstances to the power of her self; but when this fails, she too does not abandon her powers but expends them upon herself with unprecedented force and singleness of purpose. It is the last and finest expression of the unfailing energy of spirit that sustains them through inactivity and external failure:

> 'Tis sweating labour
> To bear such idleness so near the heart
> As Cleopatra this.   (I. iii. 93–5)

This absorption in the realized self is also conceived as a process of passing outside time, a process 'that shackles accidents and bolts up change':

> Eternity was in our lips and eyes,
> Bliss in our brows' bent, none our parts so poor
> But was a race of heaven. They are so still . . . (I. iii. 35–7)

Only in one earlier play, *Macbeth*, had Shakespeare given eternal validity to human experience, and there it was the eternity of damnation. Macbeth was enslaved for ever to the consequences of his deed. *Antony and Cleopatra* is the first play where experience becomes eternally significant as an enlarging or liberating force, an 'infinite virtue' (IV. viii. 17); and it is the only play where this force is generated from purely human impulse.

Failure and dishonour can thus be deliberately courted.
They take on the nature of a transcendence:

> —What should I stay—
> —In this vile world?   (V. ii. 311–12)

Antony and Cleopatra fashion their ends under the conviction that their ideal cannot be embodied on earth. To attempt
to embody it is to quarrel with reality and opt out of life.
They must fail and die to point the need for a higher sphere
of being in which their personalities may find complete
expression: 'new heaven, new earth'.

It has been commonly recognized that the imagery relating
to the 'Egyptian' order, with its celebration of life and
fecundity, carries a negative strand as well. The life-giving
Nile is associated with serpents, feasting with cloying; most
notably, light with darkness and love with death. In the last
movement, love and death become indistinguishable: love
leads to death, and death may be felt as love:

> . . . I will be
> A bridegroom in my death, and run into 't
> As to a lover's bed.   (IV. xiv. 99–101)

Love and death have become identified through their common
function: they can lead man beyond the confines of mortal
existence onto a possibly infinite course of development.

Shakespeare's presentation of man thus enters an important new phase in this play. In *Lear* or *Macbeth*, there had
been a full admission of the reality of weakness, sin, and loss,
and human strength had developed through an encounter
with these. In *Antony and Cleopatra*, these realities are
denied: there is no substantial encounter with external force,
because these forces have ceased to count, nearly ceased to
be. The self-fulfilment of the protagonists thus takes on, with
regard to their own sphere of being, a supreme reality; but to
the external world a total lack of relationship—in the normal
or orthodox perspective, a complete unreality.

In the last analysis, the aspiration of Antony and Cleopatra
possesses only a poetic or verbal validity, conveyed through
the charged, hyperbolic imagery. By a grand but fantastic
hypothesis, rhetoric is postulated as reality, and the normal

lines of experience are refracted to suit this enlarged, ideal dimension.[28] The eroticism is carried above the reach of common moral values by being linked to cosmic and high philosophic concepts; but these concepts have become counters for the imagination, wrenched from the systems to which they belonged. Thus, while they raise exalted associations and evoke a strong emotional response, they overthrow our sense of scale and order. Antony and Cleopatra's love cannot be placed in a firm philosophic setting.

So too, vice, foible, and pettiness are transformed into fiery life not through any basic revaluation of norms, but simply by the emotional intensity at which such traits are shown to work. Hence these transformations cannot be fully valid; they appear as brilliant emanations from very different moral material. We are witnessing a *tour de force* that may temporarily expel the moral sense, but does not overthrow it in a radical or absolute manner.

It is important to realize this obverse to the idealism of the play: it grows in a moral and metaphysical vacuum, a universe peopled by emanations of Antony and Cleopatra's fancy. The near-incompatible 'Renaissance alternatives' have clashed again. Human power has been vindicated by eschewing all sense of total order and tangible achievement. This humanity is basically ineffectual, futile, even cynical. It is impossible to embody: the lovers' triumph induces simultaneously a despair of the world.

The later tragedies offer the alternative heroisms of stone or water, of petrifaction or deliquescence; death can be shown to seal the opposite magnificences of Timon and Antony, but in neither case can it conceal the price that has been paid—the abandonment of the good ordinariness of a life lived among compromises, or the loss of a sense of reverence for the unknown in destiny, a sense of submission to the immanence of higher powers.[29]

From *Lear* through *Macbeth* to *Antony and Cleopatra*, Shakespeare has isolated the pure energy of the human spirit, rejecting all previous formulations of experience. In the last plays, this energy is accommodated within a valid world-order. At the same time, it is attuned to the irreducible values of common humanity.

9. *The Last Plays*

In *Lear, Macbeth,* and *Antony and Cleopatra* we have Shakespeare's strongest presentations of morally creative energy.
Man achieves most in these plays, though the achievement is
invalid in absolute terms. The last plays show a radical change
of perspective. Shakespeare still asserts the beauty and dignity
of human life, even at times its miraculous strength; but this
is placed in a new relation to its environment. Man is no
longer central and solitary, guiding his own destiny: his virtue
reflects a higher pattern of order, faith, and providence.

Today we shy away from reading these plays entirely in
terms of cosmic design and heaven's bounty. Given the
extremism of earlier interpretations along these lines, this is
an understandable reaction. It is proper to redress the balance
by emphasizing the role of man in these plays—his power and
virtue, even his problems and failures. But Shakespeare's total
purpose will emerge only when the two lines of interpretation
are coalesced, for they both yield important truths about
the plays.

We may start by considering their romance-like structures,
which strike most readers and critics even today. In the last
plays, substantially more than in Shakespeare's earlier work,
effects far exceed the cause or occur entirely without cause;
coincidences, improbable in themselves, occur in still more
improbable succession; and fantastic if not openly supernatural events provide crucial turning-points in the action.
There is no parallel in the great tragedies, with the possible
exception of Lear's division of his kingdom.

The effect of this freer structure is to loosen the link
between human action and human destiny. In *Lear, Macbeth,*
and *Antony and Cleopatra,* man had found the motive force
of his being within himself; it is now transferred back to an
external necessity.

It may appear inept to apply the word 'necessity' to a
professedly arbitrary course of events. But that is precisely
the paradox of these plays—a paradox that it shares in common
with all romantic narrative. There is no reason why the events
should occur as they do; yet they could not have happened
otherwise, for they are controlled by a benevolent providence.

In *Pericles*, this romantic providence masquerades most simply as chance working through time. In *The Winter's Tale*, it is the vital power manifested in 'great creating nature' and controlling human lives as well. In *The Tempest*, there is the more numinous power to which Prospero allies himself by the ambiguous compound of his magic. In *Cymbeline*, the power is still more difficult to define: the figure of Jove is patently a dramatic symbol, not an adequate mythic or philosophic embodiment. But undeniably here too a superior power guides the characters to fulfilment through a near-tragic pain and disorder that, in retrospect, appears a necessary preparation for the close. A pattern of apparent death and rebirth is one of the most celebrated features of these plays.

Every sort of character undergoes this revival after apparent death: young virgin-heroines like Marina, Perdita, or Miranda; older suffering heroines like Thaisa and Hermione; Imogen, who may belong to either category; or, in *The Tempest*, such varied characters as Prospero, Ferdinand, Alonso, Antonio, Gonzalo, Stephano, Trinculo, and even Ariel, released from the cloven pine.

In all these cases, the characters are apparently playing an entirely passive role. Even Prospero was strangely powerless to prevent himself from being cast out to sea, and only 'Providence divine' saved him and his daughter. But if we look more deeply, we shall find in every character a moral power or quality that is somehow associated with the process of death and revival. The association takes various and often obscure forms. It is seldom if ever the direct cause. For Alonso or Antonio, indeed, the 'sea-change' functions simply as punishment and reform. In most cases there is a subtler purpose; but in some way it serves to change or fulfil the character's moral nature.

I shall look at some of these changes in the characters, with their affinities to the larger movements of the plays. This will illustrate both the nature of man and his place in a greater scheme, as Shakespeare depicts them in the final stages of his art.

Sometimes in these plays a great spiritual energy radiates from the individual. In the young heroines it may assume an almost magical strength. The best instance is Marina's chastity in the brothel-scenes in *Pericles*. This is as different as could be from Isabella's warped self-protection in *Measure for Measure*. For Marina, chastity is a liberating, fulfilling ideal: it makes her realize the full strength of her personality and influence the lives of others. When she is first brought to the brothel, her reactions savour of martyred innocence:

> If fires be hot, knives sharp, or waters deep,
> Untied I still my virgin knot will keep.   (IV. ii. 147-8)

But in the encounter with Lysimachus, and still more with Boult a little later, she changes from passive to active, emanating a moral power that affects the lives of other men.

But it is not her unaided strength all the same. She calls for aid to Diana (IV. ii. 149)—the reigning goddess of the play, significantly enough. Moreover, Marina is associated with music, and music in this play points to a divine harmony:

> She sings like one immortal, and she dances
> As goddess-like to her admired lays; . . . (V, Prologue, 3-4)

These are wooden lines, but the idea comes to life when Marina sings to rouse Pericles. This is later taken up by the music of the spheres.

The heroine's chastity is less important in the other plays, but the idea remains. In Perdita's case, we have just three brief lines spoken by Florizel (IV. iv. 33-5). (Perhaps we should add Leontes' words in V. i. 230-1.) But Miranda's chastity is clearly if ineptly emphasized by Ferdinand's disconcerting query at their first meeting—'If you be maid or no?' (I. ii. 427). Later, Prospero raises the subject with a vehemence that the context scarcely demands:

> If thou dost break her virgin-knot before
> All sanctimonious ceremonies . . .
>   . . . barren hate,
> Sour-eyed disdain, and discord, shall bestrew
> The union of your bed with weeds so loathly
> That you shall hate it both.   (IV. i. 15-16, 19-22)

These passages disturb the texture of the drama; but they indicate Shakespeare's continuing concern with chastity as an important symbol for the strength of man's moral being.

In *Cymbeline*, Imogen's chastity is of obvious importance. The whole plot turns upon it. But Shakespeare does not

present it with such concentrated power as in *Pericles*. Only
once does it acquire a special imaginative quality: in the bed-
room scene, where Imogen's sleeping figure diffuses an
influence that nearly overpowers Iachimo:

> Cytherea,
> How bravely thou becom'st thy bed! fresh lily,
> And whiter than the sheets!   (II. ii. 14–16)

We touch the penumbra of a virtue as magical as in any medieval romance. But in the rest of the action, Imogen's chastity
remains well to the hither side of the miraculous. It is more a
datum, a premiss behind the plot, whereas Marina's chastity
was the driving impulse behind a part of the action. Moreover, in Marina's chastity lay her strength. Imogen's, on the
contrary, leaves her peculiarly vulnerable: it creates the evil
confusion of the play instead of resolving it. Her final triumph
is due to the providence of the play working upon the virtuous
compound of her moral nature; but her chastity is no more
than an element in this compound, whose more remarkable
components I shall consider later on.

On the whole, in *Cymbeline*, Shakespeare places less value
on chastity than on another quality emblematic of the excellence of man: innate royalty of nature. For Shakespeare this
is clearly linked to royalty of birth. Guiderius and Arviragus
display a nobility of spirit despite their wild upbringing.
Guiderius, seemingly a 'rustic mountaineer', vanquishes
Cloten. The ill-clad but gentle-born Posthumus defeats
Iachimo in battle. In the latter scene there is also doubtless
the sense of Britannic excellence, part of the patriotic theme
of the play.

There have been many attempts to link this theme of
royalty to specific political figures and events. We may ignore
these, as also the obvious links with points of political theory
like the divine right of kings. But we must look at the matter
in its most general implications. Just as the theme of chastity
assumes a moral dispensation, the theme of innate royalty
assumes a set order of existence: man at the top, and the king
as the highest-born perfection of mankind. The human
hierarchy is validated by a natural hierarchy, the generative
principle governing the Great Chain of Being. The order may
permit a gratifying degree of human excellence at its summit;

but it remains an order, supported all through by external referents.

In the tragedies man defied the external order, or asserted himself in the apparent absence of such an order. In the last plays, human virtue is shown as reflecting universal principles. The moral centre has once more passed outside man.

The theme of royalty creates a special problem. This is clearly expressed by D. G. James, though we may disagree with his general view of the plays. The narrow ideal of royal virtue contradicts the more general celebration of human virtue, a beauty 'for which kingships are well lost'.[30]

The contradiction shows clearly in *The Winter's Tale*. Here too royal birth is an important factor, as in any pastoral plot resolved by the discovery of the heroine's royal origin. The precedence enjoyed by Perdita among the shepherd company obviously owes much to her inborn superiority. Polixenes, himself a king, spots this at once (IV. iv. 158). Tellingly, Perdita's royal spirit shows most clearly when she defends her lowly nurture with un-proletarian fire:

> I was not much afeard; for once or twice
> I was about to speak and tell him plainly
> The self-same sun that shines upon his court
> Hides not his visage from our cottage, but
> Looks on alike.   (IV. iv. 434–8)

Yet there are difficulties. The young shepherd-clown, exulting in his new-found royal connections, declares himself a gentleman born 'any time these four hours' (V. ii. 131). At first sight, this points a direct contrast between innate and upstart nobility; but the joke may cut both ways. If royalty is so easily assumed, can it be associated with any inborn virtue at all? More profoundly, if the lost princess Perdita can so easily suit herself to rural life, flourish there and realize the noble potential of her nature, can it be judged inferior to the truly royal life? In *Cymbeline* the issues were simpler: Guiderius and Arviragus had chafed against their cramped, ignoble life. In *The Winter's Tale* the rural setting is happy and fulfilling. This raises new questions.

Shakespeare has given a moral turn to the common pastoral tension between rustic and courtly, humble and noble: the primordial human virtues and the finished perfection of

mankind. The two are finally reconciled in the figure of
Perdita. The power of nature that reigns over her being allies
her to both these milieux.

To some extent the other young heroines share this
affinity with nature. Marina is seen with flowers at Lychorida's
grave. More prominently, at the supposed burial of Imogen
by Belarius and her brothers, her life and death are strongly
linked to the cycle of the seasons, with a consequent hint of
regeneration:

> ARVIRAGUS.   With fairest flowers,
> Whilst summer lasts and I live here, Fidele,
> I'll sweeten thy sad grave. . . .
> Yea, and furr'd moss besides, when flow'rs are none,
> To winter-ground thy corse—   (IV. ii. 219–21, 229–30)

All this suggests another way in which human virtue is placed
within the workings of a superior order—this time, the cycle
of nature. The connection appears most clearly in *The
Winter's Tale*.

The pattern of the seasonal cycle, the basis of the archetypal vegetation-myth, is inexplicably strong in this play; and
it controls the course of Perdita's life. 'Blossom, speed thee
well!' says Antigonus as he lays the infant on the ground (III.
iii. 46). When we next see her, it is as a flower maiden. Plants
and flowers provide a ready image for her utterly pure and
unforced spirit. She displays a deep intuitive affinity with
pristine nature, by whose rhythms the entire action is controlled. For Perdita, to be a child of nature is itself to be in
touch with a transcendent source of pure strength. Her moral
energy is rendered exceptional not by effort, but by a spontaneous growth coequal with her very terms of being, and
fostered by the power that grants this being itself.

The action of the last plays takes place in what, for want
of a better word, we may call the symbolic mode. Human
character and action stand for, or work for, larger forces and
entities in the universe. Chastity, royalty, affinity with nature
—all reflect the movement of these larger forces in a sort of
shadow-play. Human virtue is 'innate' in the sense of being
instilled by the creating, nurturing power of a moral universe.
If at times this virtue approaches the superhuman, it is because

a divine power has made it so, to assist in the birth of a superior order of things.

There is indeed another pattern of experience in these plays that does not so readily answer to this account; yet it may finally be seen to conform. Few characters, after all, grow up like Perdita in heaven's benediction. More often than not they have to await their happiness over long periods of time: they must hold out through wandering, bereavement, danger, and injustice. Even the younger heroines like Marina and Imogen undergo these trials; and it forms the staple experience of Thaisa and Hermione, or for that matter of Pericles too. What sustains them is a resigned fortitude, a maturing capacity to absorb and outlast experience. Pericles recognizes in the young Marina the image of his own hopeless strength:

> Like Patience gazing on kings' graves, and smiling
> Extremity out of act.   (V. i. 137–8)

This is so in spite of Marina's victorious strength of character and her enterprise in supporting herself.

Imogen does not lack mettle either. She eagerly assumes a page's disguise and perseveres in her course: 'I should be sick, / But that my resolution helps me' (III. vi. 3–4). But her attitude is basically a wise passiveness, a ready adaptation to circumstances rather than a desire to control them. Among the earlier romantic heroines, her prototype is obviously Viola rather than Rosalind. (Critics have recalled *Twelfth Night* in connection with the last plays.) There is the same waiting upon time, the same capacity to colour the course of events more by suffering than by doing.

This implies moral power, not an abdication of responsibility. This is true of all the characters who suffer and wait in these plays. In Act II of *The Winter's Tale*, the accused Hermione faces her charges with marvellous strength and dignity. The wretched first half of *Pericles* will not afford any such view of the hero. In any case, his afflictions are not so sharply focused in a single predicament, but are unfolded by destiny over a long period. But for him too, as for Thaisa, the rewards of fortune come after he has acquired a stoic strength that takes him beyond such reward: 'What I have been I have forgot to know' (II. i. 71).

Here if anywhere in the last plays we find an independent moral strength in man, growing even as external support fails him. One is tempted to quote Edgar's 'Ripeness is all', and relate *Pericles* to the tragedies as preserving at least a vestige of their heroic ideal.

But the structure of the play prevents any such equation. The course of romantic providence precludes any concentration upon the hero's mental state. We are swept on to the happy ending: the traditional order is reinstated. With Imogen and Hermione, the order has never been seriously questioned. Through their seemingly hopeless adversity, they are sustained by the strength of normal moral values. There is no question of the utter desolation of spirit experienced by Lear or Macbeth.

Hermione sees herself as victim to a disturbance of the moral order:

> There's some ill planet reigns.
> I must be patient till the heavens look
> With an aspect more favourable.   (II. i. 105-7)

She inveighs against Leontes as the immediate cause of the disturbance, but does not question the order itself, or the values inspired by faith in that order. She still upholds not only honour above life but pity above revenge (III. ii. 107-9, 121). In any case the oracle soon vindicates her stand, so that the evil confusion can be charged to Leontes alone.

Imogen is more agitated when she hears of Posthumus' jealousy. But she too gauges the extent of man's evil with remarkable restraint, implicitly denying its ubiquity even as she seems to declare it:

> . . . thou, Posthumus,
> Wilt lay the leaven on all proper men:
> Goodly and gallant shall be false and perjur'd
> From thy great fall.   (III. iv. 59-62)

Her sorrow is an unbearable personal affliction, but no more. She does not dismiss the support of orthodox morality, but rather calls upon it. The outcome of the play vindicates this stand.

Even where the plays expose sin and evil passion, they differ radically from Shakespeare's earlier works. Posthumus' jealousy promises a deep misanthropic vision like Timon's, and extraordinary energy realized in the very act of hate:

> We are all bastards,
> And that most venerable man which I
> Did call my father was I know not where
> When I was stamp'd.   (II. v. 2-5)

But this passes into a noble and simple repentance—and a repentance born of plain charity and humility, even before he learns of Imogen's innocence (see V. i. 1 ff.). He expiates his offence through self-denigration as a poor soldier, and later by his conduct in the execution scene. There is a final outburst of repentance after Iachimo's confession (V. v. 209 ff.). But already Jove has granted his favour to Posthumus in a dream. The Spirit of the First Brother even suggests that Posthumus is more sinned against than sinning:

> The graces for his merits due,
> Being all to dolours turn'd ...   (V. iv. 79-80)

In the final dispensation, the evil is cast out and forgotten, and Posthumus wins the due reward of a brave warrior and romantic hero.

Leontes's jealousy takes the same course. It is perhaps more disturbing than Othello's or Posthumus' in its total lack of substance; but it comes and goes like a great fever, leaving Leontes in the latter part of the play as a noble and virtuous figure. He retains the deep memory of his past fit; but it is made pure by repentance, a return to the lines of orthodox virtue. In Othello, folly and magnanimity are simultaneous. In Leontes, wrath and folly are totally expelled before goodness can triumph.

In the last plays, characters may develop by suffering at the hands of evil, but never by incorporating it within their being in the agonizing synthesis achieved by the tragic heroes. At the opposite end of the spectrum, the love or charity pervasive in these plays is radically different from that achieved by, say, Lear on the heath. That was born out of a driving need for moral survival in a universe indifferent to moral values and thus inevitably hostile to man. In the last plays, human love confirms the design of providence and may function as its agent.

In most of these plays, the benevolent act of a minor
character initiates the movement of survival and regeneration.
Pisanio spares Imogen in *Cymbeline*, the Shepherd rescues
Perdita in *The Winter's Tale*, Gonzalo aids Prospero in *The
Tempest*. Even the villains are governed by a moral sense.
Iachimo's repentance would be unthinkable in Iago: contrast
Iachimo's

> I am glad to be constrain'd to utter that
> Which torments me to conceal.   (V. v. 141–2)

with Iago's

> From this time forth I never will speak word.
>   (V. ii. 307)

Repentance, pity, and mercy play an important part at the
close of these plays. Imogen forgives Posthumus, Posthumus
Iachimo, Cymbeline Belarius, Polixenes Florizel, Hermione
Leontes, Prospero Antonio. 'Pardon's the word to all', as
Cymbeline declares (V. v. 422).

By the very completeness of their spiritual design, the last
plays demand less of the obscure resources of the mind. They
depict an established course of moral evolution, guided by
extra-human forces that enshrine standard spiritual values.
The characters may suffer, and respond heroically to that
suffering. But this heroism does not have to provide its own
justification: it is vindicated by the total pattern of the play,
in a world seen to be governed by virtuous power. It is a
noble subjugation of man to a greater design.

For all his unique reconciliation of the discordant elements
in the Renaissance philosophy of man, Shakespeare too falls
prey to its basic division. He can assert the full power of man
only by disorganizing the world-order, or denying it an
absolute validity, or ignoring it altogether. Or else he can
bring man into total harmony with that order by curtailing
the exercise of the powers most distinctively his own. The
last plays adopt this latter course.

Even this harmony tends to fly apart in *The Tempest*.
The basic design of death and revival remains: 'Those are
pearls that were his eyes.' In fact, one may say that this
design is emphasized; the actual action covers only the

redemptive movement, the earlier action of evil being narrated
in flashback:

> 'Tis far off,
> And rather like a dream than an assurance . . .   (I. ii. 44-5)

Our difficulties begin with the fact that the play contains
so much else that is dreamlike and doubtfully real. The
happy unfolding of the action is obscured by visions, am-
biguities, and deceptions. The courtiers are shipwrecked by a
tempest of a harrowing visionary quality:

> Not a soul
> But felt a fever of the mad, and play'd
> Some tricks of desperation.   (I. ii. 208-10)

They are then caught up in a world of shifting appearances:
strange songs, strange somnolence, the apparition of the
banquet with Ariel as a harpy. They even doubt the experience of the senses—the colour of the grass and the wetness of
their garments (II. i. 50-62). Ferdinand is put through a great
trial by deception. The sudden arrest of his sword-arm is an
emblematic heightening of his helpless bewilderment (I. ii.
466). Of Stephano and Trinculo's distractions I need not
speak in detail.

The moral issues behind the main thrust of the narrative
are never in doubt; but they are asserted through these dreams
and uncertainties and in fact by their agency. We know that
Prospero is directing the fantasy to his own ends; but it is a
fantasy with no obvious support in a firm external order.
Rather it involves an external disorder—a point I shall raise
again. We have moved away from the stable 'nature' of *The
Winter's Tale*.

This bears another implication. The erring courtiers are
brought to their moral senses not by the perception of a
benevolent order but rather through terror and bewilderment.

> ALONSO.   O, it is monstrous, monstrous!
> Methought the billows spoke, and told me of it;
> The winds did sing it to me; and the thunder,
> That deep and dreadful organ-pipe, pronounc'd
> The name of Prosper; it did base my trespass.
> (III. iii. 95-9)

It is uncertain whether Alonso is referring to the tempest that wrecked them or to Ariel's 'harpy' speech immediately before these words. Kermode comments, 'Here the image is of the whole harmony of nature enforcing upon Alonso the consciousness of his guilt . . .'[31] But the power behind these images is none other than Prospero. Rather than any admonition from the deepest spirit of nature, we may detect here a sort of moral coercion. Alonso and his band are driven to repentance at a time of superhuman stress, dazing them out of full control over their being. Gonzalo's summary of the final happy outcome has an ironic meaning too:

> . . . all of us [found] ourselves
> When no man was his own.   (V. i. 212–13)

Posthumus sinned through error, and repented of his own accord when he discovered that error—in a fashion even earlier, out of simple humanity. Leontes' error was even more reprehensible; but once again its discovery brought about a self-inspired repentance. With Alonso or Antonio, there is no such direct link between wrongdoing and repentance. They must have known their guilt even when they incurred it; their repentance comes much later, through an apparently unconnected course of events; and instead of being self-inspired, it occurs through the efforts of the man they have wronged. This is obviously a less than perfect moral sequence. It diminishes man's responsibility, relies more upon justice working through external circumstances.

So much for ancient sin. Turning to young love, we again find a decline. The love of Ferdinand and Miranda is nurtured by Prospero in an artificial solitude. Florizel and Perdita had been freely attracted to each other in a normal social setting —perhaps by the generative discrimination of nature, drawing together their royal bloods. Imogen and Posthumus love with complete self-reliance, in what is perhaps best described as the interaction of two virtuous spirits. Marina reforms and wins Lysimachus through the near-miraculous influence of her virtue. By contrast, the love of Ferdinand and Miranda appears externally induced and controlled. Miranda woos Ferdinand with idyllic *naïveté*, and he responds with romantic zeal; but Prospero at once reminds us that he is overlooking their love (I. ii. 419). For all their ardour, they are curiously passive creatures.

All this places an overwhelming importance on the role of Prospero. It may be argued that though the other characters in *The Tempest* do not work out their own destiny, this is still controlled by none other than a man. No other hero in Shakespeare is granted such power as Prospero: he can control other men's beings and the very forces of nature. In one sense, *The Tempest* marks the climax of Shakespeare's celebration of man.

This is achieved at the cost of a more general harmony through the communion of many spirits, each independently grown to fruition, such as marks the end of *The Winter's Tale* or, less finely, of *Cymbeline*. Also, it unhappily reinvests man with dominion over external reality. The tragic heroes had exchanged this dominion for a command and understanding of their own nature. I shall later try to show how Prospero strives for the same understanding; but this runs counter to his power as magus.

Prospero's island rule displays the miracle-working omnipotence of a magical order; but being magical, it is also artificial, precarious, untenable not only in practice but perhaps also morally. He is a white magician, applying the powers of nature to good rather than evil purposes. Yet he is involved in such questionable, essentially 'black' arts as raising the dead. Sycorax is not said to practice necromancy, though she wielded other powers similar to Prospero's (V. i. 269–71). We cannot identify his magic with any moral or humane values.

In a more general way, Prospero's designs divert the natural or inherent tendencies of the forces he subjugates. Their vast power is uneasily cramped to serve a narrow human end. Ariel, the most enlightened of the attendant spirits, shows towards his master an affectionate loyalty that does seem different from his earlier obedience to Sycorax. Yet Ariel serves against his will and longs for freedom. In *The Winter's Tale* the powers of nature had entered easily, inevitably into the control of human affairs; in *The Tempest*, they are sullenly thwarted into serving them.[32]

Beneath the strain of command, Prospero's own benevolence can lapse into harshness and irritation. Above all, the power he wields is patently external to his being. Shakespeare

is at great pains to emphasize this point: in 'Lie there my art'
(I. ii. 25) or Caliban's design

> First to possess his books; for without them
> He's but a sot, as I am . . .   (III. ii. 88-9)

Paradoxically, Prospero's final understanding leads him to
the very same doubt, awe, and passivity he worked in other
people. He had built his world of visionary forms by manipu-
lating his hold upon material forces. But he increasingly contemplates the visionary quality itself, finds there a deeper
truth than in the realities he controls. He looks beyond the substance of his science to the fantasies he builds up with its aid,
fantasies which lead to nescience and the cessation of power:

> We are such stuff
> As dreams are made on; and our little life
> Is rounded with a sleep.   (IV. i. 156-8)

This much-discussed speech does not stand alone, but it
is Prospero's clearest shadowing of a world beyond form
and force. Ariel's release suggests not so much freedom as
annihilation:

> Then to the elements
> Be free, and fare thou well!   (V. i. 317-18)

'The elements' lose their function as the basis of matter and
suggest a region without feature, limit, or identity.

   Elsewhere Prospero relinquishes his command in more
orthodox but still more negative terms:

> . . . retire me to my Milan, where
> Every third thought shall be my grave.   (V. i. 310-11)

Even earlier, we may detect in him a resignation, a simple
desire to be ended with it all. His promises to free Ariel seem
to reflect his own eagerness to cast off his robes for ever.
Towards the end he shows an old man's exasperation with
the taxing climax of a long-drawn project: 'I had forgot that
foul conspiracy . . .' (IV. i. 139). At first sight, Prospero's
anger at this recollection seems to suit uneasily with the
following speech on 'this insubstantial pageant faded'. But
they both express a mind tied against its will to sordid tasks
it has long transcended in thought.

I shall turn from Prospero to Caliban, plumbing the entire scale of human existence. Yet from this opposite end of degenerate sub-humanity, Shakespeare seems to broach the same doubts and compromises on the nature of man.

In Ariel and Caliban we see the higher and lower powers of the universe: fire and air against earth and water, miracle-working spirit against recalcitrant brute force—a polarity reflected in the 'great amphibium' himself. Recent critics, however, find in Caliban something more than this stark image of unredeemed man. He is presented to varying degrees as a candidate for our sympathy, wronged by Prospero, and incorporating in himself the moral compound of human nature, good as well as bad.

This provides a useful corrective to the common earlier view; but taken by itself it creates more problems than it solves. If Caliban represents humanity, do the other characters belong to some superhuman beatific plane of existence? This scarcely seems convincing: their careers are too full of ironies and uncertainties. Yet there is obviously a marking-off in level between Caliban and the 'higher' characters. We find many ironic parallels; but the irony can work only if we grant a distinction between the two levels.

Given this distinction, however, we can see how Caliban distorts and questions the excellences of the superior characters. He is not incapable of knowledge, but his faculty for knowledge is utterly corrupt. He is a counterweight to Prospero.

> ... thy vile race,
> Though thou didst learn, had that in't which good natures
> Could not abide to be with; ...   (I. ii. 358-60)

He represents the savage man or 'cannibal' that Sceptics like Montaigne had held up as an ideal. His sordid existence disposes more effectively of Gonzalo's golden age than Antonio's or Sebastian's jibes can do. Gonzalo dreams that

> nature should bring forth,
> Of it own kind, all foison, all abundance,
> To feed my innocent people.   (II. i. 156-8)

What in fact this means comes out in Caliban's words to Stephano:

> I prithee let me bring thee where crabs grow;
> And I with my long nails will dig thee pig-nuts; . . .
>
> (II. ii. 157–8)

It is significant that, as David Young points out, Shakespeare has changed the much more sophisticated delights in the speech from *Mucedorus* that seems to lie behind Caliban's words.[33]

Caliban threatens the very ideal of natural innocence, presenting the obverse to Miranda's purity. He is wonder-struck by Stephano and Trinculo just as Miranda is by the nobler victims of the wreck: 'A most ridiculous monster, to make a wonder of a poor drunkard!' (II. ii. 155–6). Miranda's 'brave new world', we may remind ourselves, is peopled by her father's usurper and other would-be supplanters and assassins. True, it includes Ferdinand as well; but when they first meet, they are convinced of each other's divinity in a manner that implies uninformed innocence on her part, and dazed hyperbole on his, as much as their actual beauty and excellence. We may have lingering memories of this scene when we come upon Caliban's imbecile godmaking. Further, this godmaking questions man's basic religious impulse, so that a shadow seems to fall even upon the theme of providence and Prospero's final piety.

Yet we know that Caliban can use language for much more than cursing Prospero. He shows an incipient acuteness and even sensitivity. His initial devotion to Prospero may have been a bestial, doglike affection:

> When thou cam'st first,
> Thou strok'st me and made much of me, wouldst give me
> Water with berries in't . . .
> . . . and then I lov'd thee . . .   (I. ii. 332–4, 336)

But the 'sounds and sweet airs' on the island arouse in him an undoubted aesthetic response, making him yearn for a happiness beyond him. This has been universally noted, as also his final promise of reform, bending himself at last to a moral law.

> I'll be wise hereafter,
> And seek for grace.   (V. i. 294–5)

The parallel with Alonso or Antonio's repentance appears to be more than ironic. Like them, Caliban has been changed through his suffering and delusions, which have dissolved the normal patterns of his experience.

This does not materially alter our impression of the brute evil concentrated in Caliban. But it does mean that Shakespeare redeems Caliban from the absolute reprobation to which Prospero assigns him—and Miranda too, following her father:

> Abhorred slave,
> Which any print of goodness wilt not take,
> Being capable of all ill!   (I. ii. 351-3)

In the total context of the play, this evil is not reprobate. In the figure of Caliban, Shakespeare presents a tormented hope, perhaps no more than a yearning to hope, at the most degenerate level of humanity.

Caliban stands at one end of the spectrum of characters we have examined; Hamlet may perhaps be said to stand farthest removed at the other. In between comes a range of men and women all reaching out to unattainable ideals, vindicating themselves only by the effort with which they reach out and the intensity of their frustration.

In my studies of the plays, I have often compared Shakespeare's method of presenting these heroes with the methods and premisses of Sceptic thinkers and others who, in a looser and wider fashion, reflect the same concerns. A more general comparison may now be made. It has not been my purpose to illustrate 'the influence of Scepticism on Shakespeare'. Such direct and conscious influence might have occurred at certain points of his career, but to isolate them would be almost impossible and perhaps scarcely worth the labour. Efforts to track down the sources of Shakespeare's thought are invariably counter-productive: all one can legitimately attempt is a study of affinities, if only to define the frame of reference to which Shakespeare *cannot* be confined, the norms that he exceeds.

I have attempted to show that, in his supremely distinctive manner, he too was preoccupied with the doubt, gloom, and distrust of man's powers that characterize the age and find one of several expressions in an interest in formal Scepticism. Such Scepticism is linked to Shakespeare's plays not by linear influence or causality but simply as varying growths from a common soil. Similarly, the plays show the most memorable development of a common concern with man that accompanies these fears for his status and achievement. We have seen such a concern in Rabelais and Montaigne, in Burton and Donne. From the wreck of man's pride and ambition, they salvage a humble but worthy and fulfilling humanity. Shakespeare elevates this to the level of a new heroism, a reassertion of man's power that admits and transcends his limitations.

Only in the greatest painters of the Renaissance—Leonardo or Michelangelo—do we find the same tormented yet unquenchable vitality. There too, the perception of evil and weakness in man does not act as a simple limitation, but is mysteriously made the basis of a greater strength and nobility. But this new power, operating in regions beyond the charted provinces of thought, is never embodied in action, never synthesized with total reality. Michelangelo seems to suffer to the end a conflict between the titanic forms he portrays and the religious frame within which they must be immured: a conflict perhaps resolved only in the figure of Christ in the *Last Judgement* of the Sistine Chapel. Leonardo's dream of wisdom remains agonizingly unfulfilled. Yet in him, as in Shakespeare, we feel that the ideal has been captured even as it escapes man's grasp. Although not realized, it has somehow been validated, and the human spirit that can conceive of it has thereby fulfilled itself even in defeat.

Epilogue: Milton

It may be worth carrying on my study a little further, to indicate the later development of the trends I have marked and the scope for further investigation. In this brief epilogue, I shall suggest the possibilities in the works of Milton alone. More than any other author except Shakespeare, he deserves separate, extended treatment; and more than any other, he offers a distinctive synthesis of his own.

The passages on science and learning in *Paradise Lost* lay down strict traditional limits to human knowledge:

> Solicit not thy thoughts with matters hid,
> Leave them to God above, him serve and fear; . . .
> . . . heaven is for thee too high
> To know what passes there; be lowly wise:
> Think only what concerns thee and thy being;
> Dream not of other worlds . . .   (VIII. 167–8, 172–5)

Sometimes higher knowledge may be revealed by the special grace of God (V. 568–71, VII. 70–5); but only insofar as it relates to human salvation, and leads man to praise God but not to probe or question him (VII. 94–7, 111–30). To rise higher is to fall. Satan tempts Eve with the standard dream of Renaissance humanism, the release from one's allotted place in the Chain of Being:

> Look on me,
> Me who have touched and tasted, yet both live,
> And life more perfect have attained than fate
> Meant me, by venturing higher than my lot.
> Shall that be shut to man, which to the beast
> Is open?   (IX. 687–92)

Adam too finds this simple explanation for his fall—seeking 'Forbidden knowledge by forbidden means' (XII. 279).

There is also a subtler and more stimulating suggestion, however. Before the Fall, man did have knowledge of good; his disobedience only obtained for him the knowledge of evil.

> . . . let him boast
> His knowledge of good lost, and evil got,
> Happier, had it sufficed him to have known
> Good by it self, and evil not at all.   (XI. 86-9)

This draws upon the traditional distinction between *scientia* and *sapientia*. It is not knowledge of high and spiritual matters that is sinful, but of lowly material things. Man falls not by rising above ordained limits, but by stooping below his highest impulses. He is debased by seeking the knowledge of evil.

Yet this fall serves ultimately to ennoble and vindicate his faculties by drawing out their potential power. Through the struggling, painful experiences of the fallen state, he earns the knowledge he may legitimately command. The most radical feature of *Paradise Lost* is the constant suggestion of a *felix culpa*, not only in the orthodox sense (man redeemed by Christ's vicarious sacrifice) but in terms of spiritual growth in man after the Fall:

> True patience, and to temper joy with fear
> And pious sorrow, equally inured
> By moderation either state to bear,
> Prosperous or adverse: . . .   (XI. 361-4)

This is the heroic 'ripeness' of *King Lear*:

> Nor love thy life, nor hate; but what thou livest
> Live well, how long or short permit to heaven: . . .
>   (XI. 553-4)

And this, for Milton, true heroism: 'the better fortitude/Of patience and heroic martyrdom' (IX. 31-2).

Michael's discourse prescribes the nature of this 'Paradise within':

> . . . only add
> Deeds to thy knowledge answerable, add faith,
> Add virtue, patience, temperance, add love,
> By name to come called Charity, the soul
> Of all the rest: . . .   (XII. 581-5)

This is no passive acceptance of proferred grace. It is an exercise of moral energy, appearing not in specific actions but in the heroic enlargement of the spirit. Man builds up his own salvation.

One must also note how, after the Fall, there appears in

Adam and Eve what must fairly be called a superior humanity. The marble piety of their married life before the Fall is now succeeded by tenderness, pity, and a moving love. In fact, for Adam at least, the proximate impulse behind tasting the fruit is neither pride nor greed but conjugal loyalty. In the moral context, of course, this is lustful unreason:

> . . . if death
> Consort with thee, death is to me as life; . . .   (IX. 953–4)

Hence comes their fall and punishment. But afterwards in the fallen state, this same loyalty in love, mellowed through suffering to a tender mutual confidence, appears as a promising soil in which redemption may grow. Milton takes care that, after the first anger and recrimination, the fallen Adam and Eve may be invested with a special dignity, indeed with power and life:

> . . . peace returned
> Home to my breast, and to my memory
> His promise, that thy seed shall bruise our foe;
> Which then not minded in dismay, yet now
> Assures me that the bitterness of death
> Is past, and we shall live.   (XI. 153–8)

Yet, of course, they shall live only in Christ. The process of redemption commences in 'prevenient grace' (XI. 3) and is entirely set within the Christian doctrine of redemption. At the centre of the spiritual design is the second Adam, not the first. Milton achieves the finest possible synthesis of an orthodox world-view (including the doctrine of original sin) with a sense of human dignity and achievement. But each element of the synthesis tempers and moderates the other: there is nothing of the supreme assertion of human power that we find in *King Lear* or *Macbeth*—indefinable in moral or theological terms, created by an enlargement of total experience unrelated to orthodox values and probably incompatible with the Christian moral order. In Shakespeare, the human values do not crystallize into terms and principles in a definable spiritual system: they can suggest an unmeasured potential.

In Milton, such unmeasured potential appears to some extent in *Samson Agonistes*. Here we find a stronger sense of

both spiritual effort and controlling grace. Man's fate is
divinely ordained: it is God who raises man from fall, by laws
not only inexplicable to man but perhaps intrinsically irrational:

> Who made our laws to bind us, not himself,
> And hath full right to exempt
> Whom so it pleases him by choice . . .
> For with his own laws he can best dispense.(ll. 309-11, 314)

But the semi-Calvinism of the 'unsearchable dispose', and the
accompanying sense of election to grace, scarcely comprise
Milton's full and final stand. The repeated assertions of divine
control cannot take away the sense of Samson's own moral
victory—the transcendence of his blind and fallen state
through the 'temptations' posed by the visits of Manoa, Dalila,
and Harapha. (Blindness, of course, is a traditional image of
the fallen state; its occurrence in the 'autobiographical'
passages of *Paradise Lost* presents the poetic act as Milton's
own spiritual effort towards salvation.)

Again in *Samson* we have the theme of the 'better fortitude':

> O how comely it is and how reviving
> To the spirits of just men long oppressed!
> When God into the hands of their deliverer
> Puts invincible might . . .
> But patience is more oft the exercise
> Of saints, the trial of their fortitude . . .
> Either of these is in thy lot . . .
>   (ll. 1268-71, 1287-8, 1292)

Samson's distinctive 'lot', which of course the Chorus cannot
foresee, is that he combines these two modes of deliverance,
which also becomes self-deliverance involving his own death.
He destroys his sinful being and releases his pure spiritual
energy.

Even this is ascribed to 'dire necessity' (1666); but immediately after, it is presented as Samson's voluntary and self-
impelled achievement:

> With inwards eyes illuminated
> His fiery virtue roused
> From under ashes into sudden flame . . .
>   . . . Samson hath quit himself
> Like Samson, and heroicly hath finished
> A life heroic . . .   (ll. 1689-91, 1709-11)

The Phoenix-image that follows is traditionally applied to Christ. The first and second Adams, whose roles had interacted in the spiritual design of *Paradise Lost*, have here almost coalesced. Sin and victory are elements of a single spiritual movement, though not simultaneously present as in Shakespeare. Milton orders his pattern more clearly, but by destroying certain possibilities of complex experience that are realized in Shakespeare's tragic heroes.

The complement to *Samson Agonistes* lies, of course, in the treatment of Christ in *Paradise Regained*. The briefest of summaries must serve for Milton's doctrinal stand in this poem. In *Samson* man had become his own Christ, so to speak; and conversely, in *Paradise Regained* Christ is presented primarily as 'a man Of female seed', defeating Satan by moral effort, not divine power. The Temptation in the Desert is significantly chosen as the decisive commencement of the process which will end in the 'better fortitude' of the Passion and Crucifixion:

> By tribulations, injuries, insults,
> Contempts, and scorns, and snares, and violence,
> Suffering, abstaining, quietly expecting
> Without distrust or doubt, that he may know
> What I can suffer, how obey?   (III. 190–4)

Milton's Arminianism, incipient in *Samson*, is now carried to its climax: Christ himself is 'This perfect man, by merit called my Son' (I. 166).

Christ's nature is described in terms that echo both the provenance of the classical hero and the traditional concept of 'amphibious' man:

> His mother then is mortal, but his sire
> He who obtains the monarchy of heaven . . .   (I. 86–7)

Thus Christ releases the spiritual potential in man, and truly reinstates man in the 'Paradise within' (IV. 612 ff.).

The distinctive point of Christ's effort and suffering is that it vindicates man at the doctrinal or dogmatic level, 'officially' frees him from original sin and restores him to grace. It provides theological sanction for what is, however, presented as *essentially a moral process*. Each man can therefore enact the same process within himself. It would not be valid in an absolute sense, as Christ's achievement is, nor would it take on universal relevance. But it would testify to man's spiritual powers, his fitness for salvation, his capacity to enlarge his moral being.

Through all his temptations, Christ tellingly refrains from any exercise of his divinity. This is in fact the basic principle guiding his conduct. He will suffer as man, resist with the power that all men may command:

> To the utmost of mere man both wise and good,
> Not more; . . .   (IV. 535-6)

This is, of course, a deliberate witholding of his divinity: 'My time . . . is not yet come.' But thereby the Redemption is made less of a divine dispensation, more the inducement of moral regeneration in man.

Notes and References

CHAPTER I

1. On this subject, see such works as Rosalie Colie, *Paradoxia Epidemica* (Princeton, 1966), especially pp. 3-40, and Stanley E. Fish, *Self-Consuming Artifacts* (Berkeley, 1972), especially pp. 1-4.

2. Bynneman, fol. 4^r. 'Tanta autem est veritatis ampla libertas, liberaque amplitudo, ut nullius scientiae speculationibus, non ullo sensuum urgenti iudicio, non ullis logici artificii argumentis, nulla probatione evidente, nullo syllogismo demonstrante, nec ullo humanae rationis discursu possit deprehendi, nisi sola fide: . . .' (*De inc.*, a4^r.)

3. Bynneman, fol. 71^v-72^r. '. . . quo sit, ut quod aliquando vitium fuit, modo virtus habeatur: et quod hic virtus est, alibi vitium sit: quod uni honestum, alteri turpe: quod nobis iustum, aliis iniustum sit, pro cuiusque temporis, loci, status, hominum opinionibus vel legibus.' (*De inc.*, i8^r.)

4. Bynneman, fol. 160^r. '. . .tota atque omnis non nisi ex caducis infirmissimisque hominum commentis et placitis constituta, omnium quae sunt tenuissima, et ad omnem temporis, status, principis mutationem convertibilis existat: . . . (*De inc.*, x4^v.)

5. Bynneman, fol. 183^r. 'Hi enim tam pertinaces et obstinati in suis opinionibus sunt, ut spiritui sancto nullum locum relinquant, ac propriis viribus, proprioque ingenio sic innituntur atque considunt, ut nulli veritati cedant nec admittant . . .' (*De inc.*, 2a3^v.)

6. Bynneman, fol. A4^v. '. . . quam impia tyrannis, captivare ad praefinitos autores studiosorum ingenia, et adimere discipulis libertatem indagandae et sequendae veritatis.' (*De inc.*, πA8^v.)

7. Bynneman, fol. 4^v-5^r. 'Habet enim quaevis scientia certa quaedam principia quae credere oporteat, nec ullo modo queant demonstrari: quae si quis pertinacius negare velit, non habent philosophi illi quo contra illum disputent, moxque dicent contra negantem principia non esse disputandum . . .' (*De inc.*, a4^v.)

8. Bynneman, fol. 20^v. '. . . quin dicat quis idiotae pro homine animal rationale mortale, minus intelliget, quam si dixisset hominem.' (*De inc.*, c4^v.)

9. Bynneman, fol. 157^r. '. . . cum tamen ars omnis non possit naturam superare, sed illam imitatur, et longis passibus sequitur. Et multo fortior sit vis naturae quam artis.' (*De inc.*, x1^{r-v}.)

10. Bynneman, fol. 180^{r-v}. 'Nunc igitur qui caetera novit . . .tamen nihil scit, nisi sciat voluntatem verbi dei, et fecerit illam: qui omnia didicit, et hoc non didicit, frustra didicit, frustra scit omnia.' (*De inc.*, z8^v-2a1^r.)

11. Bynneman, fol. 1^r. '. . . quae ex seipsa laudem aliquam mereatur, nisi quam a possessoris probitate mutuatur.' (*De inc.*, a1^v.)

12. Bynneman, fol. 79^r. 'Optime enim unus, optime pauci, optime populus imperant, si probi sint, pessime autem si sint improbi.' (*De inc.*, k7^v.)

13. Bynneman, fol. 186^r. '. . . creavit deus omnia valde bona, in optimo videlicet gradu in quo consistere possent: is igitur sicut creavit arbores plenas fructibus, sic et animas ceu rationales arbores creavit plenas formis et cognitionibus,

sed per peccatum primi parentis velata sunt omnia, intravitque oblivio mater ignorantiae.' ('Operis peroratio': *De inc.*, 2a6ᵛ.)

14. Bynneman, fol. 4ʳ. '. . . haec est vera illa pestis, quae totum ac omne hominum genus ad unum subvertit, quae omnem innocentiam expulit, et nos tot peccatorum generibus mortique fecit obnoxios, quae fidei lumen extinxit, animas nostras in profundas coniiciens tenebras, quae veritatem damnans, errores in altissimo throno collocavit.' (*De inc.*, a4ʳ.)

15. Bynneman, fol. 183ᵛ. 'Melius est ergo et utilius idiotas et nihil omnino scientes existere, et per fidem et charitatem credere, et proximum fieri deo, quam per subtilitates scientiarum elatos et superbientes cadere in possessionem serpentis.' (*De inc.*, 2a4ʳ.)

16. Bynneman, fol. 80ʳ⁻ᵛ. 'Ac tandem omnes istae religionum leges, nullo alio fundamento incumbunt, quam suorum instituentium placitis: nec aliam insuper certitudinis regulam habent, nisi ipsam credulitatem. Considerate ab initio mundi quot sunt, quot fuerunt in religione studia, quot caeremoniae, quot cultus . . . et nondum a tot seculis homines ad rectam fidem perducere potest, religio absque verbo dei: . . .' (*De inc.*, k8ᵛ–11ʳ.)

17. Bynneman, fol. 177ᵛ. '. . . pauci admodum ex multis veri ac certi supersint.' (*De inc.*, z6ʳ.)

18. Bynneman, fol. 176ᵛ. 'Neque vero prophetae semper sunt prophetae, sive videntes, praedicentesque: neque habitus continuus est prophetia, sed donum et passio et spiritus transiens . . .' (*De inc.*, z5ʳ.)

19. Bynneman, fol. 178ᵛ. '. . . unum enim constantem simplicem et sanctum sensum habet . . .' (*De inc.*, z7ʳ.)

20. 'Tout le monde est fol. En Lorraine Fou est près Tou, par bonne discrétion. Tout est fol. Solomon dict que infiny est des folz le nombre. A infinité rien ne peut décheoir, rien ne peut estre adjoinct, comme prouve Aristoteles.' (Demerson, p. 534.)

21. '. . . deffiant de son sçavoir et capacité, congnoissant les antinomies et contrariétez des loix, des édictz, des coustumes et ordonnances, entendent la fraulde du Calumniateur infernal . . . invocqueroit à son ayde la grâce céleste, se déporteroit en l'esprit sacro-sainct du hazard et perplexité de sentence définitive et, par ce sort, exploreroit son décret et bon plaisir . . .' (Demerson, pp. 529–30.)

22. '. . . simplicité et affection syncère . . .' (Demerson, p. 529.)

23. Qui vous dict que blanc signifie foy et bleu fermeté? Un (dictes-vous) livre trepelu . . . Qui l'a faict? . . . je ne scay quoy premier en luy je doibve admirer, ou son oultrecuidance ou sa besterie: . . .' (Demerson, p. 66.)

24. 'Pleureray-je? disoit-il. Ouy, car pourquoy? Ma tant bonne femme est morte . . .'

Et, ce disant, pleuroit comme une vache; mais tout soubdain rioit comme un veau, quand Pantagruel luy venoit en mémoire.

'. . . Ho, ho, ho, ho! que suis ayse! Beuvons, ho! laissons toute mélancholie! . . .'

Ce disant, ouyt la létanie et les *Mementos* des prebstres qui portoyent sa femme en terre. . . .' (Demerson, pp. 225–6.)

25. 'D'un costé et d'aultre il avoit argumens sophisticques qui le suffocquoyent, car il les faisoit très bien *in modo et figura*; mais il ne les pouvoit souldre . . .' (Demerson, p. 225.)

26. 'Et il, voyant toutes choses aethérées et terrestres sans bezicles, discourant de tous cas passez et praesens, praedisant tout l'advenir, seulement ne voioit sa femme brimballante . . .' (Demerson, pp. 460–1.)

'Her Trippa' is commonly supposed to be Agrippa. It is ironical that Rabelais should turn against Agrippa the popular jest about the cuckolded astrologer that

Agrippa himself tells, quoting an epigram by Thomas More. (*De inc.*, f7ʳ; Bynneman, fol. 47ʳ⁻ᵛ.)

27. '. . . premier maistre ès ars de ce monde'. (Demerson, p. 735.)

28. '. . . de bon vin on ne peult faire maulvais latin.' (Demerson, p. 92.)

29. '. . . parce que gens libères, bien nez, bien instruictz, conversans en compaignies honnestes, ont par nature un instinct et aguillon, qui tousjours les poulse à faictz vertueux et retire de vice, lequel ilz nommoient honneur.' (Demerson, p. 203.)

30. 'Icelle herbe moyenante, les substances invisibles visiblement sont arrestées, prinses, détenues et comme en prison mises: . . .

Icelle moyenant, sont les nations, que Nature sembloit tenir absconses, imperméables et incongneues, à nous venues, nous à elles: . . . De mode que les Intelligences célestes, les Dieux tant marins que terrestres, en ont esté tous effrayez . . .' (Demerson, pp. 551-2.)

31. 'Quant doncques voz philosophes, Dieu guydent, accompaignens à quelque claire Lanterne, se adonnèrent à songneusement rechercher et investiger (comme est le naturel des humains, et de ceste qualité sont Hesrodothe et Homère appelez *alphestes*, c'est à dire rechercheurs et inventeurs) . . .' (Demerson, p. 916.) This is the ending to V. 47 given in Bibliothèque Nationale MS. fr. 2156, where it is actually the forty-sixth chapter. The reference to Herodotus and Homer does not appear in the translation.

32. Demerson, p. 917.

33. See Pléiade, pp. 583, 584, and 577 (Frame, pp. 453, 453, and 448); also Sextus Empiricus, *Hypotyposes*, I. 14 and Lucretius, *De Rerum Natura*, IV. 390 ff.

34. '. . . sont-ce, dis-je, nos sens qui façonnent . . . de diverses qualitez ces subjects, ou s'ils les ont telles? Et sur ce doubte, que pouvons nous resoudre de leur veritable essence?' (Pléiade, p. 584.)

35. 'La consequence que nous voulons tirer de la ressemblance des evenemens est mal seure, d'autant qu'ils sont tousjours dissemblables: il n'est aucune qualité si universelle en cette image des choses que la diversité et varieté.' (Pléiade, p. 1041.)

36. 'Si nature enserre dans les termes de son progrez ordinaire, comme toutes autres choses, aussi les creances, les jugemens et opinions des hommes; si elles ont leur revolution, leur raison, leur naissance, leur mort, comme les chous; si le ciel les agite et les roule à sa poste, quelle magistrale authorité et permanante leur allons nous attribuant?' (Pléiade, p. 559.)

37. 'Il faut accommoder mon histoire à l'heure. Je pourray tantost changer, non de fortune seulement, mais aussi d'intention. C'est un contrerolle de divers et muables accidens et d'imaginations irresoluës et, quand il y eschet, contraires; soit que je sois autre moymesme, soit que je saisisse les subjects par autres circonstances et considerations. Tant y a que je me contredits bien à l'adventure, mais la vérité, comme disoit Demades, je ne la contredy point.' (Pléiade, p. 782.)

38. 'Nostre contestation est verbale. . . . On eschange un mot pour un autre mot, et souvent plus incogneu. Je sçay mieux que c'est qu'homme que je ne scay que c'est animal, ou mortel, ou raisonnable. Pour satisfaire à un doubte, ils m'en donnent trois: c'est la teste de Hydra.' (Pléiade, p. 1046.) Note how Montaigne repeats Agrippa's use of the definition of man as a mortal reasoning animal: see above, p.8.

39. '. . . en son vray usage, c'est le plus noble et puissant acquest des hommes.' (Pléiade, p. 905.)

40. '. . . il sçavoit cela, qu'il ne sçavoit rien.' (Pléiade, p. 481.)

41. 'Car nous sommes nais à quester la verité; il appartient de la posseder à une plus grande puissance.' (Pléiade, p. 906.)

42. [L'homme] se sent et se void logée icy, parmy la bourbe et le fient du monde, attachée et clouée à la pire, plus morte et croupie partie de l'univers . . . et se va plantant par imagination au dessus du cercle de la Lune et ramenant le ciel soubs ses pieds. C'est par la vanité de cette mesme imagination qu'il s'egale à Dieu, qu'il s'attribue les conditions divines . . .' (Pléiade, p. 429.)

43. 'La philosophie ne me semble jamais avoir si beau jeu que quand elle combat nostre presomption et vanité, quand elle reconnoit de bonne foy son irresolution, sa foiblesse et son ignorance. Il me semble que la mere nourisse des plus fauces opinions et publiques et particulieres, c'est la trop bonne opinion que l'homme a de soy.' (Pléiade, p. 617.)

44. 'Ce n'est pas par discours ou par nostre entendement que nous avons receu nostre religion, c'est par authorité et par commandement estranger. La foiblesse de nostre jugement nous y aide plus que la force, et nostre aveuglement plus que nostre clervoyance. C'est par l'entremise de nostre ignorance plus que de nostre science que nous sommes sçavans de ce divin sçavoir.' (Pléiade, pp. 479–80.)

45. 'On a raison de donner à l'esprit humain les barrieres les plus contraintes qu'on peut. . . . On le bride et garrote de religions, de loix, de coustumes, de science, de preceptes, de peines et recompenses mortelles et immortelles; . . .' (Pléiade, p. 541.)

46. 'Les hommes vont ainsin. On laisse les loix et preceptes suivre leur voie; nous en tenons une autre, non par desreiglement de meurs seulement, mais par opinion souvent et par jugement contraire. . . .

. . . un mesme ouvrier y publie des reigles de temperance et publie ensemble des escris d'amour et desbauche. Et Xenophon, au giron de Clinias, escrivit contre la volupté Aristippique.' (Pléiade, pp. 967–8.)

47. 'Nous cherchons d'autres conditions, pour n'entendre l'usage des nostres, et sortons hors de nous, pour ne sçavoir quel il y fait. Si, avons nous beau monter sur des eschasses, car sur des eschasses encores faut-il marcher de nos jambes. Et au plus eslevé throne du monde, si ne sommes assis que sus nostre cul.

Le plus belles vies sont, à mon gré, celles qui se rangent au modelle commun et humain, avec ordre, mais sans miracle et sans extravagance.' (Pléiade, p. 1096.)

48. 'Paulus eodem in homine duos homines facit adeo conglutinatos, ut neuter sine altero, neque in gloria, neque in gehenna sit futurus, adeo rursum disjunctos, ut unius mors, vita sit alterius.' (Leyden, V. 16.) In Himelick's translation, the chapter-numbers run one behind those of the Leyden edition, so that this is ch. 7.

49. 'Les loix naturelles leur commandent encores, fort peu abastardies par les nostres; mais c'est en telle pureté, qu'il me prend quelque fois desplaisir dequoy la coignoissance n'en soit venuë plustost, du temps qu'il y avoit des hommes qui en eussent sceu mieux juger que nous.' (Pléiade, p. 204.)

50. Erich Auerbach, *Mimesis: the Representation of Reality in Western Literature*, translated by Willard R. Trask (Princeton, 1953; rptd. 1971), p. 311.

51. 'Ta raison n'a en aucune autre chose plus de verisimilitude et de fondement qu'en ce qu'elle te persuade la pluralité des mondes: . . . Or, s'il y a plusieurs mondes, . . . que sçavons nous si les principes et les regles de cettuy touchent pareillement les autres? . . . (P)ourqouy prenons nous titre d'estre, de cet instant qui n'est qu'une eloise dans le cours infini d'une nuict eternelle . . .?' (Pléiade, pp. 505, 507.)

CHAPTER II

1. 'Non potest igitur finitus intellectus rerum veritatem per similitudinem praecise attingere.' (Heidelberg, p. 9.)

2. '. . . consequens est omnem humanam veri positivam assertionem esse coniecturam. Non enim exhauribilis est adauctio apprehensionis veri. Hinc ipsam maximam humanitus inattingibilem scientiam dum actualis nostra nulla proportione respectet, infirmae apprehensionis incertus casus a veritatis puritate positiones nostras veri subinfert coniecturas.' (Heidelberg, p. 4.)

3. '. . . non aliter scitur, quam quod ipsa est omni scientia altior et inscibilis, et omni loquela ineffabilis, et omni intellectu inintelligibilis, et omni mensura immensurabilis, et omni fine infinibilis . . .' (Heidelberg, p. 10.) Cf. *De docta ignorantia*, I. xvi, xxiv, xxvi.

4. '. . . non aliud videtur esse creare quam Deum omnia esse.' (Heidelberg, p. 66.)

5. 'Ac si facies esset in imagine propria, quae ab ipsa multiplicatur distanter et propinque quoad imaginis multiplicationem (non dico secundum distantiam localem, sed gradualem a veritati faciei, cum aliter multiplicari non possit): . . .' (Heidelberg, p. 72.)

6. '. . . eadem secundum diversos modos essendi, existens prius naturaliter in intelligentia quam materia, non prius tempore, sed sicut ratio rem natura praecedit.' (Heidelberg, p. 94.)

7. '. . . maximum contractum, hoc est Deus et creatura, absolutum et contractum . . .' (Heidelberg, p. 124.)

8. '. . . ita ut in ipsa humanitate omnia supremum gradum adipiscerentur.' (Heidelberg, p. 127.)

9. 'Regio igitur ipsa humanitatis deum atque universum mundum humanali sua potentia ambit. Potest igitur homo esse humanus deus atque, ut deus, humaniter potest esse humanus angelus, humana bestia, humana leo aut ursus aut aliud quodcumque. Intra enim humanitatis potentiam omnia suo exsistunt modo.' (Heidelberg, p. 143-4.)

10. 'Haec autem omnino [homo] ad se ipsum reflectit, ut se intelligere, gubernare et conservare possit et sic homo ad deiformitatem appropinquet, ubi cuncta aeterna pace quiescunt.' (Heidelberg, p. 146.)

11. Charles Trinkaus, *'In Our Image and Likeness'*: *Humanity and Divinity in Italian Humanist Thought* (London, 1970), Vol. II, pp. 471-8.

12. '. . . ut quam sedem, quam faciem, quae munera tute optaveris, ea, pro voto, pro tua sententia, habeas et possideas. . . . Tu, nullis anguistiis coercitus, pro tuo arbitrio, in cuius manu te posui, tibi illam praefinies.' (Garin, pp. 104, 106.)

13. '. . . angelus erit et Dei filius . . .' (Garin, p. 106.)

14. '. . . ut tui ipsius quasi arbitrarius honorariusque plastes et fictor . . .' (Garin, p. 106.)

15. '. . . qui caro sumus et quae humi sunt sapimus . . . adeamus antiquos patres, qui de his rebus utpote sibi domesticis et cognatis locupletissimam nobis et certam fidem facere possunt.' (Garin, p. 112.)

16. Garin, p. 116; Forbes, p. 230.

17. 'Agemur, Patres, agemur Socraticis furoribus . . . ut mentem nostram et nos ponant in Deo. Agemur ab illis utique, si quid est in nobis ipsi prius agerimus; . . .' (Garin, p. 122.)

18. Psalm 84: 2. (Authorized Version.)

19. '. . . divini splendoris caligine exoculati clamemus cum Propheta: "Defeci in atriis tuis, domine," hoc unum de Deo postremo dicentes esse ipsum inintelligibiliter et ineffabiliter super id omne quod nos de eo perfectissimum vel loqui possumus vel concipere . . .' (Garin, p. 414.)

20. Garin, p. 304; Carmichael, p. 136.

21. Jayne, pp. 133-4. 'Divina vero haec species in omnibus amorem, hoc est sui desiderium procreavit. . . . unus quidem continuus attractus est a Deo incipiens,

transiens in mundum, in Deum denique desinens, qui quasi circulo quodam in idem inde manavit, iterum remeat.' (Jayne, p. 43.)

22. We may recall the Renaissance play on 'grace' and 'graces'. The three Graces were an accepted symbol of the cyclic process of Platonic love. See Edgar Wind, *Pagan Mysteries in the Renaissance* (Revised edition, Harmondsworth, 1967), Ch. III.

23. Charles Trinkaus, pp. 83 ff.

24. Nesca A. Robb, *Neoplatonism of the Italian Renaissance* (London, 1935), p. 41.

25. Quoted in Wind, p. 157.

26. Robb, p. 68.

27. '. . . intellectum qui (ut ita loquar) supernaturalium ultimum est supremumque naturalium, spiritales omnes rerum omnium formas accipere posse, omnesque evadere.' (Basle, I. 677.)

I have used *Five Questions* to illustrate this account as it affords a brief and simple exposition of certain key ideas in Ficino. For the more elaborate account in *Theologia Platonica* see Trinkaus, pp. 464-74, 487-94.

28. 'Quoniam vero effectus causae proximus evadit causae ipsi similimus, consequens est ut anima infinita quodammodo virtus sit et aeterna, alioquin ad finem nunquam proprie vergeret infinitum.' (Basle, I. 678.)

29. Jayne, p. 158. 'Sed primus hic fulgor in animae substantia per se prius informi receptus, fit obscurior, atque ad illius tractus capacitatem proprius ipsi et naturalis evadit, ideoque per eum utpote sibi aequalem, se ipsam, et quae infra se sunt, id est, corpora omnia anima videt quidem.' (Jayne, p. 60.)

30. 'Extra naturae primae ordinem positi sumus, praeter naturae ordinem proh dolor, agimus atque patimur, primus homo, quam facile primum omnino conversus ad Deum felicitatem accipere poterat, tam facile deinde illinc adversus ipsam amisit facilitatem.' (Basle, I. 681.)

31. ' . . . donec transferatur eodem, unde olim acceperat ignem, ut quemadmodum uno illo luminis superni radiolo nunc assidue stimulatur ad totum, sic toto deinde lumine penitus impleatur.' (Basle, I. 680.)

32. '. . . vel a corpore liber, vel in corpore temperato, immortali, coelesti . . .' (Basle, I. 682.)

33. 'Semper certe [ratio] ambigit et vacillat et angitur. Cum igitur nusquam quieta sit, certe nunquam dum sic afficitur, vel ipsa fine potitur optato, vel sensum praesente iam fine suo potiri permittit.' (Basle, I. 680.)

34. 'Le soing de s'augmenter en sagesse et en science, ce fut la premiere ruine du genre humain; c'est la voye par où il s'est precipité à la damnation eternelle.' (Pléiade, p. 478.)

35. 'C'est pour le chastiement de nostre fierté et instruction de nostre misere et incapacité, que Dieu produisit le trouble et la confusion de l'ancienne tour de Babel. . . . La diversité d'ydiomes et de langues, dequoy il trouble cet ouvrage, qu'est ce autre chose que cette infinie et perpetuelle altercation et discordance d'opinions et de raisons qui accompaigne et embrouille le vain bastiment de l'humaine science.' (Pléiade, p. 535.)

36. '. . . qui verra l'homme sans le flatter, il n'y verra ny efficace, ny faculté qui sente autre chose que la mort et la terre. Plus nous donnons, et devons, et rendons à Dieu, nous en faisons d'autant plus Chrestiennement.' (Pléiade, p. 536.)

37. Blackfriars, XIII. 99. '. . . in quibus homo natus est instrui . . .', '. . . quanta erat necessaria ad gubernationem vitae humanae secundum statum illum.' (Blackfriars, XIII. 98.)

38. '. . . cum . . . nihil aliud sit sapientia, quam duci ratione; contra stultitia, affectuum arbitrio moveri, ne plane tristis ac tetrica esset hominum vita, Jupiter

quanto plus indidit affectuum quam rationis? quasi semiunciam compares ad assem.' (Leyden, IV. 417.)

39. '. . . nobis quidem huc atque illuc, quo fert animi libido, vagari liberum est. . . . ut paradisum istam non magnopere desideremus, si liceat hic aeternum vivere. Infestamur morbis, et huic rei inveniet remedium humana industria. . . . nihil est, quod non expugnet pertinax industria.' (Leyden, III. i. 43.)

40. 'Angelus ille custos mutatus, atque, quod hominibus faveret, humano corpori inclusus. Caym, quum Deum incensis frugibus placare studeret, nec fumus subvolaret, certam illius iram intelligens, desperat.' (Leyden, III. i. 44.)

41. 'Si tibi corpus additum non fuisset, Numen eras: si mens ista non fuisset indita, pecus eras. Has duas naturas tam inter se diversas summus ille opifex felici concordia colligarat, at Serpens, pacis inimicus, infelici rursus discordia dissecuit, ut jam neque dirimi queant sine maximo cruciatu, neque conjunctim vivere sine assiduo bello . . .' (Leyden, V. 11-12.)

42. 'Ita fit, vt meis viribus diffisus, totus ab illo pendeam, qui potest omnia. Vbi sapientiam illius intueor, nihil tribuo meae sapientiae, verum credo omnia rectissime iustissimeque ab eo fieri, etiam si iuxta sensum humanum videantur absurda aut iniqua.' (Amsterdam, I. iii. 366, ll. 78-81.)

43. 'Exsistunt circa hoc sacramentum innumerae quaestiones, quomodo fiat transubstantiatio, quomodo subsistant accidentia absque subjecto . . . aliaeque permultae, quas inter eos sobrie tractari convenit qui sensus habent exercitatos. Vulgo satis est credere . . .' (Leyden, III. ii. 1276.)

44. 'Nec interim nihil agit nostra voluntas, quanquam non assequutura quod conatur, nisi adjutrice gratia: sed quoniam minimum hoc est, quod per nos agitur, totum Deo transcribitur . . .' (Leyden, IX. 1238.)

45. '. . . instauratio bene conditae naturae' (Leyden, VI. *4^r.)

46. 'Corpus enim ut est ipsum visibile, rebus visibilibus delectatur, ut est mortale, temporalia sequitur, ut est grave, deorsum sidit. Contra anima generis aetherei memor, summa vi sursum nititur, et cum terrestri mole luctatur . . . (P)eccatum quod‧ bene conditum erat, male depravavit: inter bene concordes dissensionis virus serens.' (Leyden, V. 13.)

47. '. . . quod detruditur in grave et hoc caliginosum corpus' (Lupton, pp. 163-4.)

48. 'Nam quodque evadit ejusmodi uti illud est in quod recipitur.' (Lupton, p. 164.)

49. '. . . animal hoc hominis . . . in hominis statu, et (ut ita dicam) in humana republica, imperium tenuisse . . .
A cujus violencia et tirannide, anima homunculusque ille interior, propter infelicem illam ruinam Adae invalidus et impotens, nullis conatibus se per se solvere et liberare potuit.' (Lupton, p. 146.)

50. See *Enarratio in Epistolam . . . ad Romanos*, Chs. VI, VII: Lupton, pp. 17-22, 146-50.

51. 'Hii sunt . . . qui . . . omnes fluctuantes corporis affectus exciverint, qui leve et obediens rationi corpus effecerint, qui firma et stabili spe . . . perseverant, qui omnia pocius vel acerbissima paciuntur . . . (Lupton, p. 152.)

52. Ibid., Ch. VIII; Lupton, p. 25. '. . . quum Deum auxiliatorem tenent . . .' (Lupton, p. 152.)

53. '. . . Christiani ac quodammodo quidem Christi vocitentur.' Ibid., Ch. VIII; Lupton, p. 155.

54. 'Intellectus autem spiritus est fides Deo; voluntas vero ejusdem est charitas et amor Dei.' (Lupton, p. 167.)

55. *De caelesti hierarchia*, Chs. I, II; *De ecclesiastica hierarchia*, Ch. I.

56. *De cael. hier.*, Ch. XII; Lupton, pp. 33-4, 186.

57. *Enarratio in Epistolam . . . ad Romanos*, Ch. VIII (Lupton, pp. 25–32, 155–7). The quotation, much modified, is from *Theologia Platonica*, Bk. XIV.

58. H. A. Mason, *Humanism and Poetry in the Early Tudor Period* (London, 1959), p. 125.

59. *Utopia*, trans. Ralph Robinson (Everyman's Library, revised edition, 1951), p. 124.

60. See Etienne Gilson, *The Christian Philosophy of St. Thomas Aquinas*, translated by L. K. Shook (London, 1957), pp. 11–14.

61. See Ockham's *Philosophical Writings*, selected, translated, and edited by Philotheus Boehner (London, 1957), p. xlvi.

62. '. . . ut id homo consequatur a Deo per suam operationem, quasi mercedem, ad quod Deus ei virtutem operandi deputavit.' (Blackfriars, XXX. 202–3).

63. Adolph Harnack, *History of Dogma*, translated by N. Buchanan *et al.* (New York, 1958), Vol. VI, pp. 279, 300.

64. Harnack, pp. 301–5.

65. This paragraph has been largely based on Gordon Leff, *William of Ockham: the Metamorphosis of Scholastic Discourse* (Manchester, 1975), pp. 490–5.

66. Maurice de Wulf, *An Introduction to Scholastic Philosophy*, translated by P. Coffey (New York, 1956), p. 136. (Originally published as *Scholasticism Old and New.*)

67. Heinrich Boehmer, *Martin Luther: Road to Reformation*, translated by J. W. Doberstein and T. G. Tappert (New York, 1957), p. 97.

68. One may note in this context that Gabriel Biel belonged to the Brethren of the Common Life.

69. The material in this paragraph is largely based on Boehmer's *Martin Luther*.

70. Eugene F. Rice Jr., *The Renaissance Idea of Wisdom* (Cambridge, Mass., 1958), pp. 124–5.

71. 2 Corinthians, 12 : 9.

72. '. . . dominatur in medio inimicorum, et potens est in mediis pressuris, quod est aliud nihil, quam quod virtus in infirmitate perficitur: . . . adeo ut crux et mors cogantur mihi servire . . . Haec est enim ardua et insignis dignitas, veraque et omnipotens potestas, spirituale imperium . . .' (Wittenberg, C3^r.)

73. 'Nec solum reges omnium liberrimi, sed sacerdotes quoque sumus inaeternum, quod longe regno excellentius . . .' (Wittenberg, C3^r.)

74. 'Praecepta docent quidem bona, sed non statim fiunt, quae docta sunt, ostendunt enim, quid facere nos oporteat, sed virtutem faciendi non donant, in hoc autem sunt ordinata ut hominem sibi ipsi ostendant, per quae suam impotentiam ad bonum cognoscat, et de suis viribus desperet.' (Wittenberg, B4^r.)

75. 'Gratia proprie significat misericordiam gratuitam, seu acceptationem gratuitam propter Christum. Nam cum dicitur, Per gratiam habemus remissionem, si sic intelligas, propter donatas virtutes habemus remissionem, plane evertes totam Pauli sententiam, et conscientiis adimes veram consolationem.' (*Loci Com.*, Basle 1561, p. 293.)

76. Battles, II. 931. '. . . hoc consilium quoad electos in gratuita eius misericordia fundatum esse asserimus, nullo humanae dignitatis respectu; quos vero damnationi addicit, his iusto quidem et irreprehensibili, sed incomprehensibili ipsius iudicio, vitae aditum praecludi.' (Munich, IV. 378–9.)

77. The resemblance has been noted by Hiram Haydn in *The Counter-Renaissance* (New York, 1950), p. 439.

78. See Basil Hall, 'The Calvin Legend' and 'Calvin against the Calvinists': both in *John Calvin* (*Courteney Studies in Reformation Theology*, Vol. I; Appleford, 1966).

CHAPTER III

1. See MP 79. 24, where belief in the simple myth of the Fall is said to characterize the 'credulous'.

2. See Geoffrey Shepherd's edition of *An Apology for Poetry* (London, 1965), pp. 12 ff.; Kenneth O. Myrick, *Sir Philip Sidney as a Literary Craftsman* (2nd edition, Lincoln, Nebraska, 1965), Ch. II: 'The *Defense of Poesie* as a Classical Oration'.

3. '. . . omnia abstrusa esse, nihil nos scire, nil cernere, veritatem in profundis puteis immersam, veris falsa miris modis adjuncta atque intorta esse . . .' (ES, VI. 672.)

4. '. . . omnes perceptiones tam sensus quam mentis sunt ex analogia hominis, non ex analogia universi.' (ES, I. 163–4.)

5. 'Notiones infimarum specierum . . . et prehensionum immediatarum sensus . . . non fallunt magnopere; quae tamen ipsae a fluxu materiae et commistione rerum quandoque confunduntur.' (ES, I. 159.)

6. 'Aedificium autem hujus universi structura sua, intellectui humano contemplanti, instar labyrinthi est; ubi tot ambigua viarum, tam fallaces rerum et signorum similitudines, tam obliquae et implexae naturarum spirae et nodi, undequaque se ostendunt. Iter autem sub incerto sensus lumine, interdum affulgente interdum se condente, per experientiae et rerum particularium sylvas perpetuo faciendum est. Quin etiam duces itineris (ut dictum est) qui se offerunt, et ipsi implicantur, atque errorum et errantium numerum augent. In rebus tam duris, de judicio hominum ex vi propria, aut etiam de foelicitate fortuita, desperandum est.' (ES, I. 129.)

7. 'Illi enim nihil sciri posse simpliciter asserunt; nos non multum sciri posse in natura, ea quae nunc in usu est via: verum illi exinde authoritatem sensus et intellectus destruunt; nos auxilia iisdem excogitamus et subministramus.' (ES, I. 163.)

8. 'Natura enim non nisi parendo vincitur.' (ES, I. 157.)

9. Rudolf Metz, 'Bacon's Part in the Intellectual Movement of His Time', in *Seventeenth Century Studies presented to Sir Herbert Grierson* (Oxford, 1938), p. 28.

10. 'Sympathiae et Antipathiae'; '[motus] multiplicationis naturae suae super aliud'; 'agens nobilius motum in alio latentem et sopitum excitat'; '*Motus Regius*, sive cohibitio reliquorum motuum a motu praedominante'. (All ES, I. 561.)

11. '. . . causas physicas . . . de *substantia coelestium* tam stellari quam interstellari . . . Eam *Astronomiam Vivam* nominabimus, ad differentiam bovis illius Promethei suffarcinati, et solummodo figura tenus bovis.' (ES, I. 552, 554.)

12. A. N. Whitehead, *Science and the Modern World* (Cambridge, 1926; rptd., 1932), pp. 52 ff. See also D. G. James, *The Dream of Learning* (Oxford, 1951), p. 14.

13. 'Spiritus omnium quae in corpore fiunt fabri sunt atque opifices.' (ES, II. 161.)

14. '. . . ex harum facultatem (experimentalis scilicet et rationalis) arctiore et sanctiore foedere (quod adhuc factum non est) bene sperandum est.' (ES, I. 201.)

15. '. . . ut faciamus intellectum humanum rebus et naturae parem.' (ES, I. 260–1.)

16. 'Ad opera nil aliud potest homo, quam ut corpora naturalia admoveat et amoveat; reliqua Natura intus transigit.' (ES, I. 157.)

17. 'Non leve quiddam interest inter humanae mentis *idola* et divinae mentis ideas; . . .' (ES, I. 160.)

18. The distinction is Bacon's own: see *Advancement*, II. viii. 6.

19. R. B. McKerrow (ed.), *The Works of Thomas Nashe* (London, 1904–10), IV. 3.

20. Morris W. Croll, 'The Baroque Style in Prose', first published in *Studies in English Philology: a Miscellany in Honor of Frederick Klaeber*, ed. K. Malone and M. B. Ruud (Minneapolis, 1929), and often reprinted.

21. Erich Auerbach, *Mimesis*, pp. 275–6.

22. Rosemond Tuve, *Allegorical Imagery* (Chicago, 1966). For Lancelot, see p. 424.

23. Castiglione, *The Book of the Courtier*, translated by Sir Thomas Hoby, Book IV. (Everyman's Library edition, London, 1948, p. 319.)

24. *The Romance of the Rose*, ll. 19907-20036, 20279-670.

25. Ibid. ll. 21695-780.

26. Edgar Wind, *Pagan Mysteries*, p. 45. See Ch. III generally.

27. Murray Roston, *The Soul of Wit* (Oxford, 1974).

28. Rosemond Tuve, *Elizabethan and Metaphysical Imagery* (Chicago, 1947), p. 408.

29. A. J. Smith, 'New Bearings in Donne: "Air and Angels"': first published in *English*, Vol. XIII (1960); see Helen Gardner (ed.), *John Donne: a Collection of Critical Essays* (Englewood Cliffs, 1962), p. 172.

CHAPTER IV

1. Cf. Wolfgang Clemen, *English Tragedy before Shakespeare*, translated by T. S. Dorsch (London, 1961), p. 124: 'What we find in an especially pronounced degree in Tamburlaine is in a lesser degree ·a characteristic of all the Marlovian heroes; for all of them language is, so to speak, a means of existing in another dimension, in that it carries them beyond the bounds of their own real existence and enables them constantly to soar beyond what is actual and present. In the language they use they are able to bring to realization what they 'will' and 'desire', but would not be able to accomplish in a real existence. It is in their language that they have a foretaste and an illusion of things which happen in dreams that never come true.'

2. The first two passages are in fact allusions to Helios–Apollo and Zeus–Jupiter, but there seem to be suggestions of Phaethon's career in both cases.

3. Helen Gardner, 'Milton's "Satan" and the Theme of Damnation in Elizabethan Tragedy', *English Studies* ('Essays and Studies'), New Series Vol. I (1948), p. 47.

4. See ll. 397, 465, 562, 634, 1740, 1940.

5. Wilbur Sanders, *The Dramatist and the Received Idea* (Cambridge, 1968), pp. 218, 234.

6. Ibid., p. 229.

7. '... au plus eslevé throne du monde, si ne sommes assis que sus nostre cul.' (Pléiade, p. 1096.)

8. A. C. Bradley, 'The Rejection of Falstaff', *Oxford Lectures on Poetry* (London, 1917), p. 266. Cf. pp. 262-3.

9. Alfred Harbage, *As They Liked It* (New York, 1947), p. 75.

10. See, for instance, John Danby, *Shakespeare's Doctrine of Nature* (London, 1949), pp. 81-101; L. C. Knights, 'The Public World: First Observations' in *Some Shakespearean Themes* (London, 1959), pp. 26-44.

11. A. P. Rossiter, *Angel with Horns* (London, 1961), p. 35.

12. Coleridge, *Shakespeare Criticism*, ed. T. M. Raysor (Everyman's Library, London, 1960), I. 35.

13. A. P. Rossiter, *Angel with Horns*, pp. 177-9.

14. A. C. Bradley, *Shakespearean Tragedy* (London, 1905), pp. 110-12.

15. Nevill Coghill notes the point. See his *Shakespeare's Professional Skills* (Cambridge, 1964), p. 114.

16. See p. 149.

17. A. P. Rossiter, *Angel with Horns,* pp. 135-6. This view has been brilliantly supported by John Bayley in 'Time and the Trojans', *Essays in Criticism* Vol. 25 (1975); see especially pp. 58, 61, 70-2.

18. This matter is finely treated by Willard Farnham in *The Shakespearean Grotesque* (Oxford, 1971), pp. 131-7.

19. The expression is J. W. Lever's: see his Introduction to the New Arden edition of *Measure for Measure* (London, 1965), p. lxxix.

20. Cf. Derek Traversi, 'Measure for Measure', *Scrutiny*, XI. 1 (Summer 1942), p. 52: 'As a character within the action his [the Duke's] self-confessed weakness, born though it is of a tolerance and understanding which events prove to have been very necessary, has contributed to the intolerable conditions of Viennese social life. As a detached 'symbol' of truth in judgment, whose entry into the remotest corners of the action is covered by his function as 'friar' and confessor, his understanding is absolute, perfect.'

21. R. W. Battenhouse, '*Measure for Measure* and Christian Doctrine of the Atonement', *PMLA* LXI (1946), pp. 1029-59.

22. Harley Granville-Barker, *Prefaces to Shakespeare: Antony and Cleopatra, Coriolanus* (Illustrated Paperback edition, London, 1963), p. 93.

23. The expression is Bradley's: see *Shakespearean Tragedy*, p. 358.

24. W. Sanders, *The Dramatist and the Received Idea*, p. 290.

25. Ibid.

26. A. C. Bradley, *Shakespearean Tragedy*, p. 84. Bradley is more cautious in his interpretation of the play in 'Coriolanus' (British Academy Annual Shakespeare Lecture, 1912).

27. H. Granville-Barker, *Prefaces to Shakespeare*, p. 91.

28. Cf. my remarks on *Tamburlaine*, pp. 114-15 above.

29. G. K. Hunter, 'The Last Tragic Heroes', *Later Shakespeare* (Stratford-upon-Avon Studies, Vol. 8, London, 1966), p. 25.

30. D. G. James, *Scepticism and Poetry* (1937), p. 220.

31. Frank Kermode (ed.), *The Tempest* (New Arden edition, London, 1962), p. 92.

32. I have drawn here on some points made by Rabindranath Tagore in an untranslated essay.

33. David Young, *The Heart's Forest: a Study of Shakespeare's Pastoral Plays* (New Haven, 1972), p. 25.

Index

À Kempis, Thomas 35, 46
Agrippa, Cornelius 5-13, 14, 18, 19, 20, 52, 53, 77, 217-19
Aquinas, St. Thomas 7, 36, 39, 42-3, 44, 77, 222, 224
   Summa contra Gentiles 42-3
   Summa Theologica 36, 42-3, 44, 77, 222, 224
Aristotle 7, 61, 173
Auerbach, Erich xv, 23, 79, 220, 226
Augustine, St. 25, 35, 44, 47, 61, 77

Bacon, Francis 66-76, 225
   The Advancement of Learning 66, 67, 70, 73, 74, 225
   De augmentis scientiarum 71, 225
   De sapientia veterum 68, 225
   Essays 67, 71-2, 72-3, 73, 74, 75
   History of Life and Death 71, 225
   Instauratio magna, Preface 69, 225
   Novum Organum 68, 69, 70, 72, 73, 225
   Sylva sylvarum 71
Battenhouse, Roy 162, 227
Bayley, John 227
Biel, Gabriel 45, 224
Blake, William 121
Boehmer, Heinrich 224
Botticelli, Sandro 93, 96
Bradley, A.C. 126, 141, 174, 185, 226, 227
Browne, Sir Thomas 76, 77, 111
Burton, Robert 76-84, 101, 111, 210

Calvin, Jean 48-50, 224
Castiglione, Baldassare 88, 226
Cervantes, Miguel de 2
Chaucer, Geoffrey 87, 90, 91, 96
Clemen, Wolfgang 226
Coghill, Nevill 227
Coleridge, Samuel Taylor 226
Colet, John 39-41, 223-4
   Commentary on Romans 39-41, 223-4
   Treatises on the Pseudo-Dionysius 41, 223
Colie, Rosalie 217
Croll, Morris 79, 226
Cusanus, Nicholas 26-9, 30, 31, 33, 62, 100, 220-1

De coniecturis 26, 28, 221
De docta ignorantia 26, 27, 28, 220-21
Idiota: de sapientia 26, 221

Danby, John 226
Dante 90
Davies, Sir John 57-60, 63, 64
De Meung, Jean, 90, 91, 95, 226
De Wulf, Maurice 224
Dionysius: *see* Pseudo-Dionysius
Donne, John 85, 96-7, 99-112, 210
   'Anniversaries', First and Second 99-102, 103, 111
   Songs and Sonets 102-12
Drury, Elizabeth 99-102
Duns Scotus: *see* Scotus, Duns

Eckhart, Meister 46
El Greco 2
Erasmus, Desiderius 2, 10, 22, 36-9, 48, 220, 222-3
   Colloquies 37-8, 223
   De libero arbitrio 38, 223
   Enchiridion militis Christiani 22, 37, 39, 220, 223
   Letters 37, 38, 223
   Paraclesis 39, 223
   The Praise of Folly 10, 36, 222-3

Farnham, Willard 227
Faust 5. *See also* Marlowe: *Doctor Faustus*
Ficino, Marsilio 29, 32-4, 37, 41, 60, 62, 86, 145, 221-2, 224
   Commentary on Plato's *Symposium* 32, 33, 221-2
   Quaestiones quinque de mente 33, 34, 222
   Theologia Platonica 29, 222, 224
Fish, Stanley E. xv, 217
Fletcher, Giles 58
Fletcher, Phineas 57-9, 63, 64

Gardner, Helen 226
Gilson, Etienne 224
Gower, John 90
Granville-Barker, Harley 173, 227
Greco, El: *see* El Greco
Greville, Fulke 63-6, 97-9

Greville, Fulke (*cont.*)
  Caelica 97-9
  Mustapha 63
  A Treatie of Humane Learning 63-6, 97
Groote, Gerhard 46

Hall, Basil 224
Harbage, Alfred 126, 226
Harnack, Adolf 44, 224
Haydn, Hiram xv, 224
Henry of Ghent 45
Herodotus 219
Homer 219
  Iliad 88
Hooker, Richard 77
Horace 54
Hunter, G.K. 227
Hus, Jan 48

Il Rosso 2

James, D.G. 197, 225, 227

Kempis, Thomas à: *see* À Kempis, Thomas
Kermode, Frank 204, 227
Knights, L.C. 226

Leff, Gordon 224
Leonardo da Vinci 2, 210
Lever, J.W. 227
Lucretius 18, 219
Luther, Martin 45-8, 224

Machiavelli, Niccolò 74
McKerrow, R.B. 76, 226
Malory, Sir Thomas 87-8
Marlowe, Christopher 113-22, 137, 165, 174-5, 176, 177, 178, 183, 184, 226, 227
  Doctor Faustus 118-22, 137, 165, 174-5, 176, 178, 183, 226
  Edward II 117-18
  The Jew of Malta 117
  Tamburlaine 113-17, 118, 119, 120, 177, 184, 226, 227
Mary, the Virgin 100
Mary Queen of Scots 89
Mason, H.A. 41, 224
Medici, Lorenzo de' 32
Melanchthon, Philip 48, 224
Metz, Rudolph 71, 225
Meung, Jean de: *see* De Meung, Jean
Michelangelo 2, 167, 210
Milton, John 211-16
  Paradise Lost 211-13, 214, 215
  Paradise Regained 215-16
  Samson Agonistes 213-15

Mirandola: *see* Pico della Mirandola
Montaigne, Michel de 1, 2, 7, 8, 13, 17, 18-24, 35, 68, 101, 106, 109, 124, 137, 151, 169, 207, 210, 219-20, 222, 226
More, Sir Thomas 41-2, 219, 224
  A Dialogue of Comfort 42
  Utopia 41-2
Mucedorus 208
Myrick, Kenneth O. 225

Nauert, Charles G., Jr. xv
Nicholas of Cusa: *see* Cusanus, Nicholas
Nietzsche, Friedrich 189

Ockham, William of 43-4, 45, 47, 48, 224

Paul, St. 22, 34, 106, 224
Philip II of Spain 89
Pico della Mirandola, Gianfrancesco 1
Pico della Mirandola, Giovanni 1, 2, 29-32, 33, 63, 166, 221
  Conclusiones 29
  De ente et uno 30-1, 32, 221
  De hominis dignitate 29-30, 32, 63, 166, 221
  Heptaplus 31-2
Pliny 77
Pseudo-Dionysius 26, 30, 41
Puttenham, George 76-7
Pyrrho 1

Rabelais, François 13-18, 21, 23, 41, 79-80, 106, 124, 128, 139, 169, 210, 218-19
Ralegh, Sir Walter 60-3
  The History of the World 60-63
  'The Sceptic' 60
  A Treatise of the Soul 61, 63
Rice, Eugene F., Jr. 47, 224
Robb, Nesca A. 222
Romance of the Rose, The: *see* de Meung, Jean
Rossiter, A.P. 137, 151, 226, 227
Rosso, Il: *see* Il Rosso
Roston, Murray xv, 99, 226
Ruysbroeck, Jan van 46

Salutati, Coluccio 32
Sanders, Wilbur xv, 120, 121, 226, 227
Scotus, Duns 43, 45
Sextus Empiricus 1, 18, 219
Shakespeare, William 3, 55, 99, 112, 122-210
  Antony and Cleopatra 173, 184, 185-92, 193
  As You Like It 199
  Coriolanus 173, 184-5

Cymbeline 194-202, 204, 205
Hamlet 122, 133, 134-46, 147, 148, 149, 150, 152, 154, 169, 189, 209
Henry IV 122-34
Henry V 131-2, 133
History Plays 122-34, 150, 163
King Lear 134, 163-4, 165-73, 176, 180, 181, 191, 192, 193, 200, 201, 212, 213
Last Plays 163, 173, 193-209
Macbeth 117, 163-4, 173-84, 184-5, 186-7, 188, 189, 190, 191, 192, 193, 200, 213
Measure for Measure 134, 154-63, 164, 167-8, 170, 172, 195, 227
Othello 163, 164-5, 201, 202
Pericles 194-6, 198-200, 204
Richard II 132-3
Sonnets 98
The Tempest 194, 195, 202-9
Timon of Athens 201
Troilus and Cressida 133-4, 146-54, 163
Twelfth Night 199
The Winter's Tale 194, 195, 197-202, 203, 204, 205
Shepherd, Geoffrey 225
Sidney, Sir Philip 52-6, 225

Smith, A.J. 226
Socrates 19, 30, 57
Spenser, Edmund 77, 84-96
   The Faerie Queene 77, 85, 87-96
   Fowre Hymnes 85-7, 93, 95
Staupitz, Johann von 46

Tagore, Rabindranath 227
Tasso, Torquato 88
Tauler, Johann 46
Theologia Germanica 46
Traversi, Derek 227
Trinkaus, Charles 29, 32, 221, 222
Tuve, Rosemond 87, 109, 226

Valla, Lorenzo 32
Vinci, Leonardo da: see Leonardo da Vinci

Whitehead, A.N. 71, 225
Wiley, Margaret xv
Wind, Edgar 222, 226
Wulf, Maurice de: see De Wulf, Maurice
Wyclif, John 48

Young, David 208, 227

Zara, Antonio 76